THE OLD VIC STORY

A Nation's Theatre 1818-1976

THE OLD VIC STORY

A Nation's Theatre 1818-1976

PETER ROBERTS

W. H. ALLEN · LONDON
A Howard & Wyndham Company
1976

For Nuria

IN MEMORY OF SYBIL THORNDIKE

to aid the R.V.H.B.F.

PRINTED & BOUND BY T. & A. CONSTABLE LTD,
HOPETOUN STREET, EDINBURGH
FOR THE PUBLISHERS, W. H. ALLEN & CO.LTD,

44 HILL STREET, LONDON WIX 8LB

ISBN 0 491 01747 2

Contents

Foreword

by

Dame Sybil Thorndike

'What has the Old Vic come to mean to you after so many years?' This was a question put to me soon after I went to see the National Theatre Company's final performance at the theatre in March 1976, *Tribute to the Lady*.

For me the words 'Old Vic' and 'Lilian Baylis' are synonymous. Of course, when I joined the first Old Vic Company in November 1914 for four years, we didn't call Lilian 'The Lady' then. And it was too soon for anybody to compile programmes that took the form of a tribute. Indeed there was nothing a bit lady-like or grand about Lilian when I arrived at the Old Vic for the first time. She came storming into Ben Greet's office and gave him what for. What an extraordinary way to treat the head of your Company, I thought. Then she turned to me and said, 'Now you're the daughter of a clergyman, aren't you? You'll do then. Church and Stage – same thing – or ought to be'.

That was how I came to the Waterloo stage for the first time in 1914. The last time was sixty years later in 1974 when we celebrated the centenary of Lilian's birth with the first performance of *Tribute to the Lady*. The best way I can recapture the spirit of the early pioneering days of the Shakespeare Company at the Old Vic is to contrast the personality of Lilian with that of another eccentric theatrical spinster I worked for, Miss Annie Horniman, who managed her own company at the Manchester Gaiety Theatre.

Now Miss Horniman wanted to do good *to* the people of Manchester. Lilian was one *of* the people of South London – a gruff South African cockney. Nobody would have dreamed of calling Miss Horniman 'Annie'. But we all called Miss Baylis 'Lil'. Miss Horniman was always very dignified, dressed with the utmost elegance, was well-educated, well-off and cared for music. Lilian did not bother how she looked, never troubled about dress, was both poor and scrappily educated. Though Lilian had a training as a musician, she enjoyed music more as a performer than a cultivated listener.

Had Lilian waited until she and her audiences were better educated or had she put off forming a Shakespeare Company until it could be done with dignity and elegance, I very much doubt whether a start would ever have been made. It was Lilian's extraordinary energy that got things going. That and the fact that she really loved people. When she was ticking them off for not supporting her new Shakespeare Company as she thought they should, she was loving them in a way that Miss Horniman was not able to love her audiences. And everything that Lilian did was done according to the will of God, even if, in her directness, she never struck you as a 'Holy Person'.

When I first went to the Old Vic it was already an historic playhouse. One was aware that this was a theatre where Kean had once played. Above all one was aware that it had flourished as a nineteenth-century melodrama theatre and it must be remembered that melodrama was true folk theatre – both of and for the people.

I had personal reasons, too, for understanding how this theatre had come to be Emma Cons' Temperance Music Hall. My sister-in-law, Elizabeth Casson had helped Octavia Hill and Emma Cons in their rent collecting work in the slums of nineteenth-century London – work that was to lead Emma Cons to the Old Vic and so enable Lilian Baylis, her niece, to lay the foundations for Britain's National Theatre Company and for its national opera and ballet companies too.

My own days at the Old Vic have been amongst the most exciting in my life. I hope that new generations of players will find this eminently workable theatre a place of just as much excitement. I wish the Old Vic a long life and a happy one.

Sybil Thorndike
April 1976

Introduction

Before offering an introductory note to this history of the Old Vic Theatre, I would like to thank the Chairman of the Old Vic Governors, Mr C. S. K. Benham, for his permission to write it and to consult for this purpose the theatre's archives and records.

Watch It Come Down by John Osborne, was the title of the last new play to be presented by the National Theatre Company before they vacated the Old Vic to move in March 1976 into their own new home on the South Bank. The uncertainty surrounding the Old Vic's future at that time rendered the title of Mr Osborne's play uncomfortable, if not portentous. Not unnaturally, the Equity-based 'Save the London Theatres Campaign' took an especial interest in the strenuous efforts then being made to ensure that this historic playhouse continued to fulfil a vital role in the cultural life of the British capital.

This profile of the Old Vic's history since 1818 is intended as a contribution to the campaign: I hope that nobody will ever have to watch the Old Vic come down. My own perception of this country's indebtedness to the Old Vic was sharpened in 1974 when I wrote and edited a souvenir book, published as part of the Lilian Baylis Centenary, to contribute to the funds being raised to save another threatened theatre, Sadler's Wells. That assignment, which involved an evocation of the Old Vic's history from 1880 to 1937, naturally led to a desire to take a wider look at what went on in this Waterloo Road theatre from its beginnings in 1818 up to the time of the opening of the National Theatre in 1976.

Many books (see Recommended Reading, p. 193) have already chronicled in much greater detail than is possible here the achievements of bygone Old Vic seasons. The bird's eye view of the theatre in these pages would not have been possible without consulting these invaluable records and without research in many other fields. I hope that a comprehensive picture of the Old Vic will emerge – not in a vacuum, but as part of the nation's cultural growing pains. Most of all, I hope that all those artists who have worked for the Old Vic or have written about their activities, will see a unique theatre survive.

I am grateful to Richard Findlater, author of *Lilian Baylis: The Lady of the Old Vic*, both for suggesting the present book and for the insights afforded by his own. I would also like to thank Frank Granville Barker, Peter Bettany, Noël Goodwin and Anne Tayler for their help in reading the first drafts of some of the following chapters.

Finally, I would like to thank the very many friends and contemporaries of Lilian Baylis for their vivid recollections of the years which made the Old Vic world famous.

Peter Roberts

I   *The Beginnings*

Who was twelve years old when Britain's first-ever public playhouse opened its doors in 1576? Who, had his body endured as well as his plays, would have been four hundred and twelve when Britain's National Theatre began to admit the public to its trio of auditoria in 1976? When a book outlining the history of the Old Vic coyly opens with two such questions, it will hardly come as a matter of astonishment that the answer to both is William Shakespeare.

But it may be a surprise – a shock even – to discover that for the first century of its existence the Old Vic had little to do with Shakespeare and the classics – and yet, these days, so many leading actors have been to the Old Vic, played Shakespeare in it and gone on to greater glories, that the names Old Vic and William Shakespeare seem as inseparable in the public mind as Buckingham Palace and England's monarch.

Surprise, therefore, at the Old Vic's world-wide reputation as the natural habitat of Shakespeare and the classics is only likely to arise if you approach its history from the past. But if you can do this and have a sufficiently bizarre turn of mind to look at the Old Vic's opening in 1818 from the point of view of somebody present at the first night of that first-ever playhouse in 1576, you would certainly be amazed at the Old Vic's twentieth-century reputation. Only if your sightlines are trained from 1976 and the unveiling of the National Theatre on the South Bank, will it be hard to associate the Old Vic with anything other than the classics.

It does take an enormous effort to look at a theatre through the eyes of some imaginery person born four centuries ago. Most of us, if we pay much attention to a theatre in the first place, merely do so to see who is appearing there and in what play. If this information proves sufficiently compelling, we will examine its auditorium in search of good seats that we can afford. If we *are* prepared to consider the building as a thing in itself, we are most likely to investigate whether the sightlines and acoustics are good from where the box-office manager proposes to accommodate us. Not many of us will want to concern ourselves with the theatre's history and have our minds weighed down with earlier performances that have been and long since gone forever.

Sadly, the history of the Old Vic is precisely about what has been and gone and can never be recaptured. The journey into its past must therefore seem melancholy at first. But it will seem less so if the historical starting point is made by conjuring up the quick rather than the dead. Since the National Theatre Company is still very much a living entity, its thirteen-year tenancy of the Old Vic from 1963 at least awakens memories that have lively rather than faded associations. And since the Old Vic and Shakespeare are still synonymous in the public mind, the first question must be to wonder if the National Theatre Company memories are as Shakespeare-filled as the days before 1963 when the Old Vic Company was still laying the foundations for a National Company. The answer to any such wondering must be a firm 'no'.

Even so, the National Theatre's thirteen-year occupation of the Old Vic can only have enhanced its world-wide reputation as the home of great English acting, especially in the revival of the classics. The National Theatre era at the Old Vic, after all, began with Peter O'Toole's *Hamlet* and it closed in 1976 with Albert Finney's version. Between these two Princes of Denmark there had been Laurence Olivier's Othello and Shylock, not to mention John Gielgud's Prospero. So nobody could complain that Shakespeare had been entirely neglected even though the National Theatre Company had an obligation to present a repertoire that also included foreign classics as well as the premières of new plays. They could grumble, of course, that in the forty-nine years of its existence, from 1914 to 1963, the Old Vic Company had given a very great deal more Shakespeare. But then the Old Vic Company had been primarily a Shakespeare repertory company which had taken only occasional excursions into other classical dramatists and which had premièred new plays even more rarely.

From the vantage point of the National Theatre and the second half of the 1970s, what, in retrospect, probably seems most remarkable about the Old Vic Company's successive seasons of Shakespeare is that they launched so many major British actors. In the male ranks, the Old Vic roll-call includes John Gielgud, Ralph Richardson, Laurence Olivier, Alec Guinness, Michael Redgrave and Richard Burton. And among actresses are Sybil Thorndike, Edith Evans, Flora Robson, Peggy Ashcroft, Claire Bloom and Judi Dench.

So many of these stars have become indelibly associated with Shakespeare at the Old Vic, it seems almost inevitable that this theatre should have prepared the ground for a National Theatre Company and provided it with a first temporary home. Yet the fact remains that when the Old Vic first opened in 1818 under the name of the Royal Coburg Theatre, it was expressly forbidden to stage Shakespeare. When it first attempted to do so the management was immediately prosecuted.

A Regency gentleman attending the formal opening of the Royal Coburg in 1818 would have been flabbergasted to learn that this was to be the first home of the Nation's theatre company. The only way to comprehend such fluctuations in the Old Vic's reputation is to cast off all twentieth-century associations and peer at its history in another context. This would be the panorama of theatre history that separates the years 1576/1818. To absorb so wide a panorama it is wise to stick to a rigid selection of strictly relevant information. That way, no reader will become bogged down in the small print of the footnotes to theatre history.

As it happens, there are two matters which conveniently link the theatre that opened in 1576 and the one we know today as the Old Vic. Since no less than two hundred and forty-two years separate the opening of 'The Theatre' as it was called in Shoreditch north of the Thames and the Royal Coburg which lay across Waterloo Bridge south of the river, such links might seem highly improbable. But in spite of the near two-and-a-half century gap, a little matter of theatre censorship spans the years to determine fundamentally the future of both buildings. And if one was opened north of the river and the other south of it, the bridges that were to cross the Thames were to bring the two theatres closer together, in more senses than one.

In Britain, at any rate, there has been no form of stage censorship quite as violent and quite as destructive as that exercised by the seventeenth-century Puritans who effectively closed all London theatres from the outbreak of the Civil War in 1642 until the restoration of the monarchy with Charles II's return in 1660. The beginnings of this Puritanism undermined 'The Theatre' in Shoreditch just as much as its consequences limited the nineteenth-century Royal Coburg across Waterloo Bridge.

The puritanical loathing on the part of the City Fathers at the popularity of Shoreditch's 'The Theatre' grew to such an extent that, twenty-one years after it had been built, its lessees pulled it down and trundled its timbers across London's then only bridge, London Bridge, and used this handy raw material to build the brightly-coloured Globe Theatre in the comparative safety of the Bankside where so many of Shakespeare's plays were given their world premières.

The reason why, some two hundred years later, the Royal Coburg was not permitted to revive these same Shakespeare plays on the same south side of the river was in fact an indirect result of that same puritanism, which gathered such momentum that London theatres were all forced to close for eighteen barren years. Charles II, on his restoration to the throne, was short-sighted enough, in his anxiety to get the theatre on its feet again, to entrust the exclusive rights to stage straight plays to what became known as the 'Patent Theatres' – or, more specifically, to Thomas Killigrew's Company which occupied the Theatre Royal, Drury Lane, and to Sir William Davenant whose company was eventually to occupy Covent Garden. So, had the Puritans never dabbled in theatrical affairs, it seems improbable that the resulting absurd and long-lived monopoly would have resulted.

As things stood when the Royal Coburg opened, the only way the new theatres could get round the monopoly still exercised by Drury Lane and Covent Garden was to set Shakespeare to music and to pretend that the performance was a musical. The parallel situation today would be that the Royal Shakespeare Company and the National Theatre Company had the exclusive right to perform Shakespeare and indeed all 'legitimate' drama whilst other theatres like the Old Vic were permitted to stage only the musical versions – *Catch My Soul* and not *Othello* itself, *Kiss Me Kate* and not the original *The Taming of the Shrew*.

So, just as surely as that original 'The Theatre' was hounded out of its Shoreditch existence, the Royal Coburg was repeatedly restricted by the result of a misguided Restoration attempt to stimulate theatrical activity and rectify the harm done to drama by Cromwell and his stage-hating followers.

The fact that 'The Theatre' gained a second lease of life by being used to build a new theatre is fascinating not just because the Globe and the Old Vic sprang up on the south side of the Thames a few miles apart. What links them more intriguingly is the relationship of their sites to the bridges that crossed the Thames.

From 975 until as late as 1749, it has to be remembered, London Bridge was the only bridge to cross the river in the capital itself. So it was no accident that the former Shoreditch playhouse should re-emerge as the Globe on the Bankside close to the site of the south exit from the old London Bridge. The thriving life of the Globe and its sister theatres owed as much to that vital bridge-link as Shaftesbury Avenue, in the twentieth century, does to the network of underground, car-parking spaces and bus-services that help to bring the West End its public. In the seventeenth century you could always be ferried across the river of course. But the existence of a bridge, as the birth of the Old Vic was to show, counted for a very great deal more as far as theatres were concerned.

When Westminster Bridge was built in 1749, it inspired Wordsworth to remark some years after its opening, 'Earth has not anything to show more fair'. On a rather more practical and mundane level, Westminster Bridge helped to encourage investment in theatre building on its south side in Georgian times just as, in Elizabethan, London Bridge had been a determining factor in the vitality of the Bankside playhouses.

The first of the new Georgian theatres was Astley's and the first of its many re-buildings took place in 1780 as a result of fashionable, and consequently profitable, equestrian displays on a field near where twentieth-century Londoners catch trains from Waterloo Station. A second theatre followed in 1782 a little further south, to be known first as the Royal Circus and then as the Surrey. Both Astley's and the Surrey were to be deadly rivals of the Old Vic in its Royal Coburg days. Indeed, the Surrey was not pulled down until 1934 and since it was only five minutes' walking distance from the Old Vic's stage door, continued to be an occasional source of exasperating competition to the Vic, even in the twentieth century.

It was a combination of the building of a third bridge, Rennie's Waterloo Bridge, and evil-doings down at the Surrey Theatre which brought the Old Vic into being. How sad, therefore, that the Surrey has disappeared. Those in search of instant theatre history could otherwise have it demonstrated to them, in the course of the few minutes' walk from Waterloo Bridge southwards to the Royal Eye Hospital in St George's Circus now on the site of the old Surrey. The walk over the latest Waterloo Bridge passes the new National Theatre on the very edge of the river, the Old Vic and the site of the Surrey – all theatres that have grown out of one another's existence.

The scenario for the appearance of the Old Vic under the Royal Coburg name has to be interwoven with the beginning of work on Rennie's Waterloo Bridge in 1809. The construction of the new bridge seems to have been a great source of satisfaction to the ground landlord of the Surrey theatre, a Mr Temple West. And it needs no genius from the world of higher economics to spell out the reason for his satisfaction. Improved communications result in the improved value of adjacent property. There is evidence that Mr Temple West was impatient for the Prince Regent and the Duke of Wellington to open Waterloo Bridge with all due formality and ceremony on the second anniversary of the Battle of Waterloo in 1817.

This evidence lies in what we know of Mr West's greed. On Lady Day, 1816, the Lease of the Surrey came up for renewal. The lessees, mindful of the improved accessibility of the theatre, offered to up their annual payment from two hundred and twenty pounds to six hundred pounds. Mr Temple West, however, demanded a new rate of four thousand two hundred pounds. This was clearly a hyperinflationary increase, even measured by twentieth-century standards of the sort that caused Britain's National Theatre to cost sixteen million pounds by the time it opened, compared to the estimated cost of seven and a half million at the start of work in 1966. Faced with a Mr Temple West and his outrageous demand, most of us would tell him to keep his theatre and go build one of our own nearer the new bridge. This is precisely what the Surrey's hapless lessees, Messrs Jones and Dunn, were forced to do.

In the twentieth century the couple would have slapped in an application to the Arts Council of Great Britain, the Greater London Council and the State Government for financial assistance. That is what the Governing Body of the National Theatre has had to do in order to ensure the finance to complete their new theatre complex. In the nineteenth century, the nearest equivalent to any such official support was an appeal for Royal Patronage to head a list of subscribers to provide capital for the new building, with the bait of a reasonable dividend on their investment and free theatre seats. Understandably, this is the course for which Jones and Dunn opted.

They were extremely fortunate in securing the evident enthusiastic collaboration of John Thomas Serres, who, as Marine Painter to the King, ensured the all-important foot in the all-important royal door. Since Serres is reliably reported to have invested two thousand pounds of his own money in the projected new theatre and afterwards to have become insolvent, his enthusiasm comes shining through the centuries. For, when the Royal Coburg eventually opened, one of the features that the management was most pleased to boast of was the long-since vanished Grand Panoramic Marine Saloon painted by Mr Serres himself.

The Serres connection allowed the promoters of the new theatre to announce that the project had the patronage of Prince Leopold of Saxe-Coburg and of his betrothed, the Princess Charlotte of Wales, only daughter of George IV and heiress presumptive to the throne. With these prestigious names to head the subscription list, the entrepreneurs were able to embark on a fund-raising campaign which took the form of a leaflet which reads as follows:

PROPOSALS FOR THE ROYAL COBURG THEATRE

'Mr Jones (late proprietor of the Royal Circus, or Surrey Theatre), having agreed for a piece of land near the foot of Waterloo Bridge, on the Surrey side, for the purpose of building a theatre, and having obtained the patronage of Her Royal Highness the Princess Charlotte of Wales and His Serene

Highness the Prince of Saxe-Coburg, proposes to dispose of a part by way of subscription as follows:

'The whole is estimated at £12,000. A subscriber of one eighth of that sum to be considered a joint proprietor. Subscribers for one share of £100 to receive interest at 5% and each share to entitle the holder to a personal free admission transferable each season. The holder of five shares to be eligible to be elected a trustee; and the holder of two shares to be entitled to vote on all occasions.

'Each subscriber to pay 25% at the time of subscribing and 25% monthly, until the whole is paid. As soon as £4,000 shall have been subscribed, a general meeting of the subscribers to be called for the purpose of framing laws for the government of the concern, and electing trustees, treasurers and other officers.

'Materials to the amount of several thousand pounds are already purchased; the whole property in scenery, dresses etc etc at the Surrey Theatre has been moved to this concern and the theatre is intended to open at Christmas next. Subscriptions are also received and further information will be communicated by Mr Jones, near the Obelisk, St George's Fields; and Mr Chippendale, solicitor to the Theatre, Great Queen Street, Lincolns Inn Fields.'

No doubt, also thanks to John Serres' royal connection, a licence was issued for the projected new theatre at the Surrey Quarter Sessions on 16 October 1816. Rudolph Cabanal, who had in fact designed the Surrey Theatre (as well as the stage of the Drury Lane theatre of that period) was appointed architect. What with royal patronage, the granting of a licence and a prestigious architect to design it, the new building seemed to be getting off to an auspicious start. But at this point a vein of what Polonius would have described as farcical-tragi-comedy becomes discernible. In its way it anticipates something of the black comedy that has gone into the century-long struggle to get Britain its National Theatre built.

It has been said of the National Theatre's Foundation Stone that it should have been made to rest on wheels. Three foundation-laying ceremonies in Bloomsbury, Kensington and on the South Bank were formally gone through on sites which, in the event, were used for other buildings. There was also to be a touch of wry comedy about the laying of the Royal Coburg's foundation stone, even though its site did prove to be the correct one. It was laid four months after the wedding of the new theatre's royal patrons and can still be read on the Waterloo Road side of the Old Vic as follows:

> 'This first stone of the Royal Coburg Theatre was laid on September 14, 1816, by his Serene Highness, the Prince of Saxe-Coburg and Her Royal Highness the Princess Charlotte of Wales, by their Royal Highness' proxy, Alderman Goodbehere.'

At least, although the royal personages were not able to put in a personal appearance, their proxy had a nice welcoming sound to his name. Unfortunately, there was nothing very welcoming about what happened to the trio of Jones, Dunn and Serres between the laying of that foundation stone and the delayed opening of the theatre. The site was discovered to be a near-swamp and only the extensive use of stones from the recently demolished Savoy Palace in the Strand enabled the actual foundations to be laid and the first disaster to be overcome. There were to be many others, with the result that the theatre did not open until 1818, by which time Princess Charlotte of Saxe-Coburg had died in childbirth. Eventually the theatre would be re-named after another heiress presumptive to the throne, Princess Victoria, and would achieve world fame under a rather vulgar abbreviation of that name.

Many of the delays in getting the National Theatre opened between 1966 and 1976 may be attributed to the spiralling cost of the venture and of the need to get the agreement of the authorities concerned to foot the increased bill. Many of the delays in getting the Royal Coburg opened were due to the slow amassing of the initial instalment of money. The rashly hoped-for opening of Christmas 1816 came and went just as surely as the many hoped-for openings of the National Theatre came and went in the early 1970s. But if, down at the Surrey Theatre, Mr Temple West was gleefully rubbing his hands at the plight of his former lessees, he could not afford to rub them for long. The Coburg was baled out by the stage-struck son of a well-to-do merchant, Joseph Glossop, who persuaded his father to advance a few hundred pounds to keep the venture going. Most significantly, it was also promoted by the Waterloo Bridge Company. Private patronage and private enterprise combined to save the day.

Notwithstanding the Glossop family's first loan, subscription income dried up early in 1817 and a further appeal had to be made to the Glossops. This proved insufficient to prevent the unpaid workmen from going on strike just before Easter 1817 and the owner of the vital scaffolding from removing it. Since the coffers of even wealthy private individuals like Mr Glossop have their limits, it was just as well that the interest of the Waterloo Bridge Company was enlisted to ensure the completion of the venture.

As far as the Company was concerned, their support was an act of enlightened self-interest. As late as 1878, a toll was still charged for crossing this bridge. A new theatre on its south side would mean increased traffic and profit for the Waterloo Bridge Company.

Commenting upon the assistance coming from this quarter, *The Times* remarked, '. . . as the Waterloo Bridge Company have taken an interest in completing this theatre, they should also take care that the road from their bridge be well lighted; and, still more, that the footpath, for a part of the way, be better fenced against the accidents of persons in the dark falling into the marches'.

Since Lambeth marsh then had the notorious reputation at night enjoyed today by Central Park in New York, *The Times'* indirect reference to this long-established resort of thieves and cut-throats reads like a perfect example of English euphemism. It also helps to show why a Regency gentleman who had been prevailed upon to attend the Coburg's first night in this disreputable quarter would have been amazed to learn that this was to be the nation's unofficial national theatre and that this, for thirteen years, was to be its natural and first temporary home.

Bearing in mind the Old Vic's twentieth-century reputation, it would seem appropriate that the theatre should open with *Hamlet* or at least with a gala evening of Shakespeare highlights. Bearing in mind that Drury Lane and Covent Garden theatres at that time still had exclusive rights to Shakespeare and were clearly most wary of this royally-named upstart on the opposite and unfashionable side of the river, the mixed bill that was in fact offered makes more sense.

A rummage amongst newspaper cuttings of the period reveals what was on offer. One advertises a performance on Saturday, 9 May 1818, which was evidently a dress-rehearsal for the following Monday's public opening night. For the Saturday performance, the Coburg Management invited 'the Nobility and Gentry', adding that 'Peace-officers will be in attendance'. Another and more elaborate proclamation for the public Monday evening opening reads,

ROYAL COBURG THEATRE

Under the immediate Patronage of
His Royal Highness Prince Leopold of Saxe-Coburg

'The above elegant Theatre WILL OPEN THIS EVENING, May 11, with the appropriate Address by Mr Munro. After which, a new melo-dramatic spectacle, called TRIAL BY BATTLE: or, Heaven defend the RIGHT. After which, a grand Asiatic ballet, called ALZORA and NERINE; or, the Fairy Gift. To conclude with a new and splendid harlequinade, called MIDNIGHT REV-ELRY; or, Harlequin and Comus. Lower Boxes, 4s, Upper Boxes 3s, Pit 2s, Gallery 1s. Doors to be opened at half-past 5, to begin at half past 6. Half-price at half past 8. Places to be taken of Mr Grub, at the box-office, from 10 till 4.'

A further snippet, taken from Thomas Allen's *History of Surrey* reveals that 'the stage is extensive and better fitted up than any minor house in England, in depth, from the lights to the wall it is 94 feet and in width, from stage door to stage door 34 feet. It gradually descends from the wall to the pit.'

If this is beginning to sound too technical for all but the scholarly theatre historian, it may be reassuring to know that a human dimension is given to the opening of the theatre by the backstage rows that the gala opening was to precipitate. And it is Mr Norman, billed as Clown in the Harlequinade at the close of the inaugural proceedings, that we have to thank for breathing life into what would otherwise read as a dusty record of unremembered artists appearing in unmemorable entertainments before a public whose identities can now only be guessed at.

Joseph Glossop, whose family had provided those vital funds when the theatre's completion was in danger, was now proprietor. As such he had chosen to place Mr Norman and his Harlequinade at the end of the evening. But Mr Norman insisted that it should be given first for the very practical reason that he was also engaged on the same evening to appear at Covent Garden and wished to be free to make a speedy and early departure across the new Waterloo Bridge to the more prestigious Patent Theatre. Mr Glossop, whose theatre was dubbed a Minor Theatre to distinguish it from the two privileged Patent Theatres of Drury Lane and Covent Garden, firmly disagreed. He even went to the length of having Mr Norman's Clown costume locked away.

Today Mr Norman would belong to the actor's Trade Union, Equity, and his stage management colleagues to the technical union, NATKE. And Mr Glossop would be a member of a Society like the West End Theatre Managers. Disputes of the kind that blew up between Glossop and Norman would be resolved according to strict regulations governing the conduct of employer and employees. But, in 1818, such disagreements were handled in a more free-for-all manner in which an appeal to the general public and the popularity of those concerned could resolve the outcome.

Mr Norman distributed 'bills' amongst the first-night audience explaining his grievance. The result was that when Mr Munro came forward to deliver his first-night address, Mr Norman ventured on stage too. The house was in uproar. William Barrymore, the Coburg's Acting Manager and author of the evening's new melodrama, *Trial By Battle*, endeavoured to put in a word. But both he and Munro were shouted down. For the sake of restoring order, Glossop capitulated and the Harlequinade was brought forward.

This was the first of many future battles fought at the Old Vic in the nineteenth and twentieth centuries. Though many of Glossop's successors were obliged to capitulate on far more significant matters than the pique of an artist like Mr Norman, what is important is that this Minor Theatre has survived its other south-side rivals, like Astley's and the Surrey, to have become a Major Theatre in a sense that would never have been believed or understood on that far-off opening night.

II   *The Great Melodrama Show*

When the centenary came to be celebrated in May 1974 of the birth of the most important Manager the Old Vic ever had – Lilian Baylis – the theatre was the scene for a royal Gala Evening. As narrator, Laurence Olivier read out the highlights of the Manager's life, pieced together in a series of loosely-linked cameos performed by some of the most eminent actor knights and dames of the British stage. Many of them, like John Gielgud and Peggy Ashcroft, had served their theatrical apprenticeship under that particular Manager. The key characters and determining events in her life were briefly and entertainingly laid before a nostalgic public.

Suppose that the year is 1980 and that the Old Vic is celebrating, with a similar Gala Evening, the centenary of its close as a Melodrama Theatre. Instead of outlining a single person's life, we have to devise, say, 'The Great Melodrama Show'. Such a gala presentation must somehow conjure up the many personalities whose activities shaped the Old Vic's history in the sixty-two colourful years from 1818 to 1880.

Clearly, this would be a much more difficult entertainment to put together. Instead of concentrating on the unifying factor of a single mammoth personality, we have to bring to life a number of lesser mortals. And instead of being able to weave their biographies around the presentation of the familiar classics of the Shakespeare, the opera and the ballet repertoire, we have the more difficult task of allying them to melodramatic spectacles and burlesques which have, for the most part, entirely vanished. If only the triumphs of the artists involved in nineteenth-century productions had been in works as universally known as, say, *Hamlet*, how much more easily their accomplishments could be invoked. And how much less remote they would seem.

Heaven forbid, however, that 'The Great Melodrama Show' should merely list the names of the hundreds of melodramas, farces, harlequinades and pantomimes which occupied the largest part of the first sixty-two years of the Old Vic's life. This would make for a wearying programme. And nothing could better set the seal of boredom on the evening than a blow-by-blow account of the convoluted plots of even the most successful of the melodramas. Nonetheless, these melodramas – and the army of theatrical personnel behind them – must constitute the entertainment's chief ingredient.

In the circumstances, it is pardonable to imagine the programme becoming a parody of melodrama. Its blacker-than-black villains and its whiter-than-white heroines easily lend themselves to the mockery of twentieth-century theatrical taste. So does melodrama's reliance on a veritable circus of animal performers, inspiring a popularity at least as great as that of a modern cinema audience for Tarzan and Lassie films. Indeed, so great was the Regency and early Victorian theatres' enthusiasm for live animals on stage that even Shakespeare and Shakespearean actors found themselves upstaged. A play like *Richard III*, for example, was 'equestrinised' in order that the King's horse, White Surrey, could be given top billing. In his introduction to *Eyewitnesses of Shakespeare*, Gamini Salgado remarks, 'in 1809 or thereabouts at the Royal Circus in London, a performance of *Hamlet* was given by a troupe of dogs; history does not, alas, record whether or not the leading role was taken by a Great Dane'.

This approach would make for a potentially hilarious evening. But it would miss a golden opportunity to attempt to re-write a chapter in the history of British Theatre – which has repeatedly turned up its literary nose at melodrama. The result is that, whether applied to a play or to a performance, 'melodramatic' is among the most contemptuous adjectives in the twentieth-century critic's dictionary. And this continues to be the case, in spite of the fact that since the 1960s books like Michael Booth's *English Melodrama* inaugurated a belated but informed study of the genre on its own terms.

Charles Dickens was only six when the Coburg opened in 1818 and he died in 1870, ten years before its nineteenth-century life as a theatre came to an end. Dickens, however, would probably make the ideal narrator for the Old Vic's 'Great Melodrama Show'. It is easy to think of several reasons for casting him in this role. It is not just that, like Scott, his novels were pirated for melodramatic presentation at the Coburg and other Minor Theatres. Nor is it merely that a novel of his, *Nicholas Nickleby*, actually refers to the Coburg by name. Nor is it entirely because we are deeply indebted to Dickens' other writings for a vivid impression of the Old Vic's nineteenth-century public. The over-riding consideration is that Dickens, however much he cringed at the manner in which his novels were served up on stage, could see melodrama in terms of a compassionate understanding of the public the genre catered for, rather than as 'great' drama enormously *manqué.*

The point which Dickens, as narrator, must make the gala audience immediately grasp is that melodrama was genuine folk drama. Like the cheap spirits that became widely available in the nineteenth century, it helped to anaesthetise the luckless sons and daughters of the Industrial Revolution against the squalor of their lives in the new and booming cities. It appealed directly and spontaneously to their untutored imaginations. Just as Elizabethan drama can only be truly understood *vis-à-vis* the broad spectrum of society for which much of it was written, so melodrama only begins to make sense when related to its public.

So Dickens' first task as narrator would be to rattle off as seductively as possible, a few vital statistics to explain the extraordinary changes that overtook London and transformed it from the charming eighteenth-century Georgian capital reflected in the pages of Boswell's *Life of Samuel Johnson* to the squalid vitality mirrored in *Oliver Twist*, published the year the young Victoria came to the throne in 1837.

Population figures speak for themselves. In 1800 London had eight thousand inhabitants. Two years after the Coburg opened, these had grown to one million, two hundred thousand. By 1880, when the theatre was almost auctioned off as a furniture depository, the capital's population was three million. By the close of the century this had increased to four and a half million.

Perhaps the deviser of 'The Great Melodrama Show' might be relied upon to write some pastiche Dickens, setting the opening of the Royal Coburg Theatre against the background of the relentless march of the Industrial Revolution. He would have to pay particular attention to its gathering momentum between 1750 and 1850 which was reflected in the population figures, not to mention the new bridges across the Thames that had brought the Minor Theatres on its south side into being. Perhaps Mr Pickwick and his cronies could deliberate entertainingly on the discovery of steam-power, inventions like Hargreaves' Spinning Jenny and the mining of coal to fuel the new factories and railway networks which transformed Britain from a stable agricultural and commercial society into the industrial workshop of the world. Maybe Mr Pickwick could point out that, until the year of Dickens' death in 1870, Britain provided the world with three-quarters of its coal. Dickens-lovers would recoil at so much alien dialogue being put into the mouth of one of their favourite characters – but the gala audience might more easily swallow the statistical pill that reveals the need for a melodrama theatre to provide an escape route for the lower orders of an industrial society.

What precise bearing does all this have on melodrama shown at the Royal Coburg, or, as it came to be called after 1833, the Royal Victoria Theatre? Well, the full impetus of the Industrial Revolution was very keenly felt in the immediate neighbourhood of the theatre. It transformed the rural, marshy and once patchily genteel territory that had been the setting for the Royal Coburg's opening years into a teeming throng of slum tenements. These provided homes for the immigrant labour brought in to build the new Waterloo Station, which opened in 1840. Dickens, as narrator, could at this point do nothing better than read from what he had written in 1850 under the title 'The Amusements of the People', published in *Household Words*.

Joe Whelks, of the New Cut, Lambeth, is not much of a reader, has no great store of books, no very commodious room to read in, no very decided inclination to read, and no power at all of presenting vividly before his mind's eye what he reads about. But put Joe in the gallery of the Victoria Theatre; show him doors and windows in the scene and that people can get in and out of it; tell him a story with these aids, and by the help of live men and women dressed up, confiding to him their inmost secrets, in voices audible a mile off, and Joe will unravel a story through all its entanglements and sit there as long after midnight as you have anything left to show him. Accordingly, whatever changes of fashion the drama knows elsewhere it is always fashionable in the New Cut . . . heavily taxed, wholly unassisted by the State, deserted by the gentry, and quite unrecognized as a means of public instruction, the higher English drama has declined. Those who would live to please Mr Whelks must please Mr Whelks to live. It is not the Manager's province to hold the Mirror up to Nature, but to Mr Whelks – the only person who acknowledges him.

How would Dickens' Mr Whelks react to the analysis of melodrama such as that made by a twentieth-century scholar like Michael Booth in his book *English Melodrama*? Obviously, somewhat negatively. Melodrama depended for its success on uninhibited identification, on Mr Whelks' hissing the villain, shouting warnings to the heroine, being exasperated at the unsuspecting hero's failure to foresee impending disaster, weeping with the Good Old Man and Good Old Woman whose function it was to recall the happier days of the heroine's childhood. Above all, it was Mr Whelks' total identification with the Comic Man – a humble member of society like himself – that kept him entertained when his act was performed in front of the drop cloth whilst elaborate set changes were made behind it.

Since, as Dickens remarked, Mr Whelks was not a thinking, bookish man, it would be uphill work to invent dialogue for him and the modern student of melodrama. But an attempt to include Mr Whelks and such a student in 'The Great Melodrama Show' ought to be worth the making. The melodrama student would have to crisply categorise the genre under the neat academic headings that have been devised for it. First, he would point to Gothic and Eastern Melodrama, set in gloomy castles and exotic Turkish palaces – the former made popular by the novels of Horace Walpole, 'Monk' Lewis and Anne Radcliffe. And, however unreceptive Mr Whelks might be to intellectual analysis, something would have to be added about the development of Nautical and Military Melodrama which drew initially on Britain's triumphs in the Napoleonic Wars, reflected to this day in names like Trafalgar Square and Waterloo Bridge. A reference to Domestic Melodrama in which the heroine ceased to be mewed up in Gothic Castles, Sultan's Palaces, Pirate's Caves and Smuggler's Dens would follow.

Trying not to bewilder Mr Whelks, the student would have to go into a little more detail over Domestic Melodrama, since it was a speciality of the nineteenth-century Old Vic. He would have to draw a comparison between the rural variety of Domestic Melodrama in which the heroine was the victim of the local squire and the city variety in which the same lady fell under the evil machinations of the factory owner or the urban landlord. In both, a footnote would be appended, explaining the appearance of the Demon Drink and its increasing importance in Domestic Melodrama – to the point that it spawned a further category in Temperance Melodrama.

It is hard to invent anything for Mr Whelks to say, to keep up his side of the dialogue, beyond a few unreceptive grunts. But the student would have to conclude with a few well-chosen words on the decline of melodrama reflected in the Old Vic's closing down as a Melodrama Theatre in 1880. The decay of melodrama would have to be chronicled with the arrival of a more sophisticated public who came to laugh at its absurdities rather than be thrilled by its plot or its spectacle. Its dying throes in a welter of Sensation Drama, petering out in the First World War, just as the Old Vic was beginning a new life as the Home of Shakespeare, would have to be mentioned. And, however bored Mr Whelks might now have become, an academic coda would have to be added on the way the stock characters of melodrama were matched by a rigid moral code. Though the categories of melodrama did alter over the years, the same ready-made types acted by artists specialising in one sort of role persisted. And villainy always got its just deserts and virtue always triumphed – after, of course, the maximum number of cliff-hangers.

However improbable it seems that a Mr Whelks would be prepared to sit out any such lecture, the deviser of 'The Great Melodrama Show' would be well advised to use the character for the purpose of reminiscences. It would seem natural for a Mr Whelks to recall how Astley's, with its circus ring, and the Surrey, with its tradition of presenting equestrian melodrama, had the edge over the Royal Victoria Theatre as far as sheer spectacle was concerned. Mr Whelks might remember that Sadler's Wells Theatre from 1804 once had a heyday as the home of Acquatic Melodrama when a tank connected to the New River enabled it to stage water shows culminating in *The Siege of Gibraltar* with a most realistically staged naval bombardment. This, too, was something the Royal Victoria could not rival, though it did try.

Mr Whelks would also be useful in indicating the great days of the Dumbshow at the Surrey and other Minor Theatres of London. Here, the legitimate dramas properly belonging only to the two Patent Theatres were acted out in mime and the law circumvented by supplying vital snippets of information on scrolls, often mis-spelt. A favourite burlesque of such scrolls could at this point be displayed. For example, 'Marry not the Lady Margaret. She is thy Grandmother.'

Mr Whelks would naturally express his excitement at the visual splendours of the entertainments offered at a Minor Theatre like the Royal Victoria. And the modern scholar would do well to listen. The transformation scenes, the ingenious traps, the realistic reproduction of famous 'views', all the manifold resources of the nineteenth-century stage carpenter and his workmates to beguile and thrill Mr Whelks offer in themselves a rich source of study. If the scholar is primarily concerned with dramatic literature, he will of course regret that the major literary figures of the century did not benefit from these technical ingenuities. He will be sad that Byron, Shelley, Keats, Scott and Dickens failed to write successfully for both the Patent and the Minor theatres and were only represented by proxy in the melodramas concocted from their works by play hacks.

At the moment when a scene between Mr Whelks and what might be grandiloquently called 'A Modern Student of Melodrama' had established the basic guide-lines of melodrama in general, the entertainment should move on to the Old Vic in particular. And this could hardly be done more effectively than by bringing back Dickens once more, to read a relevant extract from *London Labour and the London Poor*.

The long zig-zag staircase that leads to the pay box is crowded to suffocation at least an hour before the theatre is opened: but, on the occasion of a piece with a good number in it, the crowds will frequently collect as early as three o'clock in the afternoon. Lads stand upon the broad wooden bannisters about fifty feet from the ground, and jump on each others' backs, or adopt any expedient that they can think of to obtain a good place.

The walls of the well-staircase having a remarkably fine echo, and the wooden floor of the steps serving as a sounding board, the shouting, whistling and quarrelling of the impatient young costers is increased tenfold. If, as sometimes happens, a song with a chorus is started, the ears positively ache with the din, and when the chant has finished, it seems as though a sudden silence has fallen on the people. To the centre of the road, and all round the door, the mob is a ferment of excitement, and no sooner is the money-taker at his post than the most frightful rush takes place, everyone heaving with his shoulders at the back of the person immediately in front of him . . . to anyone unaccustomed to being pressed flat it would be impossible to enter with the mob. To see the sight in the gallery it is best to wait until the first piece is over. The ham-sandwich men and pig-trotter women will give you notice when the time is come, for with the first clatter of the descending footsteps, they commence their cries. . . .

There are few grown-up men that go to the Vic gallery. The generality of visitors are lads about twelve to three-and twenty, and though a few black-faced sweeps and white-brown dustmen may be among the throng, the gallery audience consists mainly of coster-mongers. Young girls, too, are plentiful, one third of whom now take their babies, owing to the new regulation of charging half-price for infants. At the foot of the staircase stand a group of boys begging for the return of checks, which they sell again of 1½d or 1d, according to the lateness of the hour.

At each step up the well-staircase the warmth and stench increase, until by the time one reaches the gallery doorway, a furnace-heat reaches out through the entrance that seems to force you backwards, whilst the odour positively prevents respiration. The mob on landing, standing on tiptoe and closely wedged together, resist any civil attempt at gaining a glimpse of the stage, and yet a coster lad will rush up, elbow his way into the crowd, then jump up on the shoulders of those before him, and suddenly disappear into the body of the gallery.

The gallery at the 'Vic' is one of the largest in London. It will hold from 1,500 to 2,000 people, and runs back to so great a distance that the end of it is lost in shadow, excepting where the little gas-jets, against the wall, light up the two or three faces around them. When the gallery is well packed, it is usual to see piles of boys on each others' shoulders at the back while on the partition board, dividing off the slips, lads will pitch themselves, despite the spikes.

The dance and comic songs, between the pieces, are liked better than anything else. A highland fling is certain to be repeated, and a stamping of feet will accompany the entire performance. But the grand hit of the evening is always when a song is sung to which the entire gallery can join in chorus. Then a deep silence prevails all through the stanzas. Should any burst in before his time, a shout 'ord-a-a-ar' is raised, and the intruder put down by a thousand indignant cries. At the proper time, however, the throats of the mob burst forth in all their strength . . . no delay between the pieces will be allowed, and should the interval appear too long, some one will shout out – referring to the curtain – 'pull up that there winder'.

This is certainly an impression of true folk theatre. It also paints a nightmare picture to the modern fireman, who is appointed to ensure that theatres today adhere to stringent local authority rules. Oddly enough, the Old Vic in the nineteenth century was never burned down. The irony is that when a number of people *were* killed in a stampede, it was as the result of a quite *false* fire alarm in the Royal Victoria Theatre.

Moving still further from the general to the particular, Dickens, as narrator, should begin to introduce key personalities in the fortunes of the Old Vic as a Melodrama Theatre. He could profitably beckon on to the stage half a dozen of the managers singing a chorus, to the appropriate Gilbert and Sullivan tune, *A Manager's Life is not a Happy One.* As each of the managers is given a verse to himself, he might divulge that, unlike the lady manager whose centenary was celebrated in 1974, he was not *just* a manager.

William Barrymore, the first, doubled up by stage-managing and writing melodramas, one of which, *Trial By Battle*, or *Heaven Defend the Right*, was premièred at the Coburg's opening night. George Bothwell Davidge, sole lessee and manager from 1826 to 1833 arrived at this pinnacle after a long spell as an actor, mostly in Highway Melodrama. Needless to say, he combined managing the theatre with acting in it. Mr Abbott and Mr Egerton, who began a seven-year stint of management in 1833 were also actors – from the Patent house of

Covent Garden, no less. David Webster Osbaldiston, manager from 1841 to 1848, was an actor too, and J. Arnold Cave, manager on his own, or in partnership, through the 1870s combined his job with the cobbling of suitable texts to revive the declining fortunes of the by-now aging theatre. Perhaps it is right to remember that the first two National Theatre directors at the Old Vic, Laurence Olivier and Peter Hall showed a similar versatility a century later – Olivier by acting and directing, Hall by finding time to direct films as well as becoming a television personality. *Plus ça change . . .*

To adopt the oversimplifications appropriate to melodrama, we could cast some of the managers as 'villains' and others as 'heroes'. The resoundingly named George Bothwell Davidge and David Webster Osbaldiston provide at least some basis from which to play double-dyed villains. And Messrs Abbott and Egerton have the best grounds for being allocated the parts of high-minded managerial heroes.

Fifteen years after its first opening in 1818, Messrs Abbott and Egerton made a decided bid to attract the attention of the same gentry and discerning public that the Old Vic's first proprietor, Joseph Glossop, had sought at the beginning of the Royal Coburg days. And, like Glossop, they made this attempt through royal patronage – in spite of the decline in the theatre and the neighbourhood in the intervening years. When Abbott and Egerton took over the management in 1833 they issued the following announcement:

> Having become Lessess of the above Theatre (we) very respectfully announce to the public that Her Royal Highness, the Duchess of Kent, has been graciously pleased to take the theatre under Her Royal Highness' immediate protection for the encouragement of NATIVE DRAMATIC TALENT, and to command that in future it shall be called THE ROYAL VICTORIA.

The enterprising couple had had the theatre redecorated and a new stage installed. Through their intervention, Waterloo Bridge was to be toll-free to patrons of the theatre and the managers arranged that two omnibuses should arrive to coincide with the 6 pm opening and with the half-price admission at 8.15 pm. Instead of employing only play hacks as house dramatists, they secured the services of Sheridan

Knowles, the respected actor/dramatist, author of *Virginius* and friend of Hazlitt and Lamb.

It was perhaps unfortunate that the two managers' first presentation should be *The King's Fool*, or *The Old Man's Curse!!!*. Although billed by a Mr Millington, it was hardly a work of native talent, being in fact an adaptation of Hugo's *Le roi s'amuse*, better known to modern audiences as the libretto for Verdi's *Rigoletto*. And when, in November 1833, the new managers secured a visit from Princess Victoria, daughter of their patron, the fourteen-year-old heiress to the throne after whom the theatre had been renamed, also saw little new of 'native talent'. The royal party was offered a stage version of *Guy Mannering*, and *Gustavus the Third*, or *The Masked Ball* – based not on Verdi's *Ballo in maschera* (which had still to be written) but on the earlier Auber/Scribe opera.

Further prestige was brought to the revamped theatre when another programme of interest to the musical historian came to be presented. Anticipating Dame Nellie Melba in the twentieth century, Paganini gave his farewell to the people at the Old Vic under the management of Messrs Abbott and Egerton.

These two high-mindedly attempted to improve the appearance of the building, its tone, its public and the quality of the mixed-bag of entertainments on offer. The reverse can be said both of George Bothwell Davidge (whose seven-year management preceded the Abbott-Egerton venture) and David Webster Osbaldiston (whose seven-year stint began immediately after our heroes' exploits came to a premature end).

If Davidge and Osbaldiston are to be cast as the managerial 'villains' of the Old Vic, in what way were they evil-doers? And, assuming that they would prefer to defend themselves rather than revel in their villainy, how are they to win 'bravos' rather than 'hisses'? Both could point to a certain amount of courage in their buccaneering ventures. They could, for example, claim with some reason to have the measure of the Old Vic's nineteenth-century public more realistically taped than Abbott and Egerton. The latter came to grief within a year and both died broken and poor men because they imagined they could successfully re-style the theatre along lines of gentility, intelligence and good breeding.

Davidge and Osbaldiston, however, recognized that this playhouse stood in the middle of one of London's roughest and most squalid neighbourhoods. Its only hope of survival lay in giving a tough local public theatrical goods that had no pretensions of passing over their heads. On the positive side, Davidge could point out that he had secured the services for two weeks of the Shakespeare superstar, Edmund Kean. And Osbaldiston, for his part, might add that his regime had inaugurated a house policy that was at least consistent in that the theatre became known as the home of domestic melodrama (more properly melodramas of domestics) like *Susan Hopley,* or *The Vicissitudes of a Servant Girl* and *Mary Clifford, the Foundling Apprentice Girl* in which the Vic's local star (and briefly later one of its lady managers), Eliza Vincent, brought tears to the eyes of the coster lads crammed into the gods.

If Abbott and Egerton paid the price of penury for their idealism, Davidge's rough and ready dealings resulted in his dying with a fortune of twenty-seven thousand pounds to bequeath. As manager at various times both of the Coburg and of its rivals, Astley's and the Surrey, he had no illusions about the public he had to cater for. He had been present in the early days of the Coburg when the theatre had the temerity to attract a fashionable public from across the river with a pageant on the life of George III, *George III, the Father of his People.* An early indication of the incompatibility of the local public and the fashionable one made itself evident during the run of this epic. The local costers amused themselves by emptying bottles on the assembled gentry below. Davidge's villainy, if thus it was, lay in accelerating the decline in the theatre's public by too readily cutting his managerial coat according to the available public cloth. To line his own pockets to the handsome tune of five thousand pounds a year, he instituted 'the shilling order system' at the Coburg. It was a means of bringing in a large audience dirt cheap. And it brought in a dirty public. One commentator remarked that 'dustmen, chimney-sweeps and greasy butchers are too much in evidence'.

Osbaldiston, in similarly accommodating the worst tastes in the theatre's vicinity, brought upon his head even harsher criticism. Charles Kingsley, in a frequently-quoted comment, described the Vic as 'a licensed pit of darkness, a trap of temptation, profligacy and ruin, triumphantly yawning night after night'. And two incidents greatly detract from the homely image of the domestic melodrama that Osbaldiston righteously cultivated, when he declared 'what is nearest to the Heart, touches us most, the Passions rise higher at Domestic than Imperial Tragedies'.

Passions certainly ran high when Osbaldiston issued his staff with seats for which, however, he charged. If his employees demurred at paying up for the favours bestowed upon them, Osbaldiston deducted the price of the 'cards' from their wages. In 1846 a comic, Thomas Fredericks, absolutely declined to pay for his 'comp' card and was sued by the Manager in the Southwark Borough Court of Request for three pounds. At the hearing, Fredericks claimed, though he lost the case, that he 'considered it as a privilege as a performer. He had been seven or eight years connected with theatricals, and always had the privilege presented him by the managers. There was no theatre in London, where the managers exhorted payment.' So it would appear Osbaldiston was even more mean than Davidge. The latter's reputation for avarice was so great, one of his former writer employees expressed waggish surprise at Davidge's dying in the early part of the evening, 'before the half-price comes in'.

A second court incident occurred during Osbaldiston's management. And it was the manager's turn, in 1847, to be convicted and charged twenty shillings for selling spirits without a licence. The real reason for the fine, however, was more complicated. In February 1847, the Lord Chamberlain circularised London managers concerning the fact that theatre saloons were admitting prostitutes free to round up their clients. Osbaldiston's fine was in fact a warning for promoting, on his premises, the oldest profession in the world.

In the light of these known facts, Osbaldiston's long-winded playbills positively radiate hypocrisy. On one of them he boasts of 'one of those Beautiful Domestic Dramas for which this Theatre has already, under the present Management, become so universally and extensively celebrated' and follows with a tribute to his Company, 'so peculiarly pre-eminent in the Representation of those Affecting Scenes of Real Life, which come so closely and so touchingly home to the Hearts of all'. Perhaps 'tarts and all' would have been nearer the mark.

At this point, Dickens should probably round off the managers' section by introducing a short dialogue between the first of them, William Barrymore and the last, J. Arnold Cave. A link does exist between them that must be seized upon. Cave chose to revive, in the early 1870s, *Trial by Battle*, the melodrama Barrymore had concocted for the theatre's first night. It was a sprawling piece not fitting the tidy categories drawn up by the twentieth-century student.

In as far as its villain, Baron Falconbridge, comes down from his castle to abduct the village maiden, it would seem to be heading in the direction of Gothic Melodrama. But the Baron is aided by a gang of smugglers (one of whom turns out to be a virtuous sailor), so the plot veers off towards Nautical Melodrama. Later, when it drew on a then contemporary attempt to revive a medieval law to settle a recent murder verdict, it anticipated later melodrama writers who eagerly seized on true life Jack-the-Ripper-type sensations on to which base blood-curdling theatrical spectacles.

The trouble with *Trial by Battle* was that however well it went on the theatre's first night in 1818, it had dated beyond acceptance by the 1870s. Old Vic habitués had, in the intervening years, become so accustomed to a miscellany of Sweeny Todd horrors that Barrymore's plot was much too tame and its highlight of a 'combat of six' was not nearly spectacular enough. An ideal cue, one might think, for Barrymore and Cave to swap impressions on the changing fortunes of melodrama at the nineteenth-century Old Vic – for the benefit of spectators of 'The Great Melodrama Show'.

A good many of them would no doubt welcome an interval at this point. It would be an excellent idea. In this way the second half of the programme could be devoted, separately, to Melodrama at the Old Vic from the standpoint of those who appeared in it, not to mention from that of those whose job it was to write the shows . . .

As w⁚ ⸴ the managers, a few artists would have to represent the many hundreds who performed at or wrote for the Old Vic in its first sixty-two years. And, if an introductory chorus has to be devised for them, it should make the point that they were not 'merely players'. Four actors – T. P. Cooke, Thomas Cobham, 'Bravo' Hicks and Eliza Vincent – would be the ideal choice to represent the silent majority of forgotten actors since these four were as much 'name' artists at the nineteenth-century Old Vic as Laurence Olivier, Albert Finney, Michael Crawford and Glenda Jackson are with a 1970s London public.

So it would be up to Cooke, Cobham, Hicks and Vincent to make the immediate point that their services at the Royal Victoria Theatre demanded the maximum versatility. In a single evening, they might be called upon to dance a highland fling and appear in a lead role of a melodrama, as well as a version of a Shakespeare play. And then they might have to earn their fee by rounding off the evening in a short farce. 'Jack of all trades and master of all' sums them up appropriately.

Of the four, T. P. Cooke is the most immediately captivating. Just as Edith Evans in the twentieth century came to be identified with the part of Lady Bracknell in Wilde's *The Importance of Being Earnest*, so T. P. Cooke, a hundred years before, was as closely associated with the part he created in the most famous of Nautical Melodramas – William, the sailor hero of Douglas Jerrold's *Black Ey'd Susan*. The difference was that whereas Edith Evans' childhood and adolescence were not those of the milieu of a Lady Bracknell, T. P. Cooke's was essentially that of a boy seafarer. Born in 1769, he claimed to have served as an eleven-year-old apprentice when Rodney defeated the Spanish off Cape St Vincent and later to have been present at the naval blockade off Brest.

Cooke certainly cultivated his nautical image as sedulously as a pop star in the 1970s plugs his own special gimmick and his latest album. The result was that Cooke was obliged to dance the hornpipe at a performance of Shakespeare. He was appearing in *Julius Caesar*, but there was no question of proceeding to the Forum and the assassination of Caesar until Cooke had given the house a chance to applaud his dancing a hornpipe. Remembering Churchill in the 1940s with his cigar and his V-sign makes it easier to appreciate the heady patriotism to which Cooke appealed – at a time when Britain took immense pride in her naval might.

Cooke was certainly versatile: from his role in the Vampire Melodrama shaped from Mary Shelley's *Frankenstein*, to his sympathetic playing of the sentimental William, in *Black Ey'd Susan* would strikingly illustrate the scope of Mr Cooke's talents in being able to switch from villain to hero. And, of course, he could hardly be allowed to leave the stage without a hornpipe, whether still dressed as a Jack Tar or Blood-Sucking Vampire.

Thomas Cobham should be introduced next as the apotheosis of the popular 'local' star. Unlike Cooke whose acting in *Frankenstein* was seen on both sides of the Thames as well as in Paris, Cobham excited feelings of neighbourhood pride. In looks he resembled the Number One star of the era, Edmund Kean. And he had the privilege of playing opposite this fiery genius when Kean ventured across the river for the week-long engagement on which occasion Coburg audiences unwisely overdid their appreciation of the local boy at the expense of the visiting celebrity. Cobham should certainly be allowed to let an extract from his Iago to Kean's Othello form a part of his contribution to 'The Great Melodrama Show'. Other extracts from his Shakespeare repertoire should also be included, for they would illustrate how rudely the Bard was chopped up to accommodate the needs of a Melodrama Theatre. The Shylock that he played was called, *The Three Caskets* or *The Jew of Venice* and billed as a 'new tragic comic melodrama founded on a most popular drama'. That should make interesting viewing, so should Cobham's Hamlet, a happy-ever-afterwards version with the Prince of Denmark reunited in nuptial bliss with Ophelia.

Cobham would be a good choice, too, for some account of the Old Vic's nineteenth-century audiences. He had a very wide experience to draw upon and could easily distinguish between two fundamental groups: the first who arrived at 6 pm and paid full admission and the second, rolling in for half-price at 8.15 pm. The second lot were by far the more extrovert and were famous for their impatience at long speeches. They liked the maximum of action and the minimum of rhetoric. An indication of the sort of action they were given could be provided with Cobham's appearance in scenes from Almar's *Wake Not the Dead* or *The Spectre Bride*. Disregarding the injunction of the play's title, Cobham appears as a nobleman who resorts to a sorcerer to summon up from the shades the bride on whom he still dotes. When first performed at the Old Vic, the management announced, with a touch of pride, that this presentation 'wished to gratify an Inflexion of Public Inclination' and added that it was 'confident that in strength of horrific effect, it transcends its predecessors'. Such a revival would certainly provide an opportunity for modern stagecraft to attempt to recreate the spooky effects so resourcefully conjured up by the more primitive nineteenth-century stage carpenter and stage lighting man.

Audience participation was an essential part of melodrama. Mr Hicks, the next contributor to 'The Great Melodrama Show', got his nickname of 'Bravo' precisely because he specialised in daring 'bravo' parts like smugglers and brigands. His *pièce de résistance* was in *Wizard of the Wave* or *The Ship of the Avenger*. In it, 'Bravo' Hicks played both the hero *and* the villain. By means of a series of quick changes, he switched from the part of the pirate smuggler to his twin brother, the naval officer, bent on the villain's destruction. In order that a modern audience might have some idea of the sheer spectacle involved, the following original stage directions, however expensive, should be reproduced.

> The villain expires on the deck of his ship, with the usual bid for sympathy – kissing his mother's portrait and hoping that it will not be noised abroad that the hero's brother (himself) was a pirate. The ship blows up and his blackened corpse is seen amid the flames. Then, in front of this, an immense fully-rigged schooner floats forward, the Hero conspicuous on the bows and the rest of the cast swarming aboard from boats.

'Bravo', Mr Hicks! And 'Bravo' to those nineteenth-century stage technicians who rendered such directions capable of realistic presentation.

Finally, representing so many other actresses of the period, the narrator must now introduce Miss Eliza Vincent. Her first traceable connection with the Old Vic dates from its Royal Coburg days when, in 1823, she was billed as 'Miss Vincent (the Infant Roscius), eight years of age, will recite *The Seven Ages of Woman*'.

By the time she had reached her late thirties, she had become manager of the theatre – one of a number of short-term managements. In the archives of the Old Vic there remains a letter of hers in a fine neat hand. It reads,

> Victoria Theatre Dec 14th, 1852, Sir, In reply to your note, I beg to say I will let you my theatre on one night, about the middle of Feb next. The Terms Tuesday £40, Wednesday 35, Thursday 32, Friday 30, Saturday 32. Yr obd Serv Eliza Vincent.

The highlight of Miss Vincent's career at the Royal Victoria was in the 1840s, before she could call it 'my' theatre but when she was the heroine of domestic melodramas presented under Osbaldiston's management. She appeared in a melodramatised version of *Martin Chuzzlewit* and *Oliver Twist*, in which the murder of Nancy was a great favourite with Old Vic audiences. Its traditional manner of presentation has been described (by E. F. Saville who played Sikes) as follows:

> Nancy was always dragged round the stage by her hair, after which Sikes always looked defiantly up at the gallery, and being answered by a loud and fearful curse, dragged her twice more round the stage. Then finally, having worked up to his climax (the yells becoming louder and more blasphemous), Nancy was smeared with red ochre, Sikes seeming to dash her brains out on the stage. Then no language could convey the outburst: a roar deafened the audience, with threats to tear sanguinary entrails from the villain's sanguinary body; and almost immediately the smiling ruffian came forward to make his bow.

That is a 'must' for Miss Vincent – even if Dickens, present at a performance of *Oliver Twist*, is reported to have laid himself flat on the floor of his box and refused to see this scene out.

Miss Vincent could also figure in an extract from one of the domestic melodramas she made famous under Osbaldiston's management. The best choice, here, would be from *Susan Hopley* or *The Vicissitudes of a Servant Girl*. The particular 'vicissitudes' could be illustrated by the 'vision' scene in which Susan sees the murder of her boss and of her brother. Another might be the one in which the ghost of Susan's brother helpfully reappears to direct the girl (and the Law) to the real assassins.

Finally, Miss Vincent should be called upon to revive Osbaldiston's last traceable presentation at the Vic. Given on 31 January 1848, it was billed as 'First Time, an entirely New Drama (in Four Acts) founded on the celebrated work of the same name, by Currery Bell, Esq. and now engaging the attention of all readers, to be entitled JANE EYRE. Like the many other readers who came across this novel when it was first published in the summer of 1847, Osbaldiston was unaware that the author's true identity was Charlotte Brontë.

During her term of management, Miss Vincent revived *El Hyder, Chief of the Ghaut Mountains.* Its cast included 'A splendidly Caparisoned Elephant'. Indeed a veritable zoo of performing animals featured in Old Vic Melodrama.

In its early years as the Coburg, the theatre was competing not only with the Surrey but also with nearby Astley's which was as much a circus as a theatre. Dogs were especial favourites and 'The Great Melodrama Show' would not be complete without some scenes from *The Dog Montargis* or *The Forest Bondy* starring Dog Bruin. This dog detective was trained to ring a doorbell to arouse the alarm. And he was also trained to 'take the seize' – theatrical terminology of the period which meant that the dog gnashed his way to the villain's throat by removing a fleshy-looking and red-stained flannel wrapped round the throat of the unfortunate actor down to impersonate the villain.

Our animal section would naturally also have to include horses, since the most famous of Equestrian Melodramas, *Mazeppa*, had its première at the Coburg in the autumn of 1823. At its first performance 'the impetuous range of the Wild Horse over the extensive platforms was admitted to be striking and unique'.

Writers of melodramas come both last and least in our story. Before introducing a couple to represent the body of those who kept the Old Vic's nineteenth-century playbills filled, Dickens might first regale 'The Great Melodrama Show's' public with a selection of 'views'. It would further accentuate his known contempt for peddlars of melodrama scripts. And these 'views' help to draw attention to the fact that Melodrama relied a good deal more on its visual than on its literary appeal. Nothing, in fact, delighted a nineteenth-century public more than to see the reproduction on stage of familiar paintings, prints and illustrations from books. The story of a melodrama was indeed frequently re-hashed to allow their introduction.

A good opening for the 'Views' section would be some scenes from *Life in London* or *Tom and Jerry* which conscientiously reproduced George and Robert Cruickshank's illustrations to the novel by Egan from which the melodrama had been wrenched. Another favourite was Wilkie's print 'Reading the will' which could be accommodated into a surprising number of melodramas. But probably the most striking contribution, to conclude this section of 'The Great Melodrama Show', would be the recreation of 'The Grand Pictorial Display of the Burning of the Houses of Parliament'. This was staged at the Royal Victoria Theatre in October 1834, only two weeks after the disaster had overtaken the Houses of Parliament across the river. In the 1970s the real thing would be instantly available on everybody's television screen. In the 1830s it took a little longer to get to the stage. But it's hard to think a blasé, horror-fed audience of television doom-watchers would not find a stage reproduction considerably more exciting.

It would, perhaps, have been embarrassing for Dickens to introduce the Old Vic's melodrama hacks. His attitude towards them is made clear in *Nicholas Nickleby* in the following passage where Nicholas has just made the acquaintance of Mr Crummles and is on the point of joining his troupe on its forthcoming engagement in Portsmouth.

'You can be useful to us in a hundred ways', said Mr Crummles. 'Think what capital bills a man of your education could write for the shop windows'.

'Well, I think I could manage that department' said Nicholas.

'To be sure you could', replied Mr Crummles . . . 'Pieces, too; why you could write us a piece to bring out the whole strength of the company, whenever we wanted one.'

'I am not quite so confident about that', replied Nicholas. 'But I dare say I could scribble something now and then, that would suit you.'

'We'll have a new show-piece out directly', said the manager. 'Let me see – peculiar resources of this establishment – new and splendid scenery – you must manage to introduce a real pump and two washing-tubs.'

'Into the piece?' said Nicholas.

'Yes', replied the manager. 'I bought 'em cheap at a sale the other day, and they'll come in admirably. That's the London play. They look up some dresses, and properties and have a piece written to fit 'em. Most of the theatres keep an author on purpose.'

'Indeed!' cried Nicholas.

'Oh yes', said the manager, 'a common thing. It'll look very well in the bills in separate lines – a real pump! Great attraction!'

Apart from drawing attention to the loving care which the managers of the period took over the playbills announcing their forthcoming attractions, this passage illustrates the managerial attitude towards their house dramatists. Far from being regarded as artists, they were very obviously utility men whose writings were not only at the beck and call of the particular resources of the company, but of the props and sets that they happened to have acquired. Both as the Royal Coburg and the Royal Victoria, the Old Vic did indeed keep an author, as Mr Crummles put it, 'on purpose'. In 'The Great Melodrama Show' the author would be represented by Mr Douglas Jerrold and Mr William Moncrieff.

But before these hard-working play devisers are brought on, Dickens' keenest thrust at their calling should be recited. It would then fall to the two to defend their occupation. In the relevant passage of *Nicholas Nickleby*, Nicholas, having gained a little experience in providing Mr Crummles' troupe with scripts, remarks, 'If I were a writer of books and you a thirsty dramatist, I would rather pay your tavern score for six months – large as it may be – than have a niche in the Temple of Fame with you for the humblest corner of my pedestal.'

Messrs Jerrold and Moncrieff's main line of defence would have to be that, as play devisers for the Coburg and other Minor Theatres, they worked very hard indeed for very little money. Sometimes they were called upon to be responsible for an entire evening's entertainment. This involved a bewildering miscellany of works – a melodrama, a Shakespeare adaptation and a short farce or burlesque just for good measure. The couple, on behalf of many other scribblers who toiled for the Coburg, or the Royal Victoria as it became, would be obliged to point out that no effective system of royalty payment safeguarded their labours. Managers, buccaneering in spirit like Davidge, often took great risks with the work of their dramatists. But if a smash hit was the outcome, it was the management and not the dramatist who benefited. None of the Coburg's house dramatists left a sum anywhere near the twenty seven thousand pounds that Davidge had managed to acquire.

The classic example of the unfairness of paying a house dramatist an outright fee, as opposed to the royalty system is provided by Tom Taylor and his *The Ticket-of-Leave Man*. For his play, Mr Taylor received an outright fee of two hundred pounds for a script that turned out to be so popular in the late nineteenth century it could be described as *The Mousetrap* of its day, in popularity if not content. By 1860 the iniquities of the fee-payment system had become so evident that Dion Boucicault had successfully managed to pioneer the royalty system. This meant that his *The Colleen Bawn,* was to net him a cool ten thousand pounds compared to Mr Taylor's mere two hundred pounds.

Unfortunately for Messrs Jerrold and Moncrieff, the Copyright Bill of 1832 only gave limited protection to plays written after 1833 and must be seen more as a milestone towards the goal achieved by Boucicault than an effective safeguard in itself.

Douglas Jerrold was the Coburg's house-dramatist in 1825 at the age of twenty-two. He would undoubtedly make a good case for the theatrical calling so despised by Dickens. Having served as a midshipman from the age of ten, Jerrold had as much practical experience, when writing the Nautical Melodrama, *Black Ey'd Susan* as the actor T. P. Cooke who made such a success in it. What is curious is that so wily a manager as Davidge should allow this long-surviving hit to be written at the Coburg but to be premièred at the rival Surrey Theatre. Since Jerrold thought Davidge the meannest man alive, it is clear that there was no very warm relationship between manager and house-dramatist. Jerrold, who worked on alternate weeks for the Coburg, was also writing for Sadler's Wells as well as being involved in journalism. He might well rebutt the slur cast on his calling in *Nicholas Nickleby* by pointing out how hard a writer of melodrama programmes had to work in order to make a living. He could also point out that whilst Dickens' novels were written in as many months as the author found necessary, a writer of melodrama was obliged to run up a script in a matter of hours to suit everybody's convenience except his own.

At least Moncrieff seems to have got on better terms with Davidge at the Coburg than Jerrold. There is a sense of fun shared by writer and actor-manager when Davidge directed and appeared in Moncrieff's *The Napoleon of Humble Life* or *Gypsy Jack.* This was a burlesque of a spectacle presented at Covent Garden which idolised Napoleon. In the Moncrieff version, Davidge, as Gypsy Jack, 'appeared in costumes which were a travesty of the various historical portraits of Napoleon'.

Let's round off with the words used by Jerrold to define melodrama for a Royal Commission set up to investigate the stage of nineteenth-century theatre. In Jerrold's words, 'a melodrama is a play having a great many telling situations with a physical rather than a mental appeal'. How tactful.

And what better way to end 'The Great Melodrama Show' than to project the famous Penny Plain, Tuppence Coloured Toy Theatre illustrations of melodramas which were once so well-known to our great-great-grandfathers but which today are almost entirely forgotten.

MR HICKS, AS ROBERT MACAIRE.

London Pub by J. REDINGTON, 208, Hoxton Old Town & sold by J. WEBB, 78, Brick Lane St Luke

Mr Hicks as Robert Macaire – tuppence coloured.

An Old Vic 'Green Leaflet' for the Old Vic and
Sadler's Wells, autumn 1931.

THE OLD VIC — SADLERS WELLS

The Old Vic.
Telephone:
HOP 3424
and 3425
Box Office
Open 10a.m.
to 10 p.m.

THE OLD VIC
WATERLOO ROAD, S.E.1
Founded by Emma Cons, 1880.

SADLERS WELLS
ROSEBERY AVENUE, E.C.1
Founded 1683. Re-opened 1931.

Sadlers Wells.
Telephone:
Clerkenwell
1121, 1122.
Box Office
open 10 a.m.
to 10 p.m.

Lessee and Manager of both Theatres: LILIAN BAYLIS, C.H., M.A. Oxon. (Hon.)

Conductors: AYLMER BUESST, LAWRANCE COLLINGWOOD,
CHARLES CORRI, CONSTANT LAMBERT and PERCY PITT.

Producer of Plays: HARCOURT WILLIAMS. Producer of Operas: SYDNEY RUSSELL.
Musical Director for Plays: HERBERT MENGES. Leader of Orchestra: VERNON CORRI.
Choreographist and Prima Ballerina: NINETTE DE VALOIS.

SEASON 1931-2

The Old Vic	Sadlers Wells.
Nightly (except Tuesdays)	Nightly (except Mondays).
PLAY MATINEES, WEDNESDAYS & SATURDAYS	PLAY MATINEES, THURSDAYS & SATURDAYS
OPERA MATINEES SATURDAYS ONLY	OPERA MATINEES SATURDAYS ONLY

The Old Vic

Mon., Sept. 14, 7.45. Opening Night of Opera Season, SAMSON AND DELILAH [Saint Saens]. 1st time by Vic-Wells Company.
Tues., 15, closed.
Wed., 16, 7.45. THE MAGIC FLUTE (Mozart).
Thurs., 17, 7.45. CARMEN (Bizet).
Fri., 18, 7.45. IL TROVATORE (Verdi).
Sat., 19, 2.50. THE MAGIC FLUTE (Mozart)
Sat., 19, 7.45. THE BOHEMIAN GIRL (Balfe).

Mon., Sept. 21, 7.45. RIGOLETTO (Verdi).
Tues., 22, 7.45. NIGHT OF BALLET.
Wed., 23, 7.45. SAMSON AND DELILAH.
Thurs., 24, 7.45. LOHENGRIN (Wagner).
Fri., 25, 7.45. THE MAGIC FLUTE (Mozart).
Sat., 26, 2.30. THE MARRIAGE OF FIGARO.
Sat., 26, 7.45. RIGOLETTO.

Mon., Sept. 28, 7.45.
Tues., 29 closed.
Wed., 30, 2.30.
Wed., 30, 7.45.
Thurs., Oct. 1, 7.45. } KING JOHN.
Fri., 2, 7.30.
Sat., 3, 2.30.
Sat., 3, 7.45.

Mon., Oct. 5, 7.45.
Tues., 6, closed.
Wed., 7, 2.30.
Wed., 7, 7.45.
Thurs., 8, 7.45. } KING JOHN.
Fri., 9, 7.45.
Sat., 10, 2.30.
Sat., 10, 7.45.

Mon., Oct. 12, 7.45. LA TRAVIATA (Verdi).
Tues., 13, closed.
Wed., 14, 7.45. MADAM BUTTERFLY (Puccini).
Thurs., 15, 7.45. THE BOHEMIAN GIRL.
Fri., 16, 7.45. } RIGOLETTO.
Sat., 17, 2.30.
Sat., 17, 7.45. CARMEN.

Mon., Oct. 19, 7.45. CAV. RUSTICANA and PAGLIACCI.
Tues., 20, 7.45. ASSOCIATION LECTURE on FOLK DANCING, by Douglas Kennedy, with Demonstration.
Wed., 21, 7.45. CARMEN.
Thurs., 22, 7.45. FAUST.
Fri., 23, 7.45. LA TRAVIATA.
Sat., 24, 2.30. BALLET.
Sat., 24, 7.45. MARITANA (Wallace).

Sadlers Wells.

Tues., Sept. 15, 7.45. Opening Night of Shakespeare Season.
Wed., 16, 7.45.
Thurs., 17, 2.30.
Thurs., 17, 7.45. } KING JOHN
Fri., 18, 7.45.
Sat., 19, 2.50.
Sat., 19, 7.45.

Mon., Sept. 21, closed.
Tues., 22, 7.45.
Wed., 23, 7.45.
Thurs., 24, 2.30. } KING JOHN
Fri., 25, 7.45.
Sat., 26, 2.30.
Sat., 26, 7.45.

Mon., Sept. 28, closed.
Tues., 29, 7.45. SAMSON AND DELILAH.
Wed., 30, 7.45. CARMEN.
Thurs., Oct. 1, 7.45. THE MARRIAGE OF FIGARO.
Fri., 2, 7.45. CAV. RUSTICANA and PAGLIACCI.
Sat., 3, 2.30.
Sat., 3, 7.45. SAMSON AND DELILAH.

Mon., Oct. 5, closed.
Tues., 6, 7.45. RIGOLETTO.
Wed., 7, 7.45. NIGHT OF BALLET.
Thurs., 8, 7.45. SAMSON AND DELILAH.
Fri., 9, 7.45. RIGOLETTO.
Sat., 10, 2.30. MARRIAGE OF FIGARO.
Sat., 10, 7.45. IL TROVATORE (Verdi).

Mon., Oct. 12, closed.
Tues., 13, 7.45.
Wed., 14, 7.45.
Thurs., 15, 2.30. } The Taming of the Shrew
Fri., 16, 7.45.
Sat., 17, 2.30.
Sat., 17, 7.45.

Mon., Oct. 19, closed.
Tues., 20, 7.45.
Wed., 21, 7.45.
Thurs., 22, 2.30. } The Taming of the Shrew
Fri., 23, 7.45.
Sat., 24, 2.30.
Sat., 24, 7.45.

THIS PROGRAMME IS SUBJECT TO ALTERATION. SEE OVERLEAF
The general public will be admitted to Association Lectures on payment of 6d.
The Vic can be hired on Tuesday and the Wells on Monday nights, unless a performance is announced

Copy of a letter dated 1852 from Eliza Vincent,
Old Vic Manager and former melodrama actress.

The Royal Coburg Theatre (Old Vic) in 1826.

Admittance passes for the Royal Coburg and
Royal Victoria theatres dated 1829 and 1860.

T. P. Cooke in *The Pilot*.

A scene from *The Lear of Private Life*.

An 1834 programme mentioning *Looking Glass Curtain*.

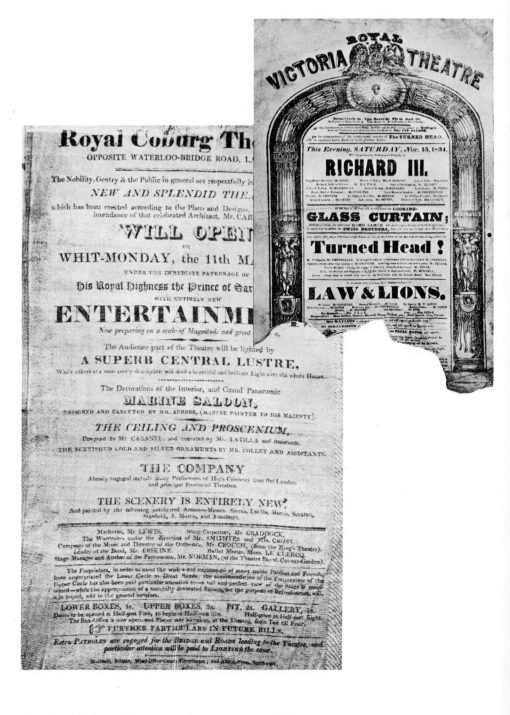

The Royal Coburg Theatre opening programme, 1818.

The Royal Coburg Theatre on its opening night in 1818.

Miss Vincent as 'Infant Roscius'.

Miſs Vincent as Goſsamer.

Paganini.

III   *Nineteenth-Century Shakespeare*

When the Old Vic Shakespeare Company was first formed during the First World War years of 1914-1918, it fell to the Company's leading lady, Sybil Thorndike, to play a number of male roles. Able-bodied men being rather more urgently needed on the battle fronts than on the stage, the shortage of actors was then understandably acute. No learned Elizabethan scholar need make the obvious comment that when Sybil Thorndike gallantly came to the rescue in her breeches parts, a Tudor wheel had turned full circle. For it is a matter of common knowledge that in Shakespeare's day the boys created the women's roles and male lips first mouthed the passions of a Juliet, Rosalind, Beatrice, Cressida, Ophelia and the rest.

Some learned recollections might, however, be welcomed in jogging wayward memories on the matter of rivalry between the adult Elizabethan players who appeared on the common stages and the boy players who graced the privileged court and private côterie theatres. The ferocity of this rivalry – and Shakespeare's own attitude towards it – is usually measured by the relevant passages of *Hamlet.* Especially to the point are Rosencrantz's scathing remarks to the Prince of Denmark about an 'aeary of children, little eyases, that cry out on the top of question, and are most tyrannically clapped for 't; these are now the fashion, and so berattle the common stages – so they call them – that many wearing rapiers are afraid of goose-quills and dare scarce come thither'.

This 'War of the Theatres' – as it was called when at its height from 1599 to 1602 – had of course long been over by the time the Royal Coburg Theatre came to open its doors in 1818. A whole galaxy of women players – from Elizabeth Barry and Nell Gwynn to Sarah

Siddons and Peg Woffington – had been and gone, consigning the Elizabethan and Jacobean boy players to oblivion. In Peg Woffington's case, Sybil Thorndike's heroic war-time endeavours at the Old Vic had even been anticipated when la Woffington numbered amongst her major successes Sir Harry Wildair in Farquhar's *The Constant Couple.*

But there remained a different War of the Theatres that had begun in 1660 and went rumbling on until 1843. It was the one resulting from the fact that Charles II, on his restoration to the throne, had, as I have mentioned in the two previous chapters, short-sightedly given two companies the exclusive right to stage Shakespeare and indeed all 'legitimate' drama. The fortunate Drury Lane and Covent Garden Theatres housing these privileged troupes had been dubbed the 'Patent Theatres' and upstarts like the Royal Coburg had to settle for being labelled 'Minor Theatres'. So the pre-Restoration rivalry between adult and children's companies had been succeeded by a post-Restoration struggle between Patent and Minor theatres. Royal Coburg Shakespeare has, therefore, to be seen very largely in the context of the battle between the Minor Theatres and Drury Lane and Covent Garden.

And yet the story of nineteenth-century Shakespeare is not merely the chronicle of freeing the plays from the stranglehold of the Patent Theatres. It is also an account of attempts to restore the texts to something approaching their original state. The date of the opening of the Coburg, 1818, is also the year in which Dr Thomas Bowdler published his ten-volume *Family Shakespeare*, in which the rude words had been softened or eradicated to spare the modest blushes of a 'family' reader. The good doctor's efforts now, however, make tame reading compared to the wholesale emendations of Restoration dramatists like Sir William Davenant and Nahum Tate whose travesties of the original texts were still very much part of Shakespeare production in the first half of the nineteenth century.

In view of the Old Vic's twentieth-century reputation with Shakespeare, it is unfortunate that, in the nineteenth century, the theatre was bold in its confrontation with the Patent Theatre but laggardly in leading the way in the reform of debased texts. Happy-ever-after Hamlets, sentimentalised King Lears and generally mutilated texts were the very stuff of Shakespeare revivals at the Royal Coburg.

Four years before the Coburg opened – on January 26, 1814 to be exact – Edmund Kean became an overnight star at Drury Lane as a result of his innovatory playing of Shylock. From then until his death in 1833, this fiery colossus was to dominate the stage of his time. And, although he only had a single, two-week engagement at the Coburg, he was to bestride any account of the theatre's presentation of Shakespeare. For it was in presenting an actor, unkindly but not altogether inaccurately, called the poor man's Kean, that the Coburg first challenged the monopoly of the Patent Theatres. Junius Brutus Booth was the actor and his engagement at the Coburg lasted from December 1819 to January 1820. Kean's own appearance at the Coburg marked, of course, the highlight of its nineteenth-century Shakespeare history. The later appearances of Kean's rival, William Charles Macready and of Kean's remarkable successor, Samuel Phelps, added some sort of coda to this great occasion with their single appearances in what would today be called charity gala performances.

Whatever the extent of his physical resemblance to Kean, Junius Brutus Booth was not quite the catch his master's voice would have been. But as an actor playing lead roles with both Patent Theatres, he was clearly a hot property. So in engaging Booth in the 1819-20 season to play Shakespeare at the Coburg, Joseph Glossop was quite clearly challenging the, by then, one hundred and fifty-eight-year-old monopoly of the Patent Companies.

In the circumstances, Glossop can hardly have been surprised that his daring to present a Patent Theatre player in Patent Theatre drama provoked a summons. As a result of information formally filed against him by the secretary to the Drury Lane Committee, Glossop was taken to court. The verdict, as could have been foreseen, went against him and he was fined fifty pounds per illegal performance, the sum to be divided between the poor of the local parish of Lambeth and the informant.

Since the Glossop family had between them by now contributed some thirty thousand pounds to ensure the building and the opening of the Coburg, this sum cannot have struck them as a colossal additional burden. But it must have dashed their hopes that the new theatre they had so generously subsidised would achieve the status equal to the Patent Theatres. That Glossop himself fully realised the principle at stake, is clear from the insertion he had put into the programme for the last night of Booth's series of appearances at the Coburg. It read:

APPEAL TO THE PUBLIC!!!

'The Proprietors gratefully embrace the present Opportunity of thanking the Public for the very liberal Support they have experienced during the Engagement of this Gentleman; at the same time they feel it their Duty to state to them, as their Patrons and Protectors, and Guardians of the Best Interests of the Drama, the Persecution to which that Engagement entered into from an earnest Desire to furnish every Gratification they could in return for the constant Encouragement extended to them from the First Opening of the COBURG has exposed them. The Proprietors of the Two Patent Theatres taking Offence at the Attraction of this Gentleman, have thought proper to institute a PROSECUTION, by way of INFORMATION, against the COBURG THEATRE for the *alleged offence of rationalizing their Performances* and bringing them within the pale of Perfection which they would claim exclusively to themselves – how just the Public will decide – at all events, assured of the COBURG THEATRE will take every means in their Power to resist this attempt at abridging their sources of Amusement, and instituting a Monopoly, which by crushing Emulation, will be fatal to the efforts of Genius and the generous Exertion of every species of Excellence!!!'

The appeal, despite its most elaborate typography and triple exclamation marks, failed to generate effective public sympathy and action. The fact that Glossop lost his case when it was heard on the King's Bench on 27 June 1821, only showed that head-on collision with the theatrical powers-that-were was not the best way of undermining them. Henceforth, in the presentation of Shakespeare and 'legitimate drama' the Coburg, like other Minor Theatres, would have to get round the system by a combination of cunning and ingenuity.

This new tack was first improbably undertaken, as far as Shakespeare was concerned, by the same Junius Brutus Booth. 'Improbably' since Booth's first writ-provoking appearances at the Coburg had also been a source of friction between actor and management. After three performances, we read, Booth rushed down to the rival Surrey theatre and signed a blank sheet of paper offering his services to the Surrey manager on any terms 'stating that he had been so ill-treated at the Coburg, that he would not play there again'.

Evidently, like Kean, Booth was capable of pique and of hasty action. Clearly he recovered, for his collaboration with the Coburg in cashing in on the popularity of his appearance in the title-role of *King Lear* at Covent Garden would not otherwise have been possible. Because of George III's apparent insanity, resulting in the Regency of 1811 to 1820, *King Lear* had been tactfully overlooked by the Patent Theatres. But once George III had died in 1820, Covent Garden was free to lift this voluntary embargo and consequently found they and Booth had a hit on their hands. William Moncrieff, the Coburg's astute runner-up of melodramas, set about cobbling a play based on Mrs Opie's novel, *Father and Daughter*, to be staged as *The Lear of Private Life*. In this Booth was prevailed upon to appear at the Coburg on the nights that he was not doing the Shakespeare *Lear* at Covent Garden.

In the Coburg version, Lear was imaginatively referred to as Fitz-Arden. A parson in a clerical hat, he lost his reason when his Cordelia-like daughter eloped, the worthy Fitz-Arden having already shown signs of instability in Lear-like prodigality reflected in his sending his curate a fiver, doubling his servants' wages and settling the debts of his parishioners. In true melodrama-style, Fitz-Arden's sanity returned at the close with the reappearance of his sorrowing daughter complete with repentant lover and one child – all this accompanied by an air from Handel's *Deborah*.

In 1826 the architectural embellishments of the Coburg, having already been improved 'on a costly scale' in 1822, were again extensively altered, both inside and out. This was to inaugurate George Bothwell Davidge's management of the theatre as its sole lessee for the following seven years. Like Glossop before him, Davidge soon looked to Shakespeare and between September 1826 and November 1828, he had succeeded in producing seven 'arrangements' of Shakespeare plays.

The length to which Davidge was obliged to go in order to avoid the sort of writ successfully served on his predecessor, Glossop, may be gleaned from the titles under which Shakespeare masqueraded on the south side of the Thames. 'A new grand serious drama founded on an ancient and well-known Romance' was compiled by H. M. Milner and billed as *The Lovers of Verona* or *Romeo and Juliet.* It was followed by *The Battle of Bosworth Field* or *The Life and Death of Richard III.* Perhaps Davidge's most inventive billing was the way he advertised *Hamlet* – 'not an alteration or adaptation of Shakespeare's admirable tragedy of the same name' but 'partly founded on the celebrated French tragedy by Ducis'. It so happened the Ducis' play was the French adaptation of *Hamlet.* In the version translated back into English, several rather interesting departures from Shakespeare's original occurred. Polonius, for example, survived the machinations at the Danish Court. So did his daughter, Ophelia, whose marriage to the equally fortunate Hamlet, resulted in the play's concluding with the coronation of the happy pair.

Clearly these were the sort of liberties that enabled Davidge to stage Shakespeare where Glossop had failed. But it was a heavy price to pay and the end-result could hardly be described as Shakespeare at all. And even by making these ludicrous adaptations, Davidge still found himself courting disaster. On announcing, for example, that he would present *Macbeth, King of Scotland* or *The Weird Sisters* Davidge was on the receiving end of a writ from the other side of the river and quickly substituted his happy-ever-after version of *Hamlet.*

In the course of these Shakespeare 'arrangements', a local favourite, Thomas Cobham, consolidated what was to be an all-too-loyal following at the Coburg with appearances as Petruchio, Richard III, Iago, Leontes and 'happy' Hamlet. There was nothing wrong in loyalty in itself. It was just that when the great Edmund Kean's two-week engagement at the Coburg began on Monday 27 June 1831, it went dangerously too far.

Davidge's coup in securing the engagement of Kean himself in five of the star's most famous roles can be gauged from the elaborate length to which the Manager went to promote the short season. His announced 'special arrangements' with regard to the seating throw a revealing light on the way the public of the period was accommodated and the shortcomings in this respect of both the large Patent and the smaller Minor theatres.

Davidge announced excitedly that the front of the pit would be fitted with 'Stalls (4s each) as at the Opera, thus enabling Ladies and

Gentlemen to be nearer the great Tragedian than when in the Boxes'. He further added his assertion that 'those of the Theatrical Public who have hitherto only witnessed the efforts of this great Tragedian in the vast spaces of the Patent Theatres, will find their Admiration and Delight at his splendid Powers, tenfold increased by embracing the present Opportunity of seeing them exerted in a Theatre of moderate Dimensions, allowing every Master look and fine Tone of the Artist, to be distinctly seen and heard. These advantages have fully proved that at no Period of his Career were the fine Talents of this inimitable Actor, displayed in such perfection as they have been during his present Engagement.'

And, after Kean's engagement, Davidge felt moved to add, 'the Proprietor of the COBURG, feels a proud Satisfaction in reflecting that the Preference for the first APPEARANCE of MR KEAN on this side of the Water (The side on which the olden Theatres once stood where Shakespeare, Massinger and Ben Jonson wrote and acted) has been given to this Theatre, and he trusts, that the style in which the different Dramas for MR KEAN's Performances have been produced have not disgraced the Distinction thus flatteringly bestowed on him'.

At what is reckoned to have been fifty pounds a performance, Kean gave Coburg audiences successively, his *Richard III*, his *Othello*, his *Macbeth*, his *King Lear*, Sir Giles Overreach in *A New Way to Pay Old Debts*, plus a repeat of *Othello*. These performances were given on Mondays, Wednesdays and Fridays of the two weeks, the actor having, as was the custom, the intervening nights off to recover from so demanding a repertoire.

The first night was a Benefit Night in favour of Davidge himself. It passed off without problems and the packed house certainly ensured that the evening was indeed beneficial to the Coburg manager himself. But the rumpus that occurred on the second night throws a vivid light on the theatregoing manners of the Minor Theatres generally and of the Coburg in particular.

On this particular night the upper reaches of the house were crowded to accommodate twelve hundred spectators – according to one authority. Even if his figure is exaggerated, we may take it that in the heat of a summer evening, the mass crammed into the gallery was far from being as comfortably placed as those in the boxes and in the new stalls 'as in the Opera' specially set up below. This may account for the locals becoming noisy and inattentive – much to Kean's understandable irritation. And, in Kean's view, they compounded their bad manners by urging on their local boy, Thomas Cobham, who was playing Iago to Kean's Othello. To liven up the evening, when Cobham appeared, they shouted 'Bravo Cobham!' with the uninhibited enthusiasm twentieth-century soccer and rugby league fans urge on the home team.

At the end of the performance, Kean was of course loudly called for. One report tells us 'after a considerable delay he came forward, enveloped in his cloak, his face still smirched, not more than half cleansed from the dingy complexion of the Moor and his eyes emitting flashes as bright and deadly as forked lightning. He planted himself in the centre of the stage, near the footlights, and demanded, with laconic abruptness, 'What do you want?' After a moment's surprise, the Coburg public is said to have volunteered, still good-naturedly, 'You! You!' Kean, after a pause, countered, 'I have acted in every theatre in the United Kingdom of Great Britain and Ireland. I have acted in all the principal theatres throughout the United States of America. But in my life I never acted to such a set of ignorant, unmitigated brutes as I now see before me.'

If Davidge had lined his pockets the previous evening, he must have been at that point wondering how much it would cost him to have his recently embellished theatre put to rights after the fights that were certain to break out. Kean, after his little speech majestically gathered up his mantle and, making a contemptuous obeisance, stalked off. A lull before the storm followed.

Fortunately, just as it was about to erupt, somebody began to shout out 'Cobham, Cobham!' The actor was conveniently placed in the wings and immediately available, with the quickness of mind to say, 'Ladies and gentlemen, this is unquestionably the proudest moment of my life. I cannot give utterance to my feelings. But to the last hour of my existence I shall cherish the remembrance of the honour conferred upon me by one of the most distinguished, liberal and enlightened audiences I ever had the pleasure of addressing.'

Kean's engagement marked the high-spot of Davidge's seven-year management of the Coburg. His reign at this theatre now had only two more years to run, as did the theatre itself under this name. And, in those remaining two years, the decline in the fortunes both of management and building were accelerated by Davidge's hauling in the public, any old how. Signs that he was over-reaching himself began to show when he became proprietor of the City Theatre in Grub Street E.C. and trundled his hard-pressed actors between the City and the Coburg in a hackney carriage fitted up as a dressing room. Harriet Smithson, the English actress unhappily married to the French composer, Berlioz, was a member of the troupe so exploited by Davidge that, had there been an actors' Trade Union like Equity at that time, it is hard to believe he would have been allowed to work his artists so ruthlessly.

More immediately damaging to the Coburg itself, however, was Davidge's expedient of issuing shilling orders. This was a way of effectively filling the house cheaply but with a public even more loutish than the one Kean had objected to. The chances of attracting Kean and a fashionable public became increasingly unlikely as Davidge's management went downhill. So it was probably just as well that the theatre was forced to close early in 1833 and Davidge's management brought to an end the first colourful era of the Old Vic as the Royal Coburg.

But it was indeed very sad that the two Covent Garden actors who succeeded Davidge in the summer of 1833 barely lasted the first year of their projected seven year management. When William Abbott and Daniel Egerton took over, it must have seemed that the hopeful elegant opening years of the theatre were to return and erase the memory of the decay that had set in under Davidge. What with the theatre being once again under royal patronage and re-named the Royal Victoria after the fourteen-year-old heiress presumptive to the throne, it must have seemed that the theatre's fortunes were at last on the mend. Retrospectively, too, the timing of the new management does not seem to have been all that premature. There was only a further ten years to go before the monopoly of the Patent Theatres was to be done away with for ever. If only William Abbott and Daniel Egerton had been able to use this decade to consolidate the theatre's reputation, its nineteenth-century history might indeed have included a Shakespearean preface to its twentieth-century achievements with the classics.

Having had the theatre again renovated, Abbott and Egerton, like Glossop before them, sought to establish the theatre's status by presenting a regular programme of Shakespeare. And they did succeed in circumventing the Patent Theatres' monopoly in the autumn of 1833 by presenting *Richard III, Othello, Hamlet, The Merchant of Venice, Romeo and Juliet* and *Macbeth*. In view of Glossop's earlier set-back of Junius Brutus Booth and with Davidge's hasty backing down from the revival of *Macbeth*, this was quite an achievement. Perhaps it was also an indication that the monopoly situation was drawing to a close. But the standard of the acting in these Shakespeare revivals does not appear to have been very satisfactory.

We are chiefly indebted to the diary of Kean's rival, William Macready, for some insight into the Shakespeare at what was now the Royal Victoria Theatre. Unfortunately, the acting seems to have been more high-minded and well-intentioned than accomplished or even waywardly exciting. On 15 August 1833, Macready confides to his diary – and posterity: 'Went to the Victoria Theatre – a very pretty salle and well-appointed – but Warde's acting was the most elaborate defiance of nature and taste I ever witnessed.' Macready was back a year later and records on 12 July 1834, 'to see *Charles I*. The play is wretchedly constructed with some powerful scenes, many passages of power and considerable effect in the sketch of Cromwell's character, which, deserving first-rate support, was consigned to the murderous hands of Mr Cathcart.'

Although in his time a manager of both Patent Theatres, Macready played an important role in freeing the London stage from their monopoly. Moreover, as an educated and cultured man, he made important Shakespearean reforms both by insisting on proper rehearsals for actors in crowd scenes and in seeking to rescue Shakespeare texts from the worst excesses of the Restoration adaptations. Macready's attitude to the endeavours of the former Coburg Theatre's attempts to achieve a new identity as the Royal Victoria is therefore of especial interest.

Unfortunately, Macready seems to have been far less impressed with this 'pretty salle' when requested by the new management to visit it as a performer. Macready had received a pressing request from the Royal Victoria's house-dramatist, Sheridan Knowles, to play in Knowles's own play *Virginius* on 28 July 1834. The evening was Knowles' Benefit – in aid of this actor-author. Macready confides to his diary (and to us) that 'after breakfast sat down to answer Knowles; I confess, though it is a great inconvenience and I feel it rather a descent to play at the Victoria, yet I am gratified in receiving this application from him . . . I answered in the kindest tones, assenting to his wish'.

On the night, however, he seems to have regretted his decision. The diary records:

> My dressing room was more inconvenient and ill-appointed than many provincial ones, and when I went on the stage, I found the wings literally choked up with people. I was rather inclined to be out of temper with this but soon recollected myself, and acted as well as I could – much of the character, Virginius, very well – really, and with heart. My reception was most enthusiastic – certainly the most of any that appeared. At the end I was called for, but declined going on and went to undress. In consequence of the continued clamour Abbott promised that I should appear at the end of the farce . . . Abbott distressed me with importunities, on personal grounds particularly, to engage for a few nights. I good naturedly but firmly resisted and I was right in doing so – how satisfactory it is to be able to say that to oneself on any occasion!

Well, however satisfactory that decision was to Macready himself, it was most unfortunate both for the new managers and the Royal Victoria Theatre itself. Abbott and his partner, Egerton, were, after all, anxious to give the playhouse the good name it lost in the course of the sharp decline at the close of the Coburg epoch. Moreover, as a truly cultivated actor with informed views on subordinating sets and costumes to the overall effect of the text at a time when the emphasis was on breathtaking spectacle, this great tragedian could have brought both weight and respected authority to the good intentions of Abbott and Egerton. How sad that this latter couple lacked the resourceful bravado of their avaricious predecessor, Davidge. Perhaps, if Macready's attitude to the Royal Victoria Theatre had been less snobbish and patronising, Egerton would not have had to pull out of the Royal Victoria management in July 1834, with Abbott following in August of that year.

Despite the set-back, the Royal Victoria still hung on at the beginning of the 1830s to its revived sense of elegance. *A Looking-Glass*

Curtain had been one of the wonders of the original Coburg under Glossop. A second one was installed and lowered for the first time after a performance of *Othello* on 29 September 1834. Also, during this period, the single centre chandelier, which had been a source of pride at the opening of the Coburg, was replaced by a number of clusters of smaller, gas-lit chandeliers. The Royal Victoria was therefore now equipped with the resources to lower the house-lights during the performance – one of the many technical innovations which were to revolutionise the nineteenth-century production of Shakespeare and indeed of all presentations.

In these circumstances it is particularly sad that the Royal Victoria, under Osbaldiston, went into the same sort of decline in the 1840s as, under the name of the Royal Coburg, it had in the 1820s with Davidge as manager. With respect to the Theatres Act of 1843, the Royal Victoria came under the authority of the Lord Chamberlain for the granting of licences. Although this act was to inaugurate an era of Royal theatre censorship which was not to be finally disposed of until the 1960s, it did at least belatedly free the British stage from the monopoly of the Patent Theatres. And indeed, under Osbaldiston's management, Shakespeare was performed at the Old Vic. Osbaldiston himself appeared as the Ghost in *Hamlet,* Jacques in *As You Like It,* Shylock in *The Merchant of Venice* and the title-role of *King Lear.* The trouble was that the theatre became better known during this period as the home of Domestic Melodrama and the incidental Shakespeare productions had no continuity or other special merit to give the Old Vic the distinction Sadler's Wells Theatre was to have in the Shakespeare field from 1843 to 1862.

Once the 1843 Act removed the Patent Theatre monopoly Samuel Phelps took over the management of Sadler's Wells and by the time he retired, the Wells had revived all but four of Shakespeare's plays, one of them, *Antony and Cleopatra* in 1849 being the first revival in one hundred years. Why should Phelps have chosen the less centrally placed Sadler's Wells as the home for the finest and most imaginative Shakespeare productions of the period? Like Osbaldiston's revivals of Shakespeare, they formed part of the period's mish-mash of lengthy melodrama and farce programmes. But Phelps at Sadler's Wells has been remembered whilst Osbaldiston at the Royal Victoria has been forgotten. A clue to Phelps' preference for the Wells may be gleaned from the fact that his single guest appearance in a charity gala performance left him with as unfavourable an impression of the Royal Victoria as Macready formed.

Phelps' appearance was in fact under Davidge's management and hence in the days when the theatre was still called the Coburg. But the audience and conditions had evidently changed very little over the years, if we judge from the relevant passage in John Coleman's *Memoirs of Phelps.* The play was *Julius Caesar* and in it Phelps played Cassius. Sheridan Knowles, for whose benefit Macready was later to appear under the Abbott/Egerton regime, played Mark Antony. Coleman recalls that the brogue of the Irish Knowles was 'as thick as butter' and rendered Mark Antony's oration over the dead Caesar practically incomprehensible. Worse, the cast being on the long side, difficulties were experienced in finding suitable actors.

The small part of Popilius was played by a popular Clown who had never been in Shakespeare in his life before. Tripping on his own toga, he had a bad attack of stage fright on his first entrance and could not remember his lines. So all he could manage, when approaching the conspirators, was 'I vish yer luck' and thereupon fled to the safety of the wings.

Whatever the reason that decided Phelps on the Wells, it was as sad for nineteenth-century Shakespeare at the Old Vic, as Macready's decision to give the Royal Victoria nothing more than a single charity performance.

With Phelps' departure from Sadler's Wells in 1862, the centre of Shakespearean activity in London could still conceivably have passed to the Royal Victoria. Irving's management of the Lyceum on the 'right' side of Waterloo Bridge did not begin until 1878 when the sumptuous era of Shakespeare as seen through the eyes of the Victorian actor-manager was inaugurated in all its glory. But the Royal Victoria's fortunes were on too low an ebb for it to preface its twentieth-century Shakespeare reputation with a nineteenth-century equivalent. It was twice up for sale in the early 1870s when its seating capacity is recorded as two thousand three hundred, compared with the near nine hundred accommodated at the end of the National Theatre's tenancy of the Old Vic in 1976.

By 1900 Shakespeare was a name that Londoners associated with Irving at the Lyceum and, to a slightly lesser extent, with Herbert Tree's management of His (now Her) Majesty's Theatre from 1888 to well beyond the turn of the century. At these theatres Shakespeare was freed both from the mutilations necessary for its presentation at the Minor Theatres in the pre-1843 era of the Patent Theatre Monopoly and what was more important, Shakespeare no longer came served up with a mixed bill that also included melodrama, short farces, fancy dancing, some singing and perhaps a hornpipe to ensure value for money.

However, the heavy-weight naturalistic trappings with which both Irving and Tree loaded their Shakespeare revivals so slowed up the presentation of his works that the Elizabethan Stage Society was founded in 1894, with the specific aim of stripping Shakespeare of the suffocating treatment he received at the hands of Irving and Tree. The aim was to revert to what the Elizabethan Stage Society imagined to have been the speed and simplicity of the original Bankside productions.   It is fascinating that the founder of this Society, one William Poel, was for two years a manager of the Royal Victoria, which, from 1880 was known no longer as a theatre but the 'Hall'. And astonishingly, Poel never once used the Old Vic to vindicate the theories of the Elizabethan Stage Society.

The explanation is quite simple. In 1880 the Royal Victoria was taken over for philanthropic work and re-named the Royal Victoria Coffee and Music Hall. It aimed to prove ordinary working-class folk with cheap non-alcoholic refreshment and a mixed bill of equally cheap and wholesome entertainment. William Poel's job was to act as clearing manager for miscellaneous but essentially uplifting recreation that ranged from respectable music-hall to lectures and from Temperance Meetings to Ballad Opera recitals. If Poel ever considered using this milieu to try out the reforms advocated by the Elizabethan Stage Society, he evidently never had the opportunity of putting theory into practice at the Royal Victoria Hall, which lacked a theatre licence.

In this way, the nineteenth century closed with the last chance lost of the Old Vic's having a Victorian equivalent to its twentieth-century work in pioneering and fostering the presentation of Shakespeare. The visits to this theatre of Kean, his imitator Junius Brutus Booth, and the guest appearances of Macready and Phelps would hardly be thought worth recalling had they not taken place in the building that was to provide a stage for Sybil Thorndike, Edith Evans, Peggy Ashcroft, John Gielgud, Ralph Richardson and Alec Guinness – amongst very many other distinguished actors.

What assessment should therefore be made of nineteenth-century Shakespeare at the Old Vic? As the Royal Coburg, it failed either to compete with or destroy the monopoly of the Patent Theatres. As the Royal Victoria Theatre, it failed to seize the opportunities available once this monopoly was broken in 1843 and bestow on the history of the Old Vic the distinction that Samuel Phelps gave to Sadler's Wells Theatre. And, as the Royal Victoria Coffee and Music Hall, it failed to provide the means and inspiration for a Shakespeare pioneer like Poel, although he actually worked on the premises. The reason for the Old Vic's failure to establish an honoured nineteenth-century Shakespeare tradition, must lie in the apparent uncertainty of successive managers to find the right public. Their aspirations to attract the smarter folk from across the river were undermined by the roughness of the neighbourhood in which the theatre was sited. The carriage trade in the boxes was quite incompatible with rough trade in the gallery. As early as 1820, when Hazlitt came to see Booth as Brutus in a revival of *Julius Caesar* he took a low view of the local public when he described it as one of 'Jew boys, pickpockets, prostitutes and mountebanks'. Since, on each facelift and re-opening, the theatre was attended by the aristocracy, Hazlitt's picture is certainly one-sided. Visitors included a number of royals, George IV's unhappy spouse, Queen Caroline, Queen Victoria's parents, the Duke and Duchess of Kent, and the young Princess Victoria herself. But there was an evident social gulf between the audience that Hazlitt talked of and the royals who over the years put in a few special appearances on festive occasions.

If the Old Vic was to make a success of Shakespeare it had to win an educated but working-class audience. So it is more than appropriate that before the Old Vic Shakespeare Company was first formed in 1914, the theatre became in part a working men (and women's) college. On the groundwork provided by this working men's college and by the philanthropic work in the Hall, Shakespeare was reborn – thanks to the work of two spinsters, an aunt and a niece, who knew little about Shakespeare or any other professional play production.

IV   *The Aunt, the Niece and the Hall*

Could a few frightened mid-Victorian watch-engravers have been responsible for the destiny of the Old Vic for the fifty-seven years from 1880 to 1937? Judge from the following story published in 1926 as a tailpiece to Cicely Hamilton's book, *The Old Vic*. In the piece Lilian Baylis writes about her aunt, Emma Cons, whom she always referred to as 'Emmie'.

> As a result of a holiday in Switzerland, Emmie discovered that the delicate business of engraving the backs of watches which, in England, was always done by men, was a women's trade over in Switzerland. The craft appealed to her artistic instincts and, on her return to London, she and some friends apprenticed themselves to a clever watch-engraver. Such was their industry or natural aptitude, that one of the friends was able to write that 'we learned in six months what usually took seven years for a man to learn'.
>
> They took a room in Clerkenwell and soon received many orders which they carried out in the spirit of artists – until the men employed in the watch-engraving trade woke up to what was happening. In spite of the fact that the girls never undercut their prices, they became fiercely jealous, because the women's work was more in demand than their own. Accordingly, they waylaid one of the messengers who collected the women-made watch-cases, set on him and nearly killed him; and manufacturers, in fear of violence, were chary thenceforth of giving their work to the girls who did not receive enough commissions and had to give up their engraving.

This tale of female persecution will seem unrelated to the Old Vic: but I happened to come across it in the early days of a six-month period of research on the author of the story, Lilian Baylis. On 9 May 1974, the

Old Vic and Sadler's Wells Theatres were to celebrate the centenary of the birth of Miss Baylis. She had in fact died the manager of both in 1937. My assignment was to write, edit and produce a souvenir book to be sold at the festival in aid of a fund to save Sadler's Wells Theatre.

It was Emmie who had been responsible for turning the disreputable Royal Victoria Theatre in 1880 into the Royal Victoria Coffee and Music Hall. So I couldn't help reflecting that if Emmie had been allowed to press on with her watch-engraving, the theatre might never have passed into her hands. And if Emma Cons had not remained responsible for the Royal Victoria Theatre until her death in 1912, its management would not have passed to her niece and god-daughter, Lilian Baylis.

The most significant point in the Baylis watch-engraving story has proved to be the comment that the women 'learned in six months what usually took seven years for a man to learn'. Put another way, Lilian Baylis is saying that anything men could do, her aunt and her aunt's friends could do better and certainly very much more quickly. And, in the course of further research, more stories followed in which aunt 'Emmie' featured as the intelligent victim of loutish male persecution.

After the watch-engraving incident, Emma Cons went on to be employed as the first woman on the payroll of a famous Whitefriars glass factory to design and to restore stained-glass windows. According to her niece, Emmie's success in this field elicited even more spiteful behaviour from her envious male colleagues. 'They would smudge the colour of her work,' Lilian Baylis wrote, 'while it was still wet and overheat the furnaces in order to crack the glass. Only the personal intervention of Mr Powell (factory manager and a friend of Emmie's) put an end to this form of persecution.'

It is intriguing that in the melodramas presented during the first sixty-two years of the Old Vic's life, women had been depicted as the nobly suffering victims of male lust, cruelty and neglect. Though they came smiling through their trials and tribulations in the end, they were exposed to every manner of male humiliation. I was soon to learn that Lilian Baylis' rude, despotic and authoritarian rule at the Old Vic was to change the women's role in those four walls. A succession of male artists, some of them with quite as violent a temperament as her own, were to be cowed by her forthright manner. And the meeker sort of male was to come to her for moral support, much as a frightened boy might turn to his mother or plucky aunt in an hour of need.

The overwhelming impression of the work of Emma Cons and Lilian Baylis at the Old Vic is one of an astonishing vitality. Somehow they found the drive to hold on to the theatre, between them, for nearly sixty years. In that same period in the nineteenth century, dozens of male melodrama theatre managers had arrived hopeful and retreated in exhausted defeat. And the managers had created nothing permanent, nor did they lay the foundation for more lasting things. Without consciously seeking to do so, Emma Cons and Lilian Baylis were to use the Old Vic as the basis on which the nation's drama, opera and ballet companies could be built. Does the explanation for their achievement lie in their being endowed with phenomenal energy, or did they perhaps derive the charge they needed from a personal compulsion to vindicate themselves and their work as emanating from women who absolutely refused to go down in a male-dominated society?

If Emmie's persecutors in the watch and glass trades were ever subsequently revenged for putting down a brave and accomplished heroine, it could be said to have happened in the terror Emmie's niece struck in the hearts and minds of the men she bossed as their employer at the Old Vic. And if aunt Emmie had been resented because of her middle-class accomplishments and connections, it was Lilian Baylis who turned the tables later when smart West End people began to want to visit and work in her shabby Waterloo Road theatre. Her theatre was for working-class people and she fiercely resented the fashionable West End invasion – however much she may have welcomed donations from this quarter to enable her enterprise to stagger on from financial crisis to financial crisis.

Lilian Baylis was a woman of many contradictions. Some have seen her strength and staying power in terms of a deeply religious Victorian spinster who happened to find an outlet for her urge to do good to the underprivileged in cultural fields, where other like-minded ladies got their fulfilment in the soup kitchens of the Salvation Army. This is a possibility – albeit an oversimplification. But it is the relationship between aunt and niece which is important.

How did the two of them come to take over the Old Vic in the first place? Born in 1838, Emma Cons was already forty-two by the time the management of the theatre (or 'Hall' as she preferred to call it) became her responsibility in 1880. Her education and training had been as an artist and, as we learn from her niece's reminiscences, she began her working life with her skills as a designer and illustrator. Thwarted in this, her childhood friendship with Victorian philanthropist, Octavia Hill, was to be a stormy but determining influence in her life. Both girls went to study with the painter John Ruskin, walking to his Dulwich home from central London. Octavia persuaded Ruskin, when his father died and left him an inheritance, to invest some of it in buying up slum property which she would manage as a contribution to improving the living conditions of the poor of mid-Victorian London. The Industrial Revolution had brought great confidence and wealth to the middle and upper classes of society, whilst leaving the rest in squalor. Octavia Hill engaged her old friend Emma as a part-time rent collector. The insight this work gave Emma Cons into the lives of those who composed the rump of Victorian society ensured that she had found her true vocation in life – just as surely as her niece was to find hers in running the Old Vic.

Emma Cons' work in managing slum property developed to the extent that she was eventually able to gain the financial help of wealthy friends to form the South London Dwellings Company and set up 'model dwellings for working folk' in Surrey Lodge, the former Manor House of a Lambeth JP, not far from the Old Vic. However, the usual explanation that Emma Cons came to the Old Vic because she discovered her Surrey Lodge tenants were beating up their wives after boozy Saturday nights at the Royal Victoria Hall gallery sounds a shade too pat and glib. The South London Dwellings Company was not formed until 1879 and Emma (and her sister Ellen) did not come to settle in Surrey Lodge until the 1880s, *after* the once-disreputable Royal Victoria had been taken over to extend her philanthropic housing work into the fields of the profitable recreation and instruction of the poor.

But alcoholism and Emma Cons' fight against it is certainly a valid link between her fortunes and those of the Old Vic. Her stand against the demon drink had pre-dated her arrival at the Old Vic by well over a decade when, in the 1870s, she enlisted the help of influential aristocrats like the Duke of Westminster and Ruskin's friend, Lord Mount Temple, to form the Coffee Tavern Company for the setting up and running of taverns where, for a penny, the poor could buy non-alcoholic beverages like tea and coffee. The aim was to provide a respectable alternative to the pub for the recreation of the whole family. This aspect of the Cons contribution to the Temperance movement, which had been gathering momentum since the 1830s, culminated in the forming of the Coffee Music Hall Company. This was the organisation which officially leased the Old Vic in 1880 at one thousand pounds per annum for eighteen years and spent three thousand pounds on the building to enable it to re-open on Boxing Day that year as the Royal Victoria Coffee and Music Hall. Among those present at the opening was Lilian Baylis, then aged five.

But she was old enough to write later, 'I can recollect standing on a chair, held by my nurse, in the Committee's box on that evening and watching the people as they rushed into the pit. Emmie's family and many of her friends were serving as stewards on the opening night, helping with tea and coffee. My own mother was one of these amateur waitresses.

'It must not be imagined that the movement to "elevate the masses" met with immediate success; on the contrary, the masses showed plainly enough that they did not want to be elevated. But less than a year after the inauguration of the ballad concerts (which was the Vic's first undoubted success), the then Prince and Princess of Wales paid a visit to Queen Victoria's own theatre for a special Irish Night.'

A further autobiographical glimpse of the young Lilian Baylis emerges with her recollection of the occasion on which Royalty 'first' came to the Vic. 'I made an appearance in public by presenting Princess Frederica of Hanover with a bouquet. Canon Horsley, at that time Chairman of the Old Vic Committee, looked after me to see that I came forward with the flowers at the right moment. A week or so afterwards, Canon Horsley half-recognized me at a children's meeting. 'Where have I met you?' he asked. I was very shy as I told him, 'Last week when I gave the Princess the flowers. I'm auntie's niece.'

This coy picture of the young Lilian Baylis offers a vivid contrast to the gruff and pushing adult who returned in 1898 to help her aunt to run the Hall and remained to oversee its activities for the rest of her life. It would not have happened, if Emmie had not been quite steadfast in her intentions when the venture first got underway. Eighteen months after its re-opening, the 'Hall' showed a deficit of two thousand eight hundred pounds and the Council running it felt the enterprise should be wound up. But Emma Cons would not hear of retreat. Even if it had lost money, the Royal Victoria Coffee and Music Hall had been a moral success and both the local clergy and the local police had attested to its beneficial effect. She won the day so that, by 1888, the freehold of the building had been purchased for seventeen thousand pounds – a condition insisted upon by the ancient charitable trust, the City Parochial Foundation, if they were to support Miss Cons' good works with an annual endowment of one thousand pounds. Three years later, in 1891, this freehold was vested with the Charity Commissioners and administered by the Governors of the Royal Victoria Hall Foundation. In the fullness of time, these benevolent gentlemen Governors were to be steamrollered by 'auntie's niece', by then a redoubtable South African cockney and no longer coy.

Emma Cons' role as the Royal Victoria Hall's honorary secretary lasted thirty-two years. Her niece's, as sole manager and lessee, a mere twenty-five. Yet all the things that have made the Old Vic famous in the twentieth century happened in the régime of Lilian Baylis and not that of Emma Cons. Was the manager who founded the nation's drama, opera and ballet company better educated than her aunt? It would seem the likeliest conclusion. But it would be the wrong one.

We have Lilian Baylis' written word for it that Emma Cons trained at the art school run by Mrs Halliday, mother of the Victorian painter Henry Halliday. And her surviving sketchbooks remain a testimony to her delicate accomplishment as an artist. Moreover her employment in her early teens in a Ladies Co-operative Guild which had been established to provide 'employment for ladies of artistic ability' supports Lilian Baylis' evidence that her aunt did not regard her skills as drawing-room accomplishments, but sought to put them to practical use.

Early evidence of Emma Cons' alert mind is to be found in her enthusiasm, at the age of thirteen, on 'reading a socialist book' and her admiration in her youth of radicals like the Rev. F. D. Maurice shows that she was 'socially aware' long before her rent-collecting days opened her eyes to the ugly realities of the social injustice of her times. Maurice's credo, which she practised from a point of view of paternalism, was that 'the principle of co-operation is stronger and truer than the principle of competition'.

Lilian Baylis' childhood and adolescence were a good deal rougher and tougher than her aunt's. Her father was a clerk with an Oxford Street store and she was the eldest of nine children Mr Baylis sired, five of whom died in infancy. Apart from being taught to play the violin she had a scrappy general education, having to deputise as mother whilst Mrs Baylis was either preparing herself to bring another little Baylis into the world or busy exercising her talents as a contralto in concert parties.

Lilian was born in Nottingham Street, Marylebone, not far from where her aunt was managing slum property. Indeed the Baylis family is recorded as having exercised its concert party talents in helping to entertain aunt Emmie's tenants. For a long period, however, they were destined to go their opposite ways.

Having attracted the attention of a small-time impresario by their successful engagements as members of 'The Gypsy Revellers', the Baylis family found themselves invited to practice their musical talents in South Africa. So, in 1891, at seventeen, Lilian accompanied her mother, father, brother William and sister Ethel in the hope of making a success of providing touring entertainment for the Gold Rush migrants in South Africa. The venture proved unsuccessful and the impresario disappeared. The family now set up on their own account, and, reverting to the original and impressive-sounding German spelling of the family name, billed themselves as 'The Konss-Baylis Family'. On the programme, Miss Lilian Konss-Baylis appears as 'Soprano, Vocalist, Violinist and acknowleged premier lady Mandolinist and Banjoist of South Africa'. Sister Ethel appeared as the 'Celebrated Juvenile Whistler'. Mother was known as 'Madame Konss-Bayliss, Contralto and Conductress'. Father who, since his days as an Oxford Street clerk, had changed his name from Edward William to Newton Baylis, is referred to as 'Bass Vocalist and Manager'. The group finally settled in Johannesburg. There her parents gained a footing in the drapery business and Lilian Baylis herself proved to be the real manager of the family by working hard and earning well as a music teacher. This South African interlude provided a tough apprenticeship that Lilian Baylis needed for the equally tough work of turning Emma Cons' nineteenth-century 'Hall' into the twentieth-century 'Home of Shake-speare and Opera in English'.

At this point, overwork and consequent illness seem to have reunited auntie's niece with auntie. In hospital in Johannesburg in 1887, Lilian Baylis was invited by her aunt to come home to London to convalesce. But on her return, Lilian Baylis found 'Emmie' also unwell through trying to cope with the 'Hall' as well as much other philanthropic work. She therefore felt it her duty to abandon South Africa in favour of 'The Hall' in the Waterloo Road. She did this, she was to claim much later, at considerable financial sacrifice. To run the Hall she was paid one pound a week. In a good teaching month in South Africa she had been earning as much as eighty pounds a month.

This explicit disclosure of financial sacrifice for the good of the Old Vic was to be a hallmark of her management of it until the day she died. Generation after generation of artists found that their salaries were knocked down to the barest minimum for 'the good of the Vic'. Her tight-fistedness became as legendary as the repeated fervour of her demands for donations, gifts, second-hand articles – anything that would enable the Old Vic to continue its work in providing the best possible entertainment for the emptiest pocket. No manager would have survived so long in wheedling money out of her patrons and her audiences whilst knocking down the salary of her artists had not that manager been Lilian Baylis. And what distinguished Lilian Baylis from any manager, before or since, was the overriding importance of her religion – Anglican High Church. In her early days at the Vic, actors coming for an audition and an interview would find themselves invited to kneel down in her office in prayer. As time went by and the enterprise grew bigger, prayers in the office with artists became more a source of legendary anecdote than a reality. But the strength of Lilian Baylis' religion certainly did not diminish. Apart from going to Mass every day on her way into the theatre, she managed to introduce her Confessor, Father Andrew, onto the premises. A white cowled figure, Father Andrew (real name Ernest Hardy) was an Anglo-Catholic priest not much liked by the Company, who were obliged to appear in the plays he wrote and which Lilian Baylis staged at the Old Vic. The nature of their relationship was speculated upon. Even long after her death, in the year of her centenary, one of Lilian Baylis' closest contempories remarked apropos Father Andrew, that 'Miss Baylis got sex and religion mixed up'.

Certainly Father Andrew and the confessional helped Lilian Baylis to cope with her own fiery temperament. When she drove herself too hard in the running of the theatre, she would slip off to a convent into retreat. But, according to another former contemporary, she would be impatient to come out of retreat and back into her office – in the wings of the stage during the day and in a box close to the stage during the performance.

At the weekends she managed to combine theatre and religion by dragooning members of her companies to visit her special charity, a Leper Colony near Chelmsford whither her artists motored on Sundays, come hail or high water. Knit the threads of a devout High Anglican with those of penny-pinching spinster who also had an egotistical need to boss and be recognized as the boss and the essential texture of Lilian Baylis' eccentric personality begins to emerge.

Her eccentricity was made the more noticeable because of the primitive conditions under which she and her artists and staff were obliged to work. The principal reason for these conditions lay in the way the aunt had sacrificed the resources of the Hall to the need of educating its public.

During Emma Cons' time at the Old Vic, Tuesday evenings were devoted to lectures. After one of these, a couple of students came up to her and suggested that the Hall's work be amplified to the extent of providing a .full-time evening institution like the Regent Street Polytechnic which had opened in 1882. The result was that in 1884 all the theatre's offices, dressing-rooms and workshops were annexed to provide the Morley Memorial College for Working Men and (significantly) Women. The college was named after the textile millionaire and Bristol MP whose vital donation of one thousand pounds had enabled Emma Cons to raise the money to buy the old theatre's lease. It did not move into its own premises until 1923, nearly ten years after the Shakespeare Company had been formed at the Old Vic.

The first two Principals of Morley College were women. If Emma Cons had been forced out of institutions where men were the bosses, the same lady ensured, in the fullness of time, that the Old Vic as 'The Hall' was a matriarchical organisation where positions of authority went to women. And Emma Cons herself practised a form of female authoritarianism as uninhibited as her niece's, if the legends pertaining to her era are to be believed. One of them was that if the variety acts in her 'respectable' music-hall threatened to turn blue she lowered the curtain at once on the offending comedian. And, if the costers up in the gallery became noisy or allowed their courting to carry them away, Emma Cons would clamber up and sort them out too.

These legends make for colourful anecdotes, particularly in what was once a Melodrama theatre where women were depicted as down-trodden creatures not capable of themselves putting in the boot. These legends also expose Emma Cons to the criticism that she attempted to solve problems arising out of social and political wrongs by simply applying abrupt, moral solutions. Yet everything of fundamental importance in Emma Cons' life suggests the contrary to be true. Her work in the slums had taught her that it was no good telling those at the bottom of the Victorian social ladder to lead cleaner lives. You had to provide living conditions in which this could be attempted. Surrey Lodge was a practical approach by a practical woman to provide this solution. And once you had provided better living conditions, she clearly grasped that you had also to provide better educational and recreational facilities. The Coffee Taverns, the Royal Victoria Coffee Music Hall and Morley College were living demonstrations of her efforts to deal with the lives of the poor in this wider context.

In these circumstances, it is hardly surprising that in the year after the London County Council was belatedly set up in 1888, Emma Cons was elected to it as one of its first Women Aldermen. Since, up till this time, the English capital had been without a proper municipal authority to provide health services (like a public water supply and civic sanitation), Emma Cons would seem to be just the right person in just the right place. But once again in her life, male prejudice intervened. Two women colleagues, because they were women, had their election as councillors to the new body challenged and they were unseated. There was nothing for Emma Cons to do but resign in protest. Since women continued to be prevented from voting (either as councillors *or* aldermen) on the LCC until 1907, Lilian Baylis was once again to be given a glimpse of her devoted aunt as the victim of male arrogance.

Bearing this in mind, it is hardly surprising that over the years Lilian Baylis surrounded herself by able female lieutenants. If she was the supreme boss – and she was certainly that – they laid down the law in their own departments. In the year of the Baylis centenary, Evelyn Mary Williams, who joined the Old Vic staff as its manager's secretary in 1921, was recollected as a figure of terror who protected the establishment's overall chief with a bossiness that struck fear in the hearts of those who got on the wrong side of her.

Mrs Kathleen Clark, who joined the Baylis retinue earlier as box-office manager in 1916 was an equally forthright and capable person – though with the saving-grace of a rich sense of humour that was still much in evidence in the mid-1970s when 'Clarkie', as she was affectionately known, was well into her eighties. And Annette Prevost who joined the Baylis administrative service in 1932 as chauffeur and companion, proved so able that she continued to play a vital role in the running of Lilian Baylis' theatres after her death to the extent that her retirement did not come until the winding up of the Old Vic Company in 1963, to make way for the National Theatre Company. When I went to research in the Old Vic Governors' Office in the mid-1970s, I discovered that her advice continued to be sought and given.

When still in harness under Lilian Baylis, this trio were always known by their surnames, Williams, Prevost and Clarkie. And the achievements of the Baylis entourage did not pass without official recognition. By 1924, when Lilian Baylis was into her fiftieth year, she was made an Honorary MA at Oxford – the first of three honorary degrees to be bestowed on the Old Vic's Manager. From 1924 onwards Lilian Baylis' eccentric end-of-season speeches were given an added dimension of funniness since they were delivered by a matron in the full academic robes of cap and gown. After 1929, she always wore a further decoration – one that indicated that she had been made a Companion of Honour.

In the course of the following chapters the extraordinary work undertaken in Lilian Baylis' female-emancipated Old Vic in the causes of drama, opera and ballet will become apparent. Before leaving Lilian Baylis herself however, it is necessary to cast a look at the many anecdotes that have grown up around her. To anyone who has had to research her life and times, the repetition of these anecdotes becomes a tiresome professional hazard. In arranging them to conclude the Baylis Centenary Festival Programme, I tried to select them in such a way that it was apparent I had chosen them as a mosaic of stories through which her true personality could filter, and not just as a rag-bag of jokes culled to mock a great if eccentric character. One of her long-time admirers has remarked that these stories diminish her and her achievements. I think that this is true unless they are carefully chosen and edited. By way of conclusion to this section of the Old Vic's history, here then is an edited choice of stories about a woman under whose auspices the Old Vic became an international name in a way that it had failed to do under the nineteenth-century melodrama managers or indeed under Emma Cons for whom the 'Vic' was a 'recreation'.

She's an absolute scream. You remember, Russell, that we always thought Miss Horniman the oddest person we had ever worked for in the theatre and so she was. But not now. Miss Baylis is much older, she has the oddest criticisms, too, and uses old-fashioned words like 'bounder'. I'm sure Shakespeare (whom she treats as a person of the theatre) is roaring at her. She runs the place exactly as we've seen people organise parish rooms. She looks like a church worker and is one. She's High Church, untidy, works like a trojan and counts 'the takings of the house' as a church worker – as if they were offertory. I'm longing for you to meet her.

Letter from Sybil Thorndike to her brother Russell, in 1914

She was a professional beggar. Rich people used to run at the sight of her – only they were not able to move fast enough.

Kathleen Clark in 1974

Miss Baylis was very exercised in her mind about a proposed production of *Henry V* which Ben Greet had told her would draw all the First World War soldiers in London. The only thing she knew about the play was The Prayer. At our first meeting, she asked me if I would kneel. Thinking she was about to ask me to play Henry, I told her that at present I could neither kneel nor walk, but that I hoped to get better soon. She then knelt down by her roll-top desk, with one hand resting upon the base of the telephone. The prayer which followed was exactly like a business talk over the telephone. The 'Dear God' she addressed seemed to be on the other end of the line. She told Him who she was and what she was praying for, and hoped that in the presence of the soldier home from the front (me), He would listen. She asked Him if it was right to do *Henry V*? It was a long cast and would need more actors. And that meant spending more money. The last sentence of the prayer was that God should send her some good actors – and, as an afterthought – she added the word 'cheap.'

Russell Thorndike

What sort of woman was Lilian Baylis? It is misleading to say that she was stout. She was thickset, but not fat. She was about five foot four inches high and moved lightly. She had trained as a dancer at one time, and was not a little proud of her lightness of movement. She had pretty, soft brown hair and gentle, rather weak eyes. She always wore spectacles, and all who met her were conscious of her slightly crooked mouth.

Harcourt Williams

Every London theatre was to give a special matinee for War Charities. Lilian Baylis did not see why, when artists and staff were giving their services free, she should pay for the lighting. 'Write to the electricity people,' she said, 'and tell them if they will deduct the cost of the performances from their bill, I shall be very glad to print it on the programme. Tell them that if they don't, I'll print that too.' The Company was happy to oblige.

Russell Thorndike

Very often during performances she would remove the seat of government from her tiny office to Box I, where she would work – screened from the audience but in full view of the stage. I remember once, during the first Act of *The Magic Flute*, she leant over the edge of the Box and addressed one of the Three Ladies with 'For God's sake, girl, throw your bosom out'.

Sumner Austin

She had little use for the conceits of the very young – but plenty for their enthusiasm.

Esme Church

When Queen Mary visited the Old Vic, Lilian Baylis pointed out the portrait of her aunt, Emma Cons, that used to hang in the foyer. Turning to the smaller portrait of George V, which also used to hang there, she explained, 'It's not quite so large as Aunt Emma's because your dear husband has not done so much for the Old Vic.'

Harcourt Williams

Once she took me into her office for ten minutes. 'I am so tired, dear,' she said. 'As soon as you are gone I am going to pray for a bit more physique. I have got a rotten body and that's the truth of it.' Do you think you will get it if you pray for it? I asked her. 'Of course, if it is right for me to have it. And it is right for me just now. I have a terrible lot to do.' I said, 'That sounds like dictation to God.' 'Oh well, He understands me, dear,' she answered. Perhaps He may even see through you, I suggested. 'So long as He helps the Old Vic, dear,' she answered, 'he can see through me all He likes'.

Hugh Walpole

Her voice was about the most disagreeable that I have ever heard issue from female lips.

Edward Dent

The body beautiful was her great topic. On this point she had no great inhibitions. I once stood with her at the back of the Old Vic circle during a ballet performance when she informed me, in clear loud tones, that a certain male dancer had a most beautiful behind.

Ninette de Valois

She had no eye for subtleties of temperament and in your dealings with her you had to take the rough with the smooth.

Robert Speaight

When Miss Baylis gave Shakespeare a trial at the Old Vic with Rosina Filippi's Shakespearean Company in residence they found to their indignation that slips were placed in the programme telling the patrons that although they might want to come and see the plays, they must clearly understand that they must not spend their Opera pennies upon them. If they couldn't afford to pay for the two shows, they must only come to one – and that one, Miss Baylis insisted, must be the Opera. Miss Filippi told Miss Baylis that it was impossible to carry on if the management thus cried 'Stinking Fish'. Miss Baylis told Miss Filippi that she had better take her Shakespeareans elsewhere.

Russell Thorndike

On the floor by the prompt corner of the Old Vic stage was a gas ring. It was not only the sole means of boiling water for the stage or dressing rooms but it had a far more important function. It kept Miss Baylis alive. She was mortal enough to require a little food during the day besides her cups of tea and it was the gas ring that prepared it. Towards the end of a long matinee the salubrious fumes of sausage, bacon or kippers would float from the prompt corner over the footlights and fill the stalls accompanied by the sound of fizzling and spitting.

Russell Thorndike

When I came to know this remarkable woman, she was already getting on in years and her extraordinary force of personality as well as her physical energy were beginning to decline. But she was already a Legend. She was a thick-set, dumpy person. I do not think she ever had been a pretty woman. In later years her features had been twisted a little, the effect, I believe of a slight stroke induced by a swimming accident. This, with a marked cockney accent and an extremely individual turn of phrase, made her an all-too-easy mark for impersonation.

Tyrone Guthrie

If I had to mention anything that I found really irritating about her it would be her dogs – long, tangle-haired creatures that left you wondering which end you were patting. She would wander round the theatre carrying these shapeless mops, one under each arm. If she wanted to point out any feature of interest a dog was dropped. It would land, yelping, on your feet – and successfully drown the observation that led to its downfall.

Ninette de Valois

I once saw her receiving Queen Mary and heard her address Her Majesty as 'dear' in a perfectly natural conversation. It was on the occasion of the Vic's Centenary Matinee. 'I'm glad you've turned up at last, dear,' she said, 'and I know it's not your fault being late, as I hear that your Dear Husband going to the Union Jack Club has held up the road. But we've got a long programme to get through and had made a start. So let's get on with things.'

Russell Thorndike

A few weeks before the opening of Sadler's Wells, Lilian Baylis had to have an operation. She took up normal working life too soon, which, coupled with the excitement of opening a new theatre, brought on a slight relapse. One day she drove me from one theatre to the other and talked about the future. As we turned up Rosebery Avenue and the square red building of the Wells came into sight, she wondered what would happen when there was no Lilian Baylis. She spoke as though she would be glad to hand over her heavy burden if only she could find the right successor. I don't think I ever got nearer the real Lilian than I did on that drive, nor was I ever so conscious of her dearness.

Harcourt Williams

The end of Temperance at the Old Vic and Sadler's Wells finally came about and showed The Lady to be a gallant loser. Once Miss Baylis had recovered from the disloyalty to Aunt Emma, to the coffee house tradition and to the triumphant overthrow of the gin palace, she decided on a large-scale campaign to reinstate gin as a financial aid to culture. Sadler's Wells Theatre was to be the first and only theatre to have a bar on both sides of the proscenium.

Ninette de Valois

A great personality, as she undoubtedly was, inevitably magnetises a quantity of satellites. Miss Baylis seemed to have more than her share; and, whilst in most respects so shrewd and sharp, she seemed oddly susceptible to flattery. I see now that this was extremely pathetic. She was an intensely affectionate and enthusiastic creature: she had never married; her position as head lady made her isolated. The incense of the adorers was her only substitute for a love and companionship which her eminent, even noble, career had precluded.

Tyrone Guthrie

Not being a mother herself, she mothered everyone she liked. She was a romantic soul and when she talked of Love hinted that she had many little romances herself. Had she married, however, the husband would have had to take a very second place to the Vic. She would have probably have made him pay for his seat too.

Russell Thorndike

She told me that when she received a letter from the Prime Minister offering her a DBE, she replied, 'None of your Dames for me! I don't want to go about the country labelled and be charged double for everything.'

Sumner Austin

By the time I returned to the Old Vic in 1936, it was established as a national institution of artistic importance. It was no longer a charitable enterprise in the slums of London. At Sadler's Wells, the opera and more particularly, the ballet, had created for themselves a similar position. As the creator and the head of these three companies, Miss Baylis was, from now until the time of her death less than two years later, not just the embodiment of an extraordinary legend peculiar to herself, but the most important theatrical manager in Britain, probably in the world.

Tyrone Guthrie

Her friend, Miss Davey, with whom she had spent all her holidays, told me just before Requiem Mass, how years ago she and Lilian had been present at the cremation of a loved relative. It was the custom in those days to have witness of the burning, and Lilian had been so caught up and thrilled by the fire. 'That's beautiful – the cleansing fire – what a splendid end to our bodies – the real part of us released,' Lilian had said. And there we left her – the fire, a symbol for her who was all fire and energy, the spirit indestructible for ever.

Sybil Thorndike

V   *Operatic Foundations*

'You would never have been here, if it hadn't been for us.'

The speaker was an eminent survivor of an Opera Company established at the Old Vic some sixty years before. The observation was addressed to Lord Harewood, Managing Director of the English National Opera Company. The place was the Company's London home at the Coliseum. The time was the early 1970s when the newly-named Company had established itself as one of the world's major opera ensembles by providing an English Wagner Ring Cycle and an English version of Prokofiev's *War and Peace* to give ample substance to its new status.

Then the speaker added, with quite unnecessary modesty, 'but of course you would. If we hadn't done it, somebody else would have'.

What is the most convincing way of establishing the importance of the unprepossessing inauguration of opera production at the once shabby Old Vic of South London? How can the claim possibly be justified that what happened there in the first years of the twentieth century *was* to mean something very important indeed for the future of opera in Britain as a whole?

Probably the first step must be to make a good case on behalf of the awesome need at that time for something important to happen. And, probably, the most graphic way to set about this is to follow the approach of Hamlet with his mother when the Prince forces her to contemplate the contrasting portraits of her noble but murdered first husband and that of her current spouse, the foul and usurping Claudius.

A similar scenario may be adopted here, though in reverse chronological order. The contrasting operatic portraits which have to be rudely thrust before the eyes of any disbelieving reader had better be the negative picture of opera in Britain in the 1870s and the positive one of the same art in the 1970s.

First, the 1970s. Even the most patriotic of British critics would have been hard put then to claim that Britain had made much of a noteworthy contribution to the history of opera – generally dated from 1600. In the intervening years, Italy had led the way of course with the four schools of *opera seria, opera buffa,* romantic opera and *verismo* opera. A succession of composers brilliantly advancing all four schools could be rolled off in the names of Monteverdi, Pergolesi, Rossini, Donizetti, Bellini, Verdi, Mascagni and Leoncavallo. And Puccini was already on the horizon with *La Bohème, Tosca, Madama Butterfly* and *Turandot* to ensure that the international opera houses continued to première new Italian works well beyond the turn into the twentieth century.

Germany, though a later starter, had given the world two reforming opera composers – Gluck in the eighteenth century and, in the nineteenth, Wagner with his passionate advocacy of music-drama culminating in the Ring Cycle. Even with his single opera, *Fidelio* of 1805, Beethoven could be no more overlooked than Mozart with masterpieces for the standard opera repertoire both to Italian and to German librettos.

At a time when the Old Vic was still a seedy and declining mid-Victorian melodrama theatre, France, too, had made an impressive beginning both with the native talents of Berlioz as well as with the imported gifts of the German-Jewish Meyerbeer. The latter's *Les Hugenots,* in particular, had helped to establish Paris as the home of Grand Opera *par excellence* in the nineteenth century. And this remained the case however much Gounod, Saint Saëns and Massenet were to leave it with a sweeter, not to say a more saccharine imprint. Even a smaller country, such as the one we today call Czechoslovakia had Smetana's *The Bartered Bride* to enchant the world. And, further East, Russia had long ago found the father of its strong national school in Glinka.

But one third of the way through the nineteenth century, Britain's operatic cupboard remained comparatively bare. Apart from the short chamber operas like *Dido and Aeneas* that Henry Purcell had managed to write in the tragically short thirty-six years of his life beginning in 1659, Britain's only claim to have contributed to the evolution of world opera would have to lie with the genre of the Ballad Opera. Commencing with the success of *The Beggar's Opera* of 1728, it was a school that was to carry English influence overseas and be reflected in the work of German composers and adapted to form their *Singspiel* operas – or spoken plays with interpolated 'songs' under which category Mozart's *The Seraglio* and *The Magic Flute* are well known examples.

Maybe the portrait of opera in Britain in the 1870s would look less bleak if there were something to set beside the massive achievements of a Wagner or a Verdi other than the charming but unimpressive native ballad operas by minor composers like Benedict, with *The Lily of Killarney*, or Balfe, with *The Bohemian Girl.*

The picture might take on a more promising aspect if there had at least been a number of strategically-placed opera houses spread over the country, offering resident companies of British artists a chance to develop in foreign opera – there being no English Rossini or English Mozart. Instead, the emphasis was on the short star-studded international seasons in London directed at a small and wealthy élite at a theatre like Covent Garden. This, significantly enough, was called the Royal Italian Opera House for most of the latter part of the nineteenth century. Here canary fanciers could drop in to hear their favourite foreign divas throw off a dazzling display of vocal pyrotechnics.

Only two chinks of light relieve the gloom cast by such a necessarily unpatriotic account of British opera in Victoria's reign. In the mid-1870s Gilbert and Sullivan began their long association which was to give us the lightweight but enduring Savoy Operas. And, in 1874, the German-born Carl Rosa founded his Carl Rosa Opera Company dedicated not only to giving opera in English but also to taking it so successfully on tour that, by 1898, it had a rival in the Moody-Manners Company which survived until 1916. Looking back from the 1970s, it is now clear that these two companies were to anticipate the Old Vic's contribution to the development of opera in English. But they did so without establishing the all-important thread of continuity that the Lilian Baylis company was to provide.

Having given the 1870s operatic picture a hurried glance, let us return, however breathless, to the 1970s portrait before taking a more careful look at opera and the Old Vic. In 1976, the year the National

Theatre moved to its own new home after thirteen years at the Vic, there was the English National Opera Company successfully filling the two thousand three hundred and fifty seats of the London Coliseum with an international repertoire of opera in English performed by British artists many of whom were known all over the world. And the English National Opera Company's regional tours, with these same artists, ensured that it respected its commitment to the country as a whole and not just to the capital. In addition, the Welsh National Opera Company (founded in 1946) and Scottish Opera (founded in 1962) were almost as firmly established, respectively, in Cardiff and in Glasgow whilst also undertaking wide regional touring commitments.

The Royal Opera House Company at Covent Garden shared its stage with the Royal Ballet. Whilst obviously less of a people's opera house, standards of orchestral playing, direction, design and lighting had been established there from 1945 which ensured the appearance on its stage, in original language productions, of international stars like a Callas and a Gobbi. Out of London, long established festival seasons at Glyndebourne and Aldeburgh helped to reinforce the impression of a thriving regional operatic network, especially with both Glyndebourne and Aldeburgh having touring ensembles which spread their work over the country in out-of-festival seasons.

How convenient it would be if all this operatic activity in the 1970s could be attributed to the stirrings of the largely amateur Vic Opera Company at the start of the century. That would, alas, be an inaccurate oversimplification. But there *is* an important link. And perhaps this may most clearly be traced with the return, after its Second World War years on the road, of Sadler's Wells Opera Company to its Sadler's Wells home in north London.

The occasion was celebrated with the triumphant world première of Benjamin Britten's *Peter Grimes*. This was to mark the beginning of a post-1945 period of impressive operatic output from Britten himself. More importantly, it also inaugurated an era when subsidised London operatic repertoire companies began to offset the tried and trusted foreign classics with a respectable number of British premières – Tippett, Rodney Bennett and Maxwell Davies at Covent Garden and Malcolm Williamson and Gordon Crosse at the Coliseum.

What has all this to do with opera at the Old Vic? The all-important connection with the Vic has to be traced through the names, or rather through the re-naming, of the companies. When the English National Opera Company first moved from Sadler's Wells Theatre to the bigger and more central Coliseum in 1968, it was still called the Sadler's Wells Opera Company – even if that important linking opera, *Peter Grimes*, was no longer in its repertoire. At Sadler's Wells Theatre, the same opera company in the early 1930s had been called the Vic-Wells Opera Company. And before the once-derelict Sadler's Wells Theatre was re-built and re-opened by the Old Vic management in 1931, that company had been simply the Old Vic Opera Company. Which brings us back both to the Waterloo Road and to the opening paragraphs of this chapter.

Lilian Baylis, writing about her aunt, Emma Cons, remarked that the Ballad Opera Recitals were the first big success of the Royal Victoria Coffee Music Hall. But Lilian Baylis had to wait until her beloved aunt died in 1912 before she was free to get a proper theatre licence and start the process of turning Emmie's 'Hall' into Lilian Baylis's 'Home of Shakespeare and Opera in English'. That she was impatient to loosen the managerial reins and to experiment must have been clear long before Emma Cons died. Between 1902 and 1910 she claimed afterwards to have made two thousand pounds from the Monday evening presentation of primitive cinema or 'picture shows' and then lost it all in putting on symphony concerts. But the passing of Aunt Emmie had to take place before the Old Vic had a theatre licence and was therefore no longer obliged to disguise its excursions into the world of opera as 'opera recitals' in order to avoid infringing the licensing laws.

That Aunt Emmie's music-hall licence for her 'Hall' involved opera performers being 'frozen' in tableaux vivants to get round the law provides a richly ironic twist in the old theatre's long battle with the licensing authorities. Those with a memory that stretches as far back as the first chapter of this book will remember that the Old Vic's first owner, Joseph Glossop, was successfully prosecuted by Drury Lane for infringing the monopoly Drury Lane and Covent Garden held on the presentation of Shakespeare. The result, for a good deal of the period up to the arrival of Emma Cons in 1880, was that successive managers had to pass Shakespeare off as melodrama and present him with musical accompaniment like the fifteen singing witches who graced nineteenth-century revivals of *Macbeth*. In her turn, Emma Cons was successfully sued in 1886 by the last of the melodrama managers, J. Arnold Cave, for presenting in her 'Hall' a stage play without a dramatic licence. Not surprisingly after this, Emma Cons had to turn the old form of licensing evasion on its head and ensure that opera performances were billed and presented as 'recitals'.

Before coming warily to grips with the unpropitious circumstances in which Aunt Emmie's opera recitals grew into Lilian Baylis' Opera in English Company, a last glance at the early history of the Old Vic would not be out of place. The reason is that the man who put up the money to ensure that the theatre was built in the first place wore two hats. In London he was Joseph Glossop and his place in these pages is ensured with the money which his family advanced the Royal Coburg to determine its opening in 1818 with Glossop billed as its first proprietor.

But in Italy Joseph Glossop was known as Giuseppe Glossop and it was not as the owner of the Royal Coburg, but as the impresario both of the Scala Milan as well as the San Carlo House in Naples. He married a singer from the San Carlo and their son, Augustus Glossop Harris, in the fullness of time, begot the Augustus Harris who was manager of Covent Garden from 1880 to 1896. In the circumstances, there is a certain piquancy in the situation that developed. Lilian's Opera in English Company set out, in what was once Glossop's theatre, to provide opera for the poorest of ordinary working people. Across the river, a descendent of Glossop's had been recently overseeing the presentation of the same art for its traditional audience of the aristocracy and the gentry.

On the face of it, neither Lilian Baylis nor the Old Vic at the start of the 1900s could present a less probable person and a less likely place for the laying of the foundations of all the busy operatic activities of the 1970s. Until 1923, all the Old Vic's workshops and dressing rooms were occupied by Aunt Emmie's Morley College. Moreover, the site of the present foyer was occupied by the working-men's cafe and restaurant, Pearce and Plenty, which could be both distinctly heard and smelt within the auditorium until the cafe's lease ran out in 1927. An anonymous reference to this cafe, written in 1922, vividly indicates the problems its presence must have posed. The writer notes, 'the benefit, however, of the new screens that have been erected at the back of the Pit to keep out the unavoidable clatter of JP Restaurant refreshment-bar, was noticed at once'.

Lilian herself was not a wealthy woman and the token salary the Royal Victoria Hall Governors paid her certainly did not give her the means of independently setting up anything like an Opera Company. When Sir Thomas Beecham began his long career as an opera impresario with a 1910 season at Covent Garden, he initially had the Beecham family fortune to draw upon. But even with these spectacular resources, the Beecham Opera Company, established in 1915, went disastrously broke in 1920. Moreover its offspring, the British National Opera Company, petered out by the end of the 1920s after brave innovatory work. Without even a modest Baylis family fortune to back it, what chances had a Baylis opera company of surviving over the same period?

The Governors of the Royal Victoria Hall certainly had no alternative Beecham-like assets to launch a fully-fledged opera company at the Old Vic. More to the point, their charter, with its obligation to provide high-class entertainment within the reach of the artisan, ensured that the Governors would never repeat the discredited formula of the nineteenth-century Melodrama Manager who periodically had the theatre done up in an attempt to attract the gentry to the unfashionable, south side of the river. So the situation did not exist whereby the Old Vic could be revamped as a south London Covent Garden in the hope that a high-paying stalls public would finance productions that could be seen more cheaply from afar by the gallery public. It had to be a People's Opera Company or nothing.

Given these unfavourable circumstances, how did Aunt Emmie's Opera Recitals actually become Lilian Baylis's Thursday performances of what she first called 'Grand Opera'? And how did these occasional Thursday evening performances develop so successfully into a People's Home of Opera in English that Lilian Baylis had to set up a second theatre in north London, Sadler's Wells, to give it permanent company status?

In the 1970s, the miracle could be pieced together by consulting the

Old Vic's Annual General Reports. And the bald, factual records that these Reports contain could be given a human dimension by talking to a number of artists who had survived the rigours of the early Vic Opera Company to become major operatic artists in the British twentieth-century scene.

Among them was Joan Cross, who joined the Vic Opera in 1923 and was still with its offspring, Sadler's Wells Opera company, to create the role of Ellen Orford in *Peter Grimes* when the Company, under her direction, returned to its home theatre in 1945. And the English mezzo soprano, Edith Coates, who joined Lilian Baylis' company in the same year, was in a specially strong position to recall the century's developments. This was because her career had taken her not only to Sadler's Wells Theatre and to Covent Garden but also to the Coliseum where she was the only member of the original Vic Opera Company to perform with the English National Opera Company and thereby to provide a living thread between the succeeding generations of companies. Moreover, Miss Coates' husband, Powell Lloyd, had the advantage of being educated in Aunt Emmie's Morley College, singing in Lilian Baylis' Vic Opera Compnay and then going on to become a director and designer when the Vic-Wells shook off the 'Vic' prefix and became Sadler's Wells Opera Company.

By collating the recollections of these artists with the relevant sections of the Old Vic Annual General Reports, it is indeed possible to piece together the process whereby the grubby amateur company at the Vic in the first years of the century led to the splendours of the 1970s reflected in the achievements of the English National Opera at the Coliseum.

Both Joan Cross and Lilian Baylis had started their musical careers by training to play the violin. Miss Cross, who appreciated Lilian Baylis' greatness as much as she relished her eccentricity, recalls that this common early background of childhood violin instruction was in fact never discussed by them. For Joan Cross, Lilian Baylis was not musically educated in the sense that the term is understood today. Lilian Baylis' operatic strength, in Miss Cross' opinion, lay rather in her instinct for attracting the people who would unstintingly devote themselves to the Baylis causes. The unpaid voluntary opera chorus of office and other workers was, accordingly, one of Lilian Baylis' most valuable human subsidies. Lacking state or municipal monies, she depended upon the free services of the volunteers who were to give up all their spare time to the promotion of the Vic Opera Company. And their enthusiasm was such that, from the beginning of the century until the opening of Sadler's Wells Theatre in 1931, generation upon generation of voluntary singers followed, to back up the principals who were paid token 'expenses only' fees.

Powell Lloyd was one of the few of the volunteers to survive the change from amateur to professional status. In the early 1920s he had haunted the Old Vic Gallery and leapt at the chance to join the chorus. But he could only afford to do so as a Civil Servant working across the river at Somerset House. Like so many of the army of volunteers, he sacrificed his lunch breaks and his paid holidays as a civil servant to the cause of working for free at the Old Vic. No doubt his eventual elevation to professional status as a tenor and later as a director and designer at Sadler's Wells was to be envied by the many colleagues who had slaved in a voluntary capacity but did not have the gifts to be able to render further service once the professional status of Sadler's Wells had been arrived at.

The experience of Powell Lloyd's wife, Edith Coates, confirms both Lilian Baylis' eccentricity and the real shortcomings of her musical education. As a larky teenager fresh from Trinity College, Miss Coates had quickly got on Lilian Baylis' 'blacklist' in 1923 as a seemingly frivolous youngster who did not take her work very seriously. For a very long period, even the remonstrances of Miss Baylis' trusted musical advisers failed to overcome the Manager's prejudice against this high-spirited mezzo. A year or two before she died, Lilian Baylis admitted, 'I made a mistake about you'. Since Miss Coates became one of the Company's most celebrated Carmens (she was later to be the first to sing the role at Covent Garden when it re-opened as an Opera House in 1945) this admission seems fair.

Other operatic collaborators have remembered Lilian Baylis' obstinacy in the opposite direction over an artist who had got on her 'whitelist'. They postponed bringing a new work into the repertoire because the Manager was determined to see the lead role taken by a singer whom she liked but whose vocal resources were manifestly not up to it. Eventually, the artist in question was allowed to audition and the results were so unsatisfactory that Miss Baylis' musical staff felt confident that even their Manager would by now see her error. Instead she marched up to the embarrassing auditionee and said, '*Lovely* dear, when can you start?'

These reminiscences make Lilian Baylis appear an improbable godmother to a successful company pioneering the twin causes of opera in English and English opera. Only some hours amongst the Old Vic Annual General Reports explains how the unlikely actually happened. For these Reports help to identify the musical lieutenants who enabled the lady general to overcome her own drawbacks. They also help to chart the stages through which the enterprise moved from inadequate but well-meaning amateur status to that of being an acclaimed professional force in the land.

Many of the Reports conclude with some words of praise for the Old Vic's musical director and conductor, Charles Corri. The following extract from the 1924–25 season Report is a good example. 'The untiring work of Charles Corri and his orchestra and of Frederick Hudson, the Stage Director, has naturally now become an accepted part of the Old Vic Opera season and without them the unbroken record of success could scarcely be maintained.'

Unremembered today, Corri was probably as much an architect of the Vic Opera as Lilian Baylis. She had with him as tempestuous a relationship as she did with her early Shakespeare directors. Mrs Clark, Old Vic Box Office Manager from 1916 to the end of the 1930s, remembered Corri in the 1970s as 'a nice South London cockney, a good family man, fond of his pint of wallop'. He had joined Lilian Baylis at the beginning of the century when Aunt Emmie was still alive and did not lay down his baton until the mid-1930s after a performance at Sadler's Wells of *Cavalleria Rusticana* and *Pagliacci*. Unlike many of Miss Baylis' long-term colleagues, he received no honour and died at the beginning of the Second World War, taking with him to the grave the full story of his contribution to the formation of the Opera Company which had begun to gather real momentum in the First World War.

In the 1970s, Joan Cross remembered Corri as 'a terrific autocrat and a terrific cockney'. She became very fond of him and when she first joined the Opera Company in the 1920s used to like to climb up to his little office. It was littered with dog-eared scores amongst which he was to be found hard at work reducing operatic scores to fit his *ad hoc* orchestra of some eighteen players. They included brother Bill (on viola) and his eldest son, Vernon, eventually one of the violinists. Of Charles Corri himself, no less a scholarly authority than the Cambridge don, Professor Edward Dent, testified to the skill of this 'autocratic cockney' in taking a score like Wagner's *Tristan and Isolde* and finding a way of scoring it down to the Vic's diminutive resources. Powell Lloyd, who had drawn a vivid sketch of a man he described as a 'reserved cockney maestro', recalled his idiosyncratic manner of conducting. It looked, apparently, rather like someone sawing away at the scores. And however reserved Corri may have been, this did not prevent him from deliberately needling performers at rehearsals.

Despite the love-hate relationship that existed between Lilian Baylis and Charles Corri, it is clear that by the time the end of his musical reign was approaching, the Manager came to value him as his many years of service entitled him to be valued. A glimpse of his importance in the structure of the organisation as late as the 1929-30 season is given by the appropriate Annual Report which reads, 'a very grave period of anxiety was experienced early in the season when Charles Corri became seriously ill, immediately after the first performance ever given of *La Tosca*. . . . Vernon Corri, the leader of the orchestra, deputised for his father in some of our more familiar operas in order to give our Conductor an extended convalescence'.

Skilful though Corri was in paring down the standard operatic classics to his substandard orchestra, it remains unclear what part he played in guiding Lilian Baylis' hand in the choice of championing operas by English composers. The Manager appears to have gone about this task – so unrewarding from the box-office point of view – in her own particular manner. The Vic's Annual General Report for the 1922-23 season reveals her at work in this field conducting her own brand of market research. The relevant passage reads, 'The Manager noticed that although both Dame Ethel Smyth and Nicholas Gatty (who conducted their works – *The Boatswain's Mate* and *Prince Ferelon* – in person at the evening performances) received very warm receptions, and although several of the greatest British musicians were present and did not stint their praise, yet not many had to be turned away at the doors, as so often happens when older works are given; she therefore put a note in the programme asking the general opinion of the audience as to what would make an ideal opera repertory for the Old Vic. Naturally in a discussion of this kind, it has to be borne in mind that the Old Vic has no "resident" opera company, and has to contend with special difficulties connected with royalties, lack of time for stage rehearsals and a chorus engaged in business during the day. The votes received split even into three classes – one-third of the audience wanted more Verdi; one-third more Mozart and one-third nothing but Wagner! So the Manager decided that it would not be possible to make any radical change in the class of operas performed without offending one section of the audience, and that the existing repertory was, on the whole, on the right lines.'

What the Report does not say is that the Manager used to harangue the audience when they failed to support the new operas by English composers that she was giving them. It would be hard to imagine the artistic directors at the Coliseum or at the Royal Opera House in London coming before a sparsely-attended new opera and ticking them off for failing to ensure that the cause of new operas by English composers had been better supported by their missing friends. And although Lilian Baylis worked before there was an Arts Council of Great Britain to channel state money the way of operatic enterprises, she freqently brought back into the Vic-Wells Opera repertoire works that were much more a *succès d'estime* than successes at the box-office.

One of the new operas to be promoted by Miss Baylis' opera company was *Macbeth*, given its première at Sadler's Wells in 1934. This was composed by Lawrance Collingwood who succeeded Charles Corri as chief conductor and musical director when the company moved to Sadler's Wells in 1931, even though it continued to return to the Old Vic until 1935.

Collingwood had first joined Lilian Baylis' opera staff in 1919 when his salary was paid for by a grant from the Carnegie Trust for one year. Having in these twelve months made himself indispensable to her, Lilian Baylis took him on her own payroll in 1920 but, characteristically, knocked the equivalent of twenty-five pence from the five pounds a week salary the Carnegie Trust had provided. An extract from the Old Vic's General Report for the 1926-27 season, when Lawrance Collingwood took temporary leave of the organisation, is revealing.

> The triumvirate which for some years has done so much for the musical side of the work here was broken this season by the departure of the Vic's valued pianist and chorusmaster, Lawrance Collingwood. In addition to his official duties, Mr Collingwood furthered the work in countless ways with his quiet personality and sound sense and by his general help to young artists. The regret felt by the management at losing so faithful a servant was balanced in some measure by the fact that the new engagement offered to him by the Gramophone Company was not only an exceedingly good one from a financial point of view, but also would only occupy about eighteen hours of his time during the week, instead of the sixty hours or so he used to give to the Vic. This will mean that Mr Collingwood's career as a composer, so rudely interrupted by his return from Petrograd during the war, can be resumed at his ample leisure.

In 1974, in his eighty-seventh year, Collingwood came out of retirement to conduct a revival of *The Marriage of Figaro* which Joan Cross, once herself a famous Countess, directed at Sadler's Wells as part of the Baylis Centenary Festival. In that centenary year, Lawrance Collingwood recollected that, unlike Charles Corri, his working relationship with the Manager had been smooth. He attributed this to his forbearance over working and financial conditions. 'I think', he said, 'that during the whole period that I worked for her, we never had a stormy encounter as I never raised the question of my salary. I simply accepted what I got. It gradually grew and I grew with it.'

In the Annual General Report from the 1930-31 season, the first official indication of Collingwood's becoming Corri's successor may be seen. In referring to the 1931 opening of Sadler's Wells and the possibility of thereby having to dispense with the services of the old faithfuls of the voluntary amateur opera chorus to enable the formation of a permanent ensemble, the Management notes:

. . . with the removal to Sadler's Wells we gained Lawrance Collingwood (once the Vic's chorus master and pianist) as second conductor; for obviously Charles Corri could not manage all the performances. . . . In forming a permanent company it was necessary to part with certain members of the opera chorus whose work had been part-time, and who by other means were earning far more than the Vic could afford to offer them for whole time services. The management would like to place on record its thanks to these old friends for their faithful adherence to the cause under very difficult conditions. Although they have no share in the triumph of permanent opera here, it was their loyalty which to a great extent made the new venture possible.

Bearing in mind that Lawrance Collingwood had completed his musical studies in St Petersburg before the October Revolution brought them to a sudden end, one can discern an indication of his interests and influence in the 1930s when the Vic-Wells repertoire dropped the old-fashioned ballad operas that belonged properly to the era of Emma Cons' 'Recitals'. In their place a bold excursion was made by the new Company into Russian and Czech opera. Under Collingwood's baton, the Vic-Wells public heard the British premières of Rimsky-Korsakov's *The Snow Maiden* and *Tsar Saltan* as well as the original Mussorsky version (in English) of *Boris Godunov*. Smetana's *The Bartered Bride* was also brought into the repertoire in English.

Evidently Lilian Baylis had at first hoped to launch permanent opera along the same repertoire lines as in Aunt Emmie's days. Balfe's *The Bohemian Girl* and Benedict's *The Lily of Killarney* were named in the first season of the permanent Sadler's Wells 1931 Company which in fact alternated between the newly opened theatre north of the river and the Old Vic. The Manager declared, 'on such "old fashioned" works as these the popularity of opera in English at the Vic was built; and there seems every reason to assume that again, at Sadler's Wells, history will repeat itself and that by such means opera will gain a preliminary hold on the people of North London, while later on more ambitious and difficult works may be presented with success.'

Lilian Baylis has been criticised for failing adequately to promote the cause of English Opera – but with the meagre resources at her disposal it is astonishing that she managed to present opera at all. It is easy to overlook the work that was presented, because these English operas by English composers have failed to win international acclaim. Certainly, Collingwood's own *Macbeth* neither proved a sure-fire winner at the box-office nor subsequently went on to be an indispensible work in the international repertoire. The same, in the long run, could be said of other operas by English composers that Lilian Baylis either revived or premièred – like those of Dame Ethel Smyth, Arthur Benjamin and Nicholas Gatty.

It may have been that the British operatic premières that the Vic Opera settled for were chosen as much for their Shakespeare associations as for their immediately discernible musical inspiration. In the 1921-22 General Report, for example, the Manager revealingly remarks that 'Nicholas Gatty's musical version of *The Tempest* was given appropriately for the first time at the Old Vic during the Shakespeare Festival Week'. But whatever the reason that operatic versions of Shakespeare like *Macbeth* and *The Tempest* were chosen, the real point is that there were no works by British composers of the stature of a Wagner or a Verdi to be launched by the Vic-Wells Opera Company or indeed by any other British National Opera Company. Lilian Baylis, sometimes belatedly, took the best of what was going. And though her personal relationship with the composer might have been stormy – (a euphemism for the dealings between Dame Ethel Smyth and the Manager) – the operas did get performed, and they were brought back into the repertoire even if, from a box-office point of view, they proved a disaster compared to a revival of say, Gounod's *Faust* or those 'old-fashioned ballad operas'.

A fair assessment of the achievement of the Vic and of the Vic-Wells Companies is that they did hold out a life-line to British composers. And this was true even at a time when the captain's operatic ship was in danger of immediate sinking in financially shallow waters. This side of the operatic enterprise at least helped to keep unreceptive ears open to British composers. And, somehow, the company that was to première Britten's *Peter Grimes* in 1945 kept going until the post-Second World War advent of state subsidy helped to inaugurate better conditions for the premières of new British operatic works.

Whatever the shortcomings and difficulties in promoting the cause of new English operas, Lilian Baylis' eccentric championship in promoting foreign opera in English at the Old Vic moved inexorably on from the slender and unpromising beginnings of the early years of the century to culminate in the 1931 Sadler's Wells opening. This great event, subsidised by that vast army of voluntary choruses and 'expenses-only' lead singers, moved King George V and Queen Mary to send the formal greeting which read, 'Their Majesties send their best wishes for the success of the new movement whereby the enjoyment of Opera will be brought within the reach of many to whom it has so far been denied.'

Lilian Baylis' successes had inevitably brought rivals. As early as the 1919-20 season, the ancient rivalry between the Surrey Theatre and the Old Vic started up again fourteen years before the venerable Surrey was finally demolished. Referring to this short-lived competition, Lilian Baylis, in the relevant Report, declares, 'In spite of competition at our very doors, our Opera season has been wonderfully successful, our audiences being overflowing, critical and greatly appreciative.'

Indeed, so over-appreciative had her public become by the 1925-26 season that the Manager records in the Annual Report:

> At the beginning of the season the Manager appealed to the Opera audiences to observe the same unwritten law that obtains with regard to the Shakespeare Company – that is to refrain from applause until the end of a scene or act, on the ground that the continuity of the plot and the feelings of the artists were often disturbed by the overwhelming applause that frequently followed some particular aria. The audience responded nobly to the appeal, and the thunder of clapping for which an Old Vic audience is famous is now almost entirely confined to the fall of the curtain, which is a great gain to the production in artistic effect.

By the 1929-30 season, the Manager was hard put to conceal her glee when a further attempt to steal her operatic thunder (and her artists) had come unstuck. 'At Christmas', the Annual Report remarks, 'the ill-fated Scala season of opera absorbed a certain number of our most popular artists for a time . . . it was nevertheless a compliment that the organisers relied so largely on singers trained at the Vic when they cast their revivals.'

Whether the singers themselves would have described their work at the Vic as 'training' is open to question. In the 1970s, Joan Cross felt that it had indeed been most valuable in the sense that the Vic and the Vic-Wells Opera Company attempted so many operas and hence leading roles had come her way which were really beyond her capabilities and would not have fallen in her path in different circumstances. Moreover, Frederick Hudson, who was stage manager (with Corri and Collingwood he made the third part of the 'triumvirate' which ran the company in the early 1920s) had, by today's standard, unorthodox methods of training. Joan Cross went to him to learn how to stand and to move but found herself instead learning passages of Shakespeare by heart. Since lead singers like Miss Cross were paid, at most three pounds a week which had to cover all their expenses, they could perhaps claim that in training their voices at the Vic in so many roles in the 1920s, they also trained the Vic audiences – not to mention its management.

Some idea of the meagre conditions under which everyone worked can be gathered from the Annual General Report's account of how the management bought up the goods and chattels of another 'ill-fated' operatic rival. The 1920-30 season Report contains the following entry:

> Scenery and dresses belonging to the British National Opera Company came into the market at the beginning of the season and the scenic director and wardrobe master spent several stuffy hours in sale rooms bidding for various properties. The set used for *Tosca* was among those offered and came in very happy time for our own production, being cut down to fit our stage. Many of the clothes thus acquired were of course equally useful to the Shakespeare Company; for instance *Tristan and Isolde* dresses were used in *Macbeth* and so on. And the wardrobe now possess an adequate supply of that very expensive item, chain-mail suits of which we never had enough for any army of imposing size.

Since Lilian Baylis' operatic venture was clearly in no way underpinned by its promotion of the works of English operatic composers, how did it manage to outlive its competitors and build up so enthusiastic an audience for the standard works of the international repertoire? How can the vast amount of work done in this field be broken up into the key stages of its development?

Even more than the Shakespeare Company, the development of the Opera in English Company had to wait upon the turning of Emma Cons' 'Hall' into something approaching a working theatre with all the resources in terms of work-rooms and dressing rooms that that implies. When Joan Cross and Edith Coates first went to the Old Vic in the early 1920s there was not even a stage door. Artists had to share the same entrance at the rear of the theatre as was used by Morley College students whose classrooms occupied what should have been their dressing and rehearsal rooms as well as their company's workshops. The removal, as a result of an eleventh-hour gift of thirty thousand pounds from Sir George Dance, of Morley College to its own premises in 1923 was therefore a milestone in the development of the potential for a permanent opera company.

After 1923, for the first time since he had arrived at the Old Vic at the beginning of the century, Charles Corri now had a 'band room exit for the orchestra under the stage'. And, when the Pearce and Plenty café lease on the foyer ran out in 1927, the next step meant the elimination of distracting restaurant noises during opera performances as well as the restitution of the old theatre's front entrance. This change, in fact, involved the virtual re-building of the Old Vic because the old theatre was found to be in such bad condition when the alterations came to be made in 1927.

As far as the Opera Company was concerned the 1927 re-building meant a temporary setback. Whilst the Old Vic was being rebuilt, the Annual General Report for the 1926-27 season notes that 'Frederick Hudson had taken a skeleton opera company recruited mainly from this theatre to various music-halls in Greater London during the closing months of last year, and great success attended this tour. But the operas had to be severely mutilated to make it possible to play them twice-nightly.' Since the repertoire for that season had included Verdi's *Il Trovatore* and *Rigoletto*, Mozart's *The Marriage of Figaro* and *The Magic Flute* as well as Wagner's *Lohengrin* and *Tannhäuser*, 'mutilated' was undoubtedly an apt word.

But the patience of the Old Vic opera enthusiasts was rewarded when the theatre re-opened, minus the old cafe at its front. The same Annual Report explains, 'as it was the success of opera at the Vic the first paved the way for drama, it was only fitting that the first week of the new theatre should be devoted exclusively to the former. . . .'

In spite of these important physical improvements, it was clear that what the Opera Company really needed to get into its stride was its own theatre. The Report for the 1929-30 season that 'opera, admittedly the most difficult of the arts, has at the Old Vic to struggle against every conceivable drawback: lack of time because principals and orchestra are not permanent and have to take other engagements: lack of space because the stage is only free on one day during the week; lack of money to cover the additions to salary for more than the bare minimum of rehearsals. So it is invariably with a sense of wonder that it can have happened at all that we look back on any opera season.' That was a clear signal for the move to Sadler's Wells. And, within five years of the move, the Vic Opera stayed at the Wells and the old Waterloo Road theatre remained the drama theatre.

Both the Vic Opera Company at the beginning of the century and the Vic-Wells Opera Company at the beginning of the 1930s had leaned at first on the popularity of the homely charms of those ballad operas like *The Bohemian Girl*, *Maritana* and *The Lily of Killarney* – then patriotically billed as 'The English Ring Cycle'. Obviously to have come so far in the first thirty years of the twentieth century, the Vic Opera Company had built up its reputation on the performance in English of more substantial standard international classics. I would like to look at the particular composers involved and the artistic partnerships that helped to build up an English public for them.

The most important partnership that was to bring the Vic Opera Company a *réclame* in informed musical circles happened in what was, for the Old Vic, a characteristically roundabout way. In the manner of Aunt Emmie, Lilian Baylis like to put work the way of women. So, in 1919, when she decided to attempt a more ambitious revival of *The Marriage of Figaro* than had been possible in the 1914-1917 war years, the Manager turned to the talented soprano, Muriel Gough. Miss Gough, however, did not accept this flattering proposal. Instead she put Lilian Baylis in touch with the baritone, Clive Carey, who had appeared in a celebrated revival of *The Marriage of Figaro* at Cambridge in 1911, translated into English by Edward Dent. The upshot was the improbable collaboration of the fastidious and scholarly Professor Dent with the brusque and untutored Lilian Baylis. Or perhaps it would be more accurate to describe the collaboration, under Lilian Baylis' management, of Clive Carey as both baritone singer and director with Edward Dent as English librettist. The result was to give the Old Vic the honour of putting Mozart firmly into the English operatic repertoire in the language the audience could understand.

The beginning of this historic collaboration is recorded in the Vic's General Report for the 1919-20 season.

> The Vic had the honour of using for the first time Edward Dent's new translation of the libretto of *The Marriage of Figaro* and his translation of *The Magic Flute* was also used at its first production here this season. Both operas aroused great interest and our grateful thanks are due to Clive Carey, the producer who spared no pains to make them a success.

The following year the Vic Opera's Mozart work was further consolidated. *Don Giovanni* was given with Dent's new English translation and with Clive Carey doubling up the singing of the title-role and sharing production honours with the Vic's then Shakespeare Company director, Robert Atkins. By November 1922 the Vic Opera Company put on what it described as a 'Mozart Festival'. Using Dent's librettos, *The Marriage of Figaro*, *The Magic Flute* and *Don Giovanni* were given during a season of three consecutive weeks. Despite the awesome limitations under which it was presented, this Mozart Festival probably did as much to consolidate the reputation of the Vic Opera Company in the early 1920s, as, on a quite different level, the Wagner Ring Cycle at the Coliseum in the early 1970s consolidated the reputation of the Vic Opera's great-grandson, the English National Opera. And the parallels between the work of the two companies in the early 1920s and 1970s are accentuated even more since the Vic Opera Company added what were called 'Wagner Festivals' and 'Verdi Festivals' to repeats of the 'Mozart Festivals'. What the Wagner Festival comprised was a season that included *Lohengrin, Tristan and Isolde* and *Tannhäuser* whilst that devoted to Verdi was taken up with the trio of *Rigoletto, Il Trovatore* and *La Traviata*.

A young generation whose operatic education in the 1970s has in part been through attendance at the English National Opera Company's subsidised productions would certainly have found these earlier presentations laughably unsophisticated in the matter of direction, design, lighting and costume. But they would have to bear in mind that the Vic Opera productions were put on with quite inadequate financial and workshop resources. If this pioneering work had not been pursued despite primitive conditions, maybe the foundations for national opera companies like the English National, Scottish Opera and the Welsh Opera Company would not even have been laid.

Certainly this work at the Vic would not have been possible, if Lilian Baylis had not brought herself to drop a regular feature of the programme of her aunt's 'Hall'. Tuesday evenings under Emma Cons (and during Lilian Baylis' early years at the Old Vic) had been devoted to lectures. These had encompassed an extraordinary miscellany of topics from 'The Mountains of Wales' to 'The Courtship of Birds' and from 'Some Volcanoes I Have Seen' to 'Our Teeth, How to Preserve Them'. During the First World War years, Lilian Baylis forced herself to throw these out so that the Opera Company could have the theatre for a single night's dress rehearsal.

In the 1970s Powell Lloyd recalled how essential this step had been in giving the Opera Company and its *ad hoc* orchestra an opportunity to improve its standards. In the war years, performances were given on alternate Thursdays only. But, as a Morley-college educated youngster, Powell Lloyd did regret the passing of the lectures, however necessary. Some of them had been given by inspiring people like the explorer, Ernest Shackelton and the advocate of female emancipation, Marie Stopes.

But the lectures could and did go on outside the auditorium. And, as the Old Vic's Shakespeare and Opera Companies became increasingly important, the talks ceased to be on the general topics that had been right for the Vic of Emma Cons and concentrated on lectures related to the new Shakespeare and Opera productions that were right for the Old Vic of Lilian Baylis.

Lectures were not the only way of building up an informed and enthusiastic public for the theatre's productions. This side of the work was wisely bolstered in the form of house magazines and groups. The first hint of consolidating the audience, as well as the random presentation of works in the opera repertoire, came in the Annual General Report of the 1919-20 season.

> This season a new social element has developed as a result of the publication of the Old Vic Magazine which forged a link between friends on both sides of the curtain as did the formation of the Old Vic Circle, a society with the object of cementing the cordial ties existing between the Old Vic workers and the audience.

Perhaps the history-conscious who attend the lunch-time talks given at the London Coliseum and who read the English National Opera Company's informative programmes will see further parallels between work done in the 1920s and in the 1970s.

Apart from the growth of the various 'Festivals', the repertoire of the Vic opera company appears, in retrospect, curious. Today's operatic rarities like Donizetti's *The Daughter of the Regiment* were regularly available at the Old Vic. But the standard Puccini works which are today regarded as bread-and-butter sure-fire box-office revivals did not arrive in the Waterloo Road until the late 1920s – *Madam Butterfly* in the 1926-27 season, *La Bohème* in the 1927-28 season and *Tosca* following a year later. Of *Butterfly*, the Manager wrote 'the past season has been remarkable for the first performance at the Vic of a Puccini opera – an event which Manager and Conductor alike have laboured to bring about for many years . . . it did not have to be nursed as has sometimes happened with operatic innovations.'

Perhaps the introduction of Puccini in the 1926-27 season may have owed something to the fact that it was in two acts of *La Bohème* that Dame Nellie Melba chose to make her Farewell to the People at the Old Vic on December 7, 1926, the diva having made her Farewell to the British gentry six months before at Covent Garden. In the Annual General Report, the Manager claimed that this was a fulfilment of a promise made to her by Dame Nellie twelve years before 'in the dark days of this theatre'. Little did Lilian Baylis know at first what she had taken on.

Like Rosina Filippi who had presumed, in 1914, to take over Lilian Baylis' theatre for the promotion of her own Filippi-led Company, Dame Nellie dared to use the same edifice as though it had no other purpose in life but to serve Melba and Puccini. Not content with insisting on bringing her own conductor in place of the Old Vic's Charles Corri, Dame Nellie insisted that the orchestra pit must be increased in size to accommodate a full-sized orchestra. The billing was to be exactly as Melba specified, the front seats were to be reserved for her friends and the Queen of Song paid out of her own pocket for the extra players and principals she commanded were to accompany her.

'That woman and I are going to have a row presently,' Lilian Baylis told Father Hutchinson, the Old Vic's chaplain, who had been brought down from his church, St John's in the Waterloo Road, to witness Dame Nellie in the throes of an arduous rehearsal. It was not until the performance was completed and the Manager had been given some medicinal brandy that Lilian Baylis began to emerge from the uncharacteristically cowed state that Dame Nellie had plunged her into. Miss Baylis' recovery was marked by her insistence that at least some of the diva's bouquets should be sent, through the good offices of Father 'Hutch', to local hospitals.

Assuming that the structural alterations to the orchestra pit were done at Melba's expense, the Annual General Report may echo the Manager having the last laugh in what had been a battle royal. 'One concrete reminder of Dame Nellie's visit,' the Report reads 'is that the orchestra pit is permanently enlarged to hold forty or more instrumentalists. Thanks are due to the London County Council for the unusual expedition with which they gave permission for this enlargement to be carried out.'

Miss Baylis also pocketed three hundred pounds for the Sadler's Wells Fund which was to go towards providing the Vic Opera Company with the sort of resources, after thirty years of heroic shoestring endeavour, that Dame Nellie had to have carried out instantly for anything so important as her Farewell.

It is unfortunate that none of Lilian Baylis' principal artists ever gained the international fame of a Melba, since their early work with the Old Vic would, in retrospect, seem doubly interesting. Alas, of this generation only Dame Eva Turner, a stalwart of the Carl Rosa Opera

Company, is remembered as the singer with an international career that was to take her to the Scala Milan and to the Met in New York. And Dame Eva achieved this status by having to make the decision to turn her back on the overworked repertoire companies like the Vic Opera Company which, in common with the Carl Rosa, could offer much in the way of sweat and tears but very little indeed by way of salary or wide recognition of vocal talents and artistry. But those fascinated by this era should listen to a record album like *Stars of the Old Vic and Sadler's Wells.* They will quickly gather that these overworked and underpaid British artists who grew up in the 1920s and 1930s were quite as talented as those who have built up an international career in the 1960s and 1970s from their beginnings with the new British subsidised national ensembles. The point is that the foundations for these companies were laid years ago by artists, most of whom have long since been forgotten. But it was their work at the Old Vic which played a vital part in ensuring that in the twentieth century Britain has at last been able to take a leading and widely respected role in world opera.

Birth of Ballet

'Ballet at the Old Vic?' queried the lady, in disbelief. 'Surely that is not worth a whole chapter?'

My questioner was a devotee of the theatre. But the devotion, like so many people's, derived from an admiration and a long experience of this venerable playhouse as the home of Shakespeare and of classical drama.

However inextricably the Old Vic's history has become entwined with the Bard and with the works of other classical writers, the drama-lover is easily persuaded to grant the opera-lover his well-deserved pages in a chronicle of the theatre's history. After all, the Opera Company at first helped to subsidise the setting up of the Shakespeare Company. And the sheer quantity of opera piled on to the Old Vic stage in the first three decades of the twentieth century must in itself make an eloquent case for considering the place as much a nursery for the nation's Opera Company as it has been for its National Theatre Company.

But when such honours have also to be shared with *ballet* a surprised reluctance manifests itself. Can it really be true that the ballet that came into being in the 1920s as a curtain-raiser to Old Vic opera was father to the mighty Royal Ballet so firmly established at the Royal Opera House by the 1970s? Because these short ballet curtain-raisers were so few and so far between, the link connecting the old Vic stage of the 'twenties and that of Covent Garden in the 'seventies must at best seem tenuous. Yet the fact that one of these ballets, *Les Petits Riens*, premièred at the Old Vic in 1928, actually inaugurated the Vic-Wells Ballet when it came to be established, mainly at Sadler's Wells Theatre in 1931, does suggest that an improbable connection is worth investigating.

Fortunately, the matter may be easily resolved by listening in to an interview conducted in Lilian Baylis' office at the Old Vic in May of 1926. It has been recorded for posterity by the interviewee, the founder of Covent Garden's Royal Ballet, in her book *Come Dance with Me.* In the mid-1920s Lilian Baylis was looking for somebody suitable to arrange the dances in her Shakespeare and Christmas productions. A number of applications and recommendations had been passed to her via her formidable secretary, Evelyn Williams, who was present that afternoon. One of the applicants, a former soloist with the exotic and expatriate Ballets Russes, directed by the magnetic Serge Diaghilev, was admitted. Although she had been born in Ireland as Edris Stannus, she had assumed the professional, French-sounding name of Ninette de Valois – notwithstanding Diaghilev's reservations about this choice of name in the years that she danced with his sensationally innovating company in Monte Carlo and Paris from 1923 to 1925.

Years later, as Dame Ninette, she was to remember, 'I was nervous yet determined to stand my ground and get as good a hearing as possible for my plans: the formation of a British Ballet through the good offices of the Old Vic.' Dame Ninette described her appeal to the Old Vic's Manager as a 'peroration'. At the end of it, Lilian Baylis could not have been more discouraging. She said that she had neither the money nor the second theatre for such a venture. There was not even an available rehearsal room – so nothing could be done at that time about such a project.

Then Dame Ninette in her autobiography goes on to explain how Lilian Baylis obtained de Valois' services for the following four years at the Old Vic by dangling in front of her the prospect of the re-opening of the derelict Sadler's Wells in 1931 and the establishment there of a permanent British Ballet Company. In the intervening years, Dame Ninette earned an average of forty pounds a year to improve the dance sequences in the Waterloo Road Shakespeare productions and to provide short ballet performances before Christmas opera revivals – like Humperdinck's *Hansel and Gretel*. De Valois was looking to the future. Lilian Baylis was also no doubt mindful of the present and of the free services that she could expect from students of the London school Ninette de Valois was then running, The Academy of Choreographic Art.

Why, on that day in May 1926, was there not already in existence a national British Ballet Company? The Royal Danish Ballet had, after all, been founded as far back as 1748 in the wake of the still earlier Paris Opera Ballet dating from 1669. And, of course, Russia's Bolshoi Ballet had been in existence since the 1780s.

The coupling of the British public and the Vic-Wells Ballet in the 1930s has been described as a marriage made in heaven. Certainly, the speed with which its offspring, the Royal Ballet, has won national and international acclaim would render such terminology appropriate. But, in that case, it would be only fair to recall some of the earlier flirtations – and serious love affairs – the people of Britain had had with the art of the dance.

Admittedly, England's romance with the art of the dance had not really got seriously underway in the fifteenth century when the rivalry between the nimble-footed courts of Renaissance Italy had resulted in a lively degree of dancing-skill becoming an essential accomplishment of any self-respecting aristocrat in what was then a far-off peninsula. When it was invaded by the French with a view to acquiring the throne of Naples, the victors brought back with them to Paris something of these newly-acquired skills, as well as Italian dancing masters, with all that they represented as status symbols.

The fact that England remained aloof from such goings on was to have long-term consequences. One of them was that if Ninette de Valois' 'peroration' on British ballet had ventured on to a technical level, Lilian Baylis would have heard Italian words like 'ballerina' and French phrases like *pas de quatre* flung across her messy Old Vic desk.

But if England's heart was not touched by the dance during ballet's first courtly phase of its history to the point of planting English words in its technical vocabulary, the art was not entirely ignored. There may have been no English equivalent of the Académie Royal de Danse. But there was the English Masque devised to entertain and to flatter the Tudor monarchs, Henry VIII and Elizabeth I, as well as the early Stuarts.

Maybe Ben Jonson's involvement with the Masque, in steering it away from the dance and in the direction of literature, was unpropitious for the future of ballet in England. But at least Inigo Jones bestowed on the Masque a visual splendour worthy of the scenic innovations previously undertaken by the Italians. It was unfortunate that the arrival of the Puritans and of Cromwell's Commonwealth abruptly terminated England's growing interest in these visual pleasures – however wordly and trivial.

Retrospectively, it is intriguing that Ninette de Valois' plea on behalf of British ballet had to be made to a twentieth-century High Church puritan. For, although Lilian Baylis was forthright in her praise of the beauty of the behinds and what she called 'the forms' of the male artists who eventually made up her Vic-Wells ballet, she exercised the sort of instant censorship to be expected of a Victorian spinster. In the early days of the Vic-Wells ballet, a female nude disappeared from the backcloth to a new ballet while choreographer and designer were at lunch. It transpired that Miss Baylis had ordered the figure to be erased forthwith.

When the theatre that Lilian Baylis managed was first built in 1818, the Victorian era and all its prudery had not even begun. And the playbills for the Old Vic when it was still called the Royal Coburg showed that in pre-Victorian London, ballet occupied a healthy and central position in the miscellaneous and marathon entertainments that the new theatre had to offer. The very first programme announced at the Royal Coburg's opening night included a 'grand Asiatic ballet, *Alzora and Nerine* or *The Fairy Gift*'. It also included a specimen of a very English version of the very Italian *commedia dell'arte*, dubbed a harlequinade, which depended so much on its performers having a good measure of virtuosity in the fields of mime and dumbshow. The first to be presented at the Coburg – *Midnight Revelry* or *Harlequin and Comus* was devised by Mr Le Clercq and danced by him and by his wife. Since both became resident superintendents as well as performers of ballet at this new theatre, clearly the art had come a long way since the Puritans had snuffed out the courtly English Masque. And since the Coburg's gallery audience were wildly enthusiastic over any artist who could turn in a good performance of dance like the hornpipe, there could be no doubt that the art had by that time appealed to the ordinary, not say the *very* ordinary, British public.

The popularity of ballet in London in the eighteenth and nineteenth centuries, makes it the more surprising that Ninette de Valois should have to be marketing its attractions to the wary but astute Lilian Baylis that Saturday afternoon in the 1920s, and also that her own dancing career could initially only find a professional outlet in Christmas pantomime (at the Lyceum in 1914).

Like other British dancers of that period who might have preferred to develop with a national company rather than with a foreign one (even so flamboyantly pioneering as Diaghilev's Ballets Russes) Ninette de Valois had to wait until the 1930s when the Camargo Society, a small but influential subscription club, threw in its repertoire with her own baby Vic-Wells Company. That, effectively, was the only available choice – apart from the brave and forward-looking group started up by another ex-Diaghilev dancer, Marie Rambert, who, in the 1920s, had begun Britain's oldest surviving dance company, Ballet Rambert. If Marie Rambert, as has sometimes been suggested, had an earlier 'peroration' about British Ballet with Lilian Baylis, both parties have kept remarkably quiet about it.

In the annals of ballet's history, London has repeatedly figured as an even more receptive city than Paris in the evolution of this art. A whole century before the Old Vic was first built, Drury Lane theatre had begun an impressive record of fostering the art of the dance. In fact, under the Drury Lane ballet master, John Weaver, the first-ever theatre ballet to convey its plot with mime and gesture was produced there. Under the title *The Loves of Mars and Venus,* it had opened at Drury Lane as far back as 1717 and had managed to convey its story without recourse to the sung or the spoken word.

Another milestone was lodged on the same Drury Lane stage when the French ballerina, Marie Sallé, premièred the ballet *Pygmalion* and for the first time offered spectators the opportunity of seeing a female dancer bold enough to throw off the absurd fashionable pannier of street and drawing-room wear and to substitute a simple and flowing muslin dress. The rigid conservatism of the Paris Opera Ballet had prevented Sallé from attempting anything so innovatory, so it was fortunate that this ballerina found in London the freedom to make a long overdue reform.

When the Vic-Wells ballet came to be formed in the 1930s, it was very hard to find good male British dancers because there was such a strong national prejudice against a man becoming a dancer. But in the days of Sallé and her rival, Marie Camargo, the dance world was dominated by the male stars. The women had been effectively prevented from offering the equivalent of male displays of dance virtuousity since the voluminous period dresses that they were obliged to wear on stage disguised the line of their bodies and inhibited movement.

Perhaps it is not surprising that the pioneering work of a foreign ballerina like Sallé in the English capital failed to sow the seeds of a permanent British Ballet Company. Why should a visiting star seek to found an English national company rather than merely use its stage and its public to further her own career and the freedom to express herself?

But David Garrick, Drury Lane's manager from 1747 to 1763, had good reason to anticipate the efforts of a Ninette de Valois. Acclaimed as the greatest and most civilised actor of his generation – and married to a dancer, Eva Marie Veigl – he was certainly much better placed to perform the service the Vic-Wells was to render the nation a couple of centuries later.

Not only did Garrick have the management of London's prime Patent Theatre with which to found such a venture, he was also a friend of Georges Noverre whose *Letters on Dancing* (1760) were so revolutionary as to bring about the abandonment of the legacies of the stately court ballets and introduced scenic and costume reforms that justly gained for Noverre the title of grandfather to modern ballet. To give Garrick his due – and perhaps rob the Vic-Wells of a *little* of its glory – Garrick did have the sense to take Noverre on his Drury Lane staff in 1775 to teach him mime as ballet master and to present at Drury Lane a version of one of Noverre's one hundred and fifty ballets, *The Chinese Festival.*

Theoretically, Benjamin Lumley, who managed Her Majesty's Theatre in the Haymarket in the middle of the nineteenth century, was as capable of anticipating Ninette de Valois' achievement as John Weaver and David Garrick had been at Drury Lane. From the dance point of view, Lumley's management of this now-vanished building close to the present Her Majesty's went from strength to strength with his seasonal presentation of the great ballerinas of the Romantic Age of ballet. By this time, of course, the ladies had rid themselves of cumbersome court dresses and were the lightly-clad and ethereal

Penny Science Lecture leaflet.

Emma Cons in her garden.

Lilian Baylis cutting *Twelfth Night* cake on the Old Vic stage.

Lilian Baylis receiving the first of her honours, an honorary Oxford MA, accompanied by her father (right) shortly before he died.

Lilian Baylis and Robert Atkins receiving congratulatory telegrams after completing their performance of all the Shakespeare plays in the First Folio at the Old Vic.

Lilian Baylis in her 'first night' robe.

Lilian Baylis with John Gielgud and Dorothy Green.

Edith Coates.   Sybil Thorndike as Aase in *Peer Gynt.*

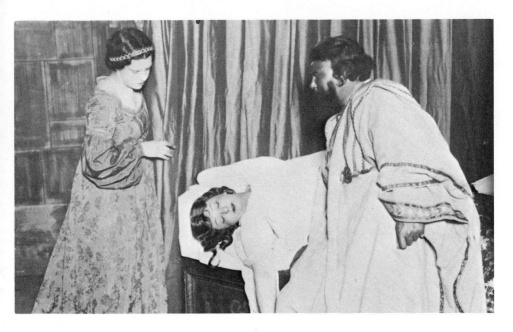

Edith Coates, Joan Cross and Arthur Cox in a Vic-Wells Opera revival of *Otello.*

Peggy Ashcroft as Viola on the re-opening of the
Old Vic in 1951.

Joan Cross with Peter Pears in the world premiere of *Peter Grimes*.

Michel Saint-Denis with students of the Old Vic School (John Vickers).

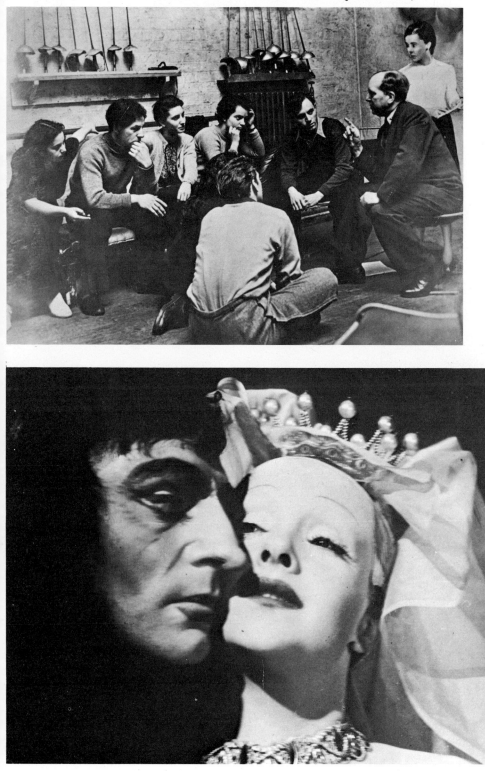

Laurence Olivier as Richard III (Old Vic at the New Theatre) (John Vickers).

Richardson and Olivier as Falstaff and Shallow (John Vickers).

creatures around whom today's standard classical ballet repertoire is built.

And Lumley seemed at first fair set to succeed in a more permanent way than Weaver or Garrick. The finest choreographer of the day, Jules Perrot, was engaged and in the six years he was in London – 1842 to 1848 – Perrot staged, amongst others, *Giselle*, one of the first ballet classics that was to go into the Vic-Wells repertoire in 1934.

So great was Lumley's success that Queen Victoria herself was among the celebrities attracted to the all-star gala programmes at Her Majesty's in the 1840s, which were then billed as 'divertissements'. Needless to say, there was no British ballerina to head the cast. Instead, legendary French and Italian dancers in the next few years were to bring the British public's love of ballet to fever pitch. It is fascinating to read how Lumley persuaded the great Fanny Elssler and Fanny Cerrito to perform in a *pas de deux* in 1843. And his tact and diplomacy in capturing the four greatest stars of Romantic ballet to appear in the famous *Pas de Quatre* in 1843 with Taglioni, Cerrito, Grisi and Grahn would make even more heartening reading if only such tact and diplomacy had been used to promote a British ballerina of equal standing.

With fashionable society and royal patronage heaped on it, surely the ballet must at this point have seemed like taking indigenous root in Britain? Since there was no Puritan revolution to put an end to this blossoming, it does seem rather lame to have to name the arrival of the Swedish Nightingale, Jenny Lind, as being responsible for a swing in the pendulum away from ballet and back to opera.

It is doubtful if so impatient and downright a person as Lilian Baylis would have welcomed further briefing on the false starts of ballet in Britain – even from so determined a tongue as Ninette de Valois'. Yet, had the Saturday afternoon talk skated over the historical perspective of British ballet, there would really have been little need to trespass much further on Miss Baylis' time beyond the obligatory mention of the Masque and the lost opportunities of following up the work of John Weaver, David Garrick and Benjamin Lumley. After these men, ballet tradition was kept alive in the less elevated spheres of the Minor Theatres like the nineteenth-century Old Vic itself where the clowning of the greatest of English clowns, Joseph Grimaldi demonstrated that

the English continued to have a healthy love of dancing and of mime –
even if this was now to be increasingly in the context of the horseplay of
the harlequinade and its successor, the English Christmas pantomime.
From here on, ballet would have to be accommodated in the rough and
tumble world of the variety and music halls of which the Old Vic had
become, in 1880, such an unusual Temperance version.

We should hastily mention the two rival Leicester Square variety
theatres where ballet had to survive to make its way into the London of
the twentieth century. Of the two, the Alhambra, which was
demolished in 1936, was the larger. Between 1890 and 1910, its resident
ballet companies were strengthened by a resident musical director,
George Jacobi, who provided fifty ballet scores in twenty-six years of
service. Unfortunately a British *prima ballerina assoluta* was still not on
the horizon so his music was danced to by imported Italian stars of
whom the best-known, Pierina Legnani, was famed for the technical
feat of performing no less than thirty-two *fouettés*. This display of
virtuosity was permanently incorporated in the choreography of *Swan
Lake* and, in the fullness of time, was performed by the Vic-Wells' first
English ballerinas, Markova and Fonteyn.

The smaller Empire Theatre in Leicester Square, which was pulled
down the year the Old Vic was rebuilt in 1927, offered the petite Danish
ballerina, Adeline Genée, the opportunity to build up a regular public of
worshippers from 1897 to 1907 in a miscellany of ballet items of which
the best-known was her interpretation of Swanilda in *Coppélia*.
After her dancing days were over, Adeline Genée was to become
President of the London Royal Academy of Dancing and a leading
light in the formation of the important Camargo Society from 1930 to
1933.

Looking closely at the missed chances of vanished ballet epochs in
London of times gone by and then at Lilian Baylis' Old Vic in the
mid-1920s, the beginnings of British ballet at this theatre do not now
seem so unlikely. The failure of ballet to take permanent root in Britain
earlier can be fairly attributed to two main causes. The first was a lack of
a first-class national school to feed its pupils into a permanent company
occupying a permanent theatre devoted to the promotion of national
ballet. The second was that, however enthusiastic a British public had
shown itself to be when something exciting did happen for ballet in

London, this public was either subjected to the fickleness of what was considered fashionable viewing or else was obliged to enjoy dancing in the unelevated context of variety shows, *faute de mieux*. This inconsistency did not make for a reliable and loyal public.

Now Lilian Baylis had been working at building up a regular and loyal public for the Old Vic since 1896. And, as far as the theatre arts were concerned, this particular public had been brought up on the emergent Opera in English and Shakespeare Companies. The family feeling in the audience had further been nurtured by social groups like the Old Vic Circle and its related magazines and programmes. Because they were essentially a homely, working-class audience, these people were less susceptible to the vagaries of theatrical fashion. And, because they were brought up on regular Shakespeare and opera productions, they were more likely to be receptive to the formation of a permanent ballet company than an audience who thought of ballet as part of a variety bill.

On the other side of the Old Vic footlights, Ninette de Valois had a school of her own already formed. Once she had her hands on Lilian Baylis' second theatre, the venture would have to be backed by throwing the resources of her private Academy of Choreographic Art behind a much bigger school. The latter would have to have the status, resources and aims of a national institution where generation after generation of British dancers could be trained to inspire British choreographers to devise British ballets, exploiting their gifts in new works which would supplement the repertoire of the standard international classics with British works.

Fortunately, even before anything so ambitious could be embarked upon, Ninette de Valois already had at the end of a telephone Britain's first own ballerina, willing and ready, to be involved in the new enterprise. As a fourteen-year-old, Lilian Alicia Marks had joined Diaghilev's troupe in Monte Carlo. But, as only a Russian or at least a French-sounding name was at that time acceptable in ballet circles, Alicia Marks had become Alicia Markova. She was already set for international stardom as a result of her adolescent career in France when Diaghilev's sudden death in 1929 put an end to his company and provided a temporary set-back in the development of this British dancer. France's loss was to be Britain's gain.

In 1974, the year of the Baylis Centenary Festival, Dame Alicia recalled, 'I went to the Old Vic initially as a guest in ballets that de Valois had choreographed for me. At that time, they were considered quite modern as they were works in which I often danced bare-footed. I adored doing them and next season came back again when Miss Baylis asked me if I would "throw in my fortunes with hers".'

The most enlightening feature of Markova's recollections is in her memories of the enthusiastic receptiveness of the early Vic-Wells audiences. The loyalty of the ordinary local gallery public had in those days been an inspiration and had rendered the shoestring pioneering days infinitely rewarding.

Perhaps this cannot be over-emphasised. The ballet school that came into existence with the opening of Sadler's Wells at the beginning of the 1930s would serve no purpose if there had not been a loyal and dependable public on which to launch the pupils' professional careers. The folly of staging ballet outside the variety hall for an *ad hoc* West End public at that time had been all too cruelly demonstrated as recently as 1921. Diaghilev had brought a lavish new production of *The Sleeping Beauty* to the Alhambra Theatre. Although it included a succession of now legendary artists – including Spessivtseva, Lopokova, and Nijinska – the production lost a fortune in its three months' sparsely-attended run.

There was no fortune to spend on the Vic-Wells ballet. It grew out of the needs of its sister opera and Shakespeare companies. But it thrived on the unfashionable public Lilian Baylis had been haranguing and badgering money out of since the beginning of the century. To the bright young artists of the new Vic-Wells public, she probably seemed by now a remote and perhaps quaintly old-fashioned matriarch. But the fact that this frumpish, eccentric and bespectacled spinster was manager of two theatres that commanded a permanent and fiercely enthusiastic audience was to prove a determining factor in ensuring that the Vic-Wells ballet was not just another entry in the ledger of lost opportunities that hitherto constituted the one unifying thread in the history of British ballet.

It would, however, be wrong to suggest that it was a case of instant conversion. Ninette de Valois, in her autobiography, recalls having just left the stage after performing *Spectre de la Rose* with another former

Diaghilev artist, Anton Dolin. There was an immediate summons to visit the Baylis office and the exhausted dancer was asked on arrival, 'What are you going to do about it? We are losing money on these matinees'. The impropriety of hurling such a question at a ballerina who had just given her public her all seems to have penetrated even Lilian Baylis' thick skin. The enquiry was brushed aside and the dancer offered a placatory cup of tea.

The genesis of the new company – and the surprise of its runaway success once Sadler's Wells was added to the Old Vic – can be pieced together by dovetailing the recollections of its pioneers with the more idiosyncratic prose of the Old Vic General Reports. That for the 1925-26 season gives some insight into the tutorial waters on which Ninette de Valois was to float her enterprise. 'A satisfactory feature of the season', Lilian writes, 'has been the increase of opportunity for gaining stage experience afforded students of the Shakespeare Company. Besides the customary voice-production classes under Dr Aikin and the dancing classes under Miss Jean Anderton, the students have given performances for charity, either for some object dear to the Manager or for churches in the vicinity of the Waterloo Road . . . though some of these entertainments have necessarily been rather frivolous in character they have all been useful in teaching the students how to face an audience.'

By the time the 1926-27 Report was written, Miss Anderton had disappeared although Dr Aikin was still instructing. The Report reads:

> Dr Aikin has again given the Shakespeare students weekly classes in voice production and Ninette de Valois has continued her weekly dancing classes, and the arrangement of such dances as are required in the plays.

Something much more ambitious than 'dances' is at last referred to in the 1928-29 Report. In it the Manager declares:

> In spite of the fact that the unprecedented number of three new operas were added to the repertory during the past season, perhaps its most far-reaching and important events were concerned with the Old Vic's first tentative efforts at founding a school of English ballet.

Such a development of the operatic side of the work had always been an ideal that the Manager has set in front of her; and in the indomitable hands of Ninette de Valois this ideal has been translated into an achievement. By their appreciation and support, the audiences have not only justified the extra trouble and expense involved by this new departure but have made considerable development of the scheme possible in the coming season. . . .

From the following year's Report we learn that Ninette de Valois' illness had prevented a projected new ballet from coming into existence when expected. But in the 1928-29 season she had managed to give *Les Petits Riens* (to Mozart) and *The Picnic* (to Vaughan Williams' *Charterhouse Suite*).

Given as a curtain-raiser to the matinee performance of *Hansel and Gretel, The Picnic* was a financial success and was repeated the following season with the same opera. A hint of what was to come, once Sadler's Wells had opened, can be gleaned from the 1929-30 Report. The extract reads:

. . . an entirely new and delightfully-dressed ballet, *Homage to the Beauties of Vienna* to Schubert was apparently a great success with the audience who gave the happiest signs of appreciating more and more this new development of the Vic's work. We are extremely proud of the way in which Miss de Valois' Lieutenant, Rosalind Patrick, has strengthened and improved the ballets incidental to the various operas.

With the opening of Sadler's Wells in 1931, the Report for the 1931-32 season was in a position to take a more widely historical view of the Vic-Wells offspring. Under a heading 'Ballet', new to the Reports, the one issued for this season states:

The performances which were so popular in England some hundred years ago were in a sense swallowed up by the nineteenth-century vogue for opera. There is a fine sense of justice in the idea that Opera may be the medium through which a native school of Ballet – one moreover which should give a great opportunity to British musicians and scenic artists – should be established.

That the ballet company was still thought of at this stage as very much
an offshoot of the Opera Company is confirmed by a further extract
from the same Report.

> The new (ballet) school has its headquarters in the large Association
> Room at Sadler's Wells Theatre and is under the direction of Ninette
> de Valois and her assistant, Ursula Moreton. Students receive all
> their training in the theatre and are given a chance of stage experience
> when – as in *Aida* and *Carmen* for instance – a large ballet, exceeding
> the number of those regularly engaged for Vic-Wells operas, is
> required . . . for the first time the ballet music in the third act was
> inserted in some of the performances of *Faust* and this time, danced
> as a separate number in the three complete evenings of ballet, proved
> one of the most popular features.

Just as the various re-namings of the original Vic Opera Company leads
to the English National Opera, so the pedigree of the Royal Ballet at the
Royal Opera House can be traced back to the Vic-Wells Ballet. The
curtain-raiser ballets first performed before opera at the Old Vic in the
late 1920s clearly provided the basis for the repertoire of the Vic-Wells
ballet when it was set up at the beginning of the 1930s at Sadler's Wells
and at the Old Vic. But when both the opera company and the ballet
company were established at Sadler's Wells, the ballet company came
to be known quite sensibly as the Sadler's Wells Ballet. And this is the
name the Company still had when it moved in 1946 to the Royal Opera
House in Covent Garden where, ten years later, a royal charter enabled
it and the school to be re-christened the Royal Ballet *tout court.* Thus the
lineage from the Old Vic to Covent Garden, speculated upon at the start
of this chapter, seems in retrospect, as clear as the one in the previous
chapter that leads from the Vic Opera Company to the English
National Opera at the London Coliseum.

But when the Ballet began to swiftly develop in the early 1930s, the
Management seems to have been somewhat taken off guard. Lilian
Baylis writes:

> The success of these three first performances constituted one of the
> surprises of the season, because it had not been expected that this

newest extension would become immediately so popular. That it is taken seriously, and even with enthusiastic approval, by those who have won their laurels in this difficult school, is proved by the appearances of Anton Dolin and Lydia Lopokova with the Vic-Wells ballet in an honorary capacity, and by the fact that Constant Lambert, one of the few Englishmen who has written music for the Diaghilev ballet, consented to conduct at all three performances at a greatly reduced fee.

It is unfortunate that none of the early works Ninette de Valois choreographed for the Old Vic stage survived in the Vic-Wells repertoire to become British classics. If only *Les Petits Riens* had survived like the same choreographer's *Job* or *Checkmate*, the road from the Old Vic to Covent Garden would certainly be more clearly signposted. As Ninette de Valois' first ballet for the Old Vic and the first to be given by the Vic-Wells ballet at Sadler's Wells, *Les Petits Riens* would seem to occupy a key historical position. But, in the mid-1970s, Ninette de Valois recalled 'those earlier ballets at the Old Vic could not survive because I did not have a proper company then'. The choreographer had to cut her cloth to the material provided by the available dancers. In those preparatory days it naturally could not be made to stretch very far.

The fact that those early curtain-raiser ballets were conducted by the veteran Charles Corri whose place in the orchestra pit went back to the Old Vic of Emma Cons does provide an intriguing link in the Old Vic story. By then Corri was certainly past his workman-like best and, without rehearsal time, his still modest orchestra could hardly be expected to do more than rough justice to a score like Vaughan Williams' *Charterhouse Suite*. Dame Ninette was to recall that Dr Vaughan Williams' rejoinder at her apologies for the execution of her score for her ballet, *The Picnic*, had been 'Better a bad performance, my dear, than no performance at all'. It was this cheerful motto that the Old Vic had been obliged to accept in so many departments to lay the foundations that it did.

On the whole, the pioneers appear to have been relieved when the unavoidable frustrations in trying to create ballet with the inadequate resources at the Old Vic came to an end. Markova recalled, 'I preferred dancing at the Wells and thought it a sensible decision when the ballet company eventually settled there . . . at the Vic there was so little space, we used to have to take everything in a suitcase – just as though we were doing one night stands somewhere.'

Of course the early ballet days at the Vic should not be measured from the point of view of those on its stage like Ninette de Valois and Markova. Frederick Ashton who was to become the new company's choreographer and developer of the talents of its dancers right through to the 1970s at the Royal Opera House had reason to be grateful to the Old Vic as a young and eager habitué of its gallery in the 1920s. He was to remember, 'I went to see as many of the Shakespeare and opera productions as I could. A little later, with the chance to dance in the ballet sequences of Lilian Baylis' Shakespeare and opera productions, I seized on them – at five shillings a show. At that time there was a terrific prejudice about a man becoming a dancer and even my own parents were reluctant to go further than confessing that I was 'on the stage'.

There is a labyrinthine thread that weds the early history of ballet at the Old Vic both with the Royal Ballet at Covent Garden and with post-Second World War Shakespeare at the Old Vic theatre itself. One of the male dancers who was boldly to overcome the prejudice against male dancers (sometimes in works choreographed by Ashton) provides this thread. As leading male dancer with the Sadler's Wells Ballet in the late 1930s, he moved on in the 1940s to become also the Company's leading choreographer at a period when Ashton was away on war service. In two words this thread is Robert Helpmann.

To recall Helpmann's early career merely in terms of his services to the Sadler's Wells Ballet is to miss the connection with the Old Vic. Shortly before the beginning of the Second World War, Helpmann formed a close personal and professional association with an actor who was performing bit parts with the Old Vic Company before the 1939 declaration of war. In time, the bit-part actor was to become, from 1953 to 1961, the next-to-last director of the Old Vic Shakespeare Company. And, during his artistic directorship of the company, Helpmann was to become involved with the Shakespeare productions both as actor and director. In particular, Helpmann undertook overseas tours which were of great importance in providing the Old Vic with monies towards the cost of building, in the 1950s, its workshop Annexe. These were to provide resources undreamt of in the early days of ballet at the Old Vic and it is hard to believe that a National Theatre Company could have successfully operated a repertoire of plays at the Old Vic from 1963 to 1976 without the benefit of these workshop facilities.

Michael Benthall was the name of the once small-part actor turned Old Vic Shakespeare director. Significantly, he was author of the scenarios for two of Helpmann's ballets of the 1940s – *Miracle in the Gorbals* (1944) and *Adam Zero* (1946). 'Theatricality' was an important factor in Helpmann's personality as a dancer, choreographer and actor. Benthall, clearly, would have found it hard to collaborate with Helpmann had he not shared an appreciation of the importance of this quality.

Evidence that he in fact did so is provided not only in his work at the Old Vic but specifically in an interview he gave. In this interview Benthall remarks, 'To treat Shakespeare's plays principally as vehicles for the verse is to destroy their vitality in the theatre; concentration on the verse at the expense of other factors is admirable at a poetry reading, but it has nothing to do with theatre, the prime function of which is to stimulate, excite, amuse or exhilarate an audience.'

It has been remarked that this approach to Shakespeare production resulted sometimes in the plays' being choreographed rather than directed. Ballet, certainly, could stimulate, excite, amuse or exhilarate without, in the flamboyance of its visual impact, obscuring the spoken word. Some might, therefore, argue that the way ballet at the Old Vic in the late 1920s snaked back to influence Shakespeare in the 1950s was not always in that great writer's best interests. What cannot, however, be denied is that the theatre that came to be known for so long as the Home of Shakespeare was also, for a brief period of its history, the nursery for an indigenous British ballet at the most critical moment of its belated birth.

VII   *Sense of Direction*

'Remember the lines and don't bump into the furniture.' This is the practical advice that Noël Coward was fond of handing out to earnest-minded students in search of some elevated deliberations on play direction.

The reason that Coward's advice to the players is recalled here has nothing to do with the fact that he happened to direct a revival of his own *Hay Fever* at the Old Vic in 1964 for the National Theatre Company. At this point it is remembered quite simply as an illustration of the way thoroughly professional Englishmen of the theatre have preferred to get to grips with the day-to-day side of their work, instead of delivering thesis-inspiring reflections open to endless interpretation – and, indeed, misinterpretation.

In the circumstances, it is hardly surprising that there is no single, mighty theatrical guru under whose teachings successive generations of Old Vic directors can be conveniently grouped.

In post-Second World War London, theatregoers had plenty of opportunity to contrast the necessarily pragmatic approach of Old Vic Shakespeare directors with that of a number of foreign visiting companies fortunate enough to have had a dynamic teacher and a reasonable subsidy to give their work a long-standing ensemble approach which the Old Vic Company had lacked.

The best illustration of such a permanent company approach was probably provided by the Moscow Art Theatre on their visits to Sadler's Wells Theatre and to the World Theatre Seasons at the Aldwych. On these occasions, Moscow Art Theatre Chekhov still showed, in its meticulous naturalism, the unmistakable hand of the company's nineteenth-century co-founder, Stanislavsky, some of whose teachings were codified in *My Life in Art* and *An Actor Prepares*, first published in the early 1920s.

The visit to the World Theatre season of the New York Actor's Studio, also with Chekhov, seemed in its uninhibited exposure of 'The Method', to be a travesty of what Stanislavsky had been after. But, like or loathe the end product, the Actor's Studio work did carry the imprimatur of a closely-knit group and demonstrated a unity of approach that had evolved only after long preparatory exercise.

Audiences at the Comédie Française productions – of Molière and of Marivaux in particular – were also given a demonstration of a consistent overall house-style. Detractors could claim, of course, that such 'style' was little more than a set of period mannerisms and stage business the result of the accumulation of centuries of tradition rather than of fresh directorial insight into French classics. But, whatever the detractors claimed, the revivals certainty offered evidence of a cohesion in the company's approach to its repertoire that a succession of *ad hoc* Shakespeare Companies at the Old Vic could not be expected to evince overnight or, indeed, over half a century.

A further and perhaps even more illuminating contrast to Old Vic practice was provided by another company visiting London – Bertolt Brecht's Berliner Ensemble at the Palace in 1956. Brecht's Marxist outlook and his lengthily-rehearsed anti-illusionist method of staging a play like *Mother Courage* made such an impact on a young generation of English directors that the Ensemble's visit continued to reverberate in the British theatre many years after – even when it came to the staging of Shakespeare.

If the London Old Vic were obliged to summon up a dramatic theorist to set besides a Stanislavsky or a Brecht, whose names could be pressed into service as the Company's intellectual founding fathers? The first must be William Poel who founded the Elizabethan Stage Society which, between 1894 and 1905, put into practice his advocacy of a return to the simplicities of the original Elizabethan staging of Shakespeare. And yet, Poel's work with Shakespeare is hardly equivalent of Stanislavsky's with Chekhov. Poel's writings were to become considerably less celebrated than Stanislavsky's and the Poel influence came to be exercised in Shakespeare at second-hand and with other innovators in mind at the Old Vic.

One of these 'other innovators' was a former actor with the Elizabethan Stage Society, Harley Granville Barker. His five-volume *Prefaces to Shakespeare*, published between 1927 and 1947, have ensured that his name is certainly better known than Poel's. The latter's theories had to be elaborated upon in fit-up halls under primitive conditions and came across as well-intentioned but rather fustian exercises. Granville Barker had the advantage of having been a lead actor and director at the Royal Court at the beginning of the century when the premières of plays by Shaw, Galsworthy and Ibsen translations brought the enterprise (and those involved with it) the sort of avant-garde *réclame* the Royal Court was to recapture in the 1950s and 1960s with the first performances of plays by Osborne, Wesker and Bond.

More to the point, as a result of his experiences as actor and director at the Royal Court, Granville Barker had published, along with William Archer, *A National Theatre: Scheme and Estimates* in 1907. This is relevant to the Old Vic theatre since the story of the Old Vic Company, from the point of view of its directors, is in fact the tragedy of the Old Vic Company itself failing to become the *de facto* National Theatre when it had for so long been acclaimed as the unofficial one. It had to settle, in 1963, for seeing its company wound up and its theatre and workshops used as the temporary home of the National Theatre Company for which, in forty-nine years, it had laid the foundations but had not itself grown into. The founding of an Old Vic Studio under Michel Saint-Denis in 1946 had suggested that an *ad hoc* seasonal Shakespeare repertory company was indeed preparing itself for the status of an ensemble. In the event, however, this consolidating studio work was to come to nothing.

At least the earlier influence of Poel and Granville Barker had a more positive long-term effect on the development of the staging of Shakespeare at the Old Vic in the 1920s and the 1930s. Granville Barker's *Prefaces* were certainly important. But the early innovating Old Vic Shakespeare directors may not have taken his writings so much to heart had Granville Barker not put his ideas into practice with epoch-making revivals of *The Winter's Tale, Twelfth Night* and *A Midsummer Night's Dream* at the Savoy between 1912 and 1914.

To the ingenuous observer looking back from the 1970s, it might seem logical that Granville Barker should have been the Old Vic's first director much as Stanislavsky was the Moscow Art Theatre's overlord. The fact is that the 1914 revival of *The Dream* was Granville Barker's last full-scale production in the British theatre. Under the influence of a second and a wealthy wife, he hyphenated his name and withdrew to the world of the study whence *The Prefaces* (and some translations) emerged over the years. Only an actor, like John Gielgud, acutely aware of Granville Barker's position as a 'Lost Leader' managed to coax practical advice from a man of the theatre who had become a man of the study. Even more disappointing was Poel's own involvement with the Old Vic Shakespeare Company. When Poel did return to the Old Vic in 1917, it was not as a Shakespeare director but as a Lecturer, delivering himself of a single talk, 'Stage Costumes in Shakespeare's Day'.

A collaboration between the scholarly Granville Barker and the unlettered Lilian Baylis seems as unworkable as the pooling of resources of the Cambridge don, Professor Edward Dent, and the same lady. It was Shakespeare's loss at the Old Vic that the former partnership never came into being.

Consider how a national opera company somehow managed to emerge from Lilian Baylis' enterprises. Consider how adroitly Ninette de Valois used these same enterprises to found the national ballet company. Then consider the extent of the loss that resulted from Barker's clear ideas for the setting up of a National Theatre never having been grafted on to Lilian Baylis' desire to serve up good drama productions for poor people. But a difficult collaboration that might have had far-reaching consequences never went beyond Granville Barker's remarking, 'Queer woman, Miss Baylis. I don't think that she knows anything about these plays. But she's got something.'

To understand why Poel and Granville Barker's approaches to the staging of Shakespeare were innovatory and therefore important for the development of Old Vic Shakespeare directors, it is necessary to glance at the stately edifice of nineteenth-century Shakespeare production in the hands of the late Victorian actor-managers. For it was against their slow-moving, plush and over-loaded approach to the plays that Poel and Granville Barker's reforms were aimed, both in theory and in practice.

There is little space – and less point – for detailed cataloguing here of the way the Victorian actor-managers for so long determined the presentation of Shakespeare. In London the two essential reference names are of course Henry Irving, just across the river from the Old Vic at the Lyceum from the 1870s to 1902, and Beerbohm Tree at Her Majesty's from 1888 to 1914. And of the actor-managers in the provinces, the vital name is Frank Benson whose touring company was to take the Irving-Tree Shakespeare traditions throughout the country for thirty-three years from 1883.

What were the most salient features of the actor-manager Shakespeare revivals? First, of course, these were productions built round the star personality of the actor-manager himself and, though they provided valuable experience for young actors, they certainly were not ensemble companies in the sense that the term is understood today. It must also be remembered that they sustained the tradition of speaking the verse with a slow rhetorical magnificence that audiences in the 1970s would find amusing rather than impressive. Even more snail-like was the pace of the productions. This resulted from the need to build up and then dismantle vast naturalistic settings which lovingly recreated Shakespearean settings in scholarly and antiquarian detail. The texts themselves had to be mutilated partly in deference to Victorian prudery, partly to ensure that the actor-manager himself was given appropriate limelight, and partly to enable actors to perform short scenes before a drop-cloth whilst the background for the highlights of the drama were being carefully assembled behind them. In Irving's case, the search for visual impact at the Lyceum did involve important lighting reforms. But the overall effect could hardly be more further removed than what careful scholarship has taught of the swiftness and the simplicity of the original Elizabethan staging of the plays. Many of the first generation of Old Vic actors grew up with this actor-manager tradition and, in Benson's touring version, a reputation was acquired for the promotion of new acting talent much of which went on to the Vic. But the Old Vic's slender resources ensured from the beginning that, in the Waterloo Road, the tide turned away from the ponderous splendours of Lyceum and Her Majesty's Theatre Shakespeare.

An important feature common to the actor-managers had been that 'lead' Shakespeare roles did not come to an actor until comparatively late in life – and remained in his repertoire almost to the end of his days. Irving was approaching forty when he was first seen in London as

Hamlet. and Benson was still playing the Prince of Denmark when approaching his seventieth year. Now Lilian Baylis' impoverished Old Vic Shakespeare Company in the 1920s was greatly to benefit from this senior citizen tradition in the playing of Shakespeare's great roles. For the contrast provided by their entrusting the same parts to actors who may have lacked experience but who had the compensation of youth, vitality and enthusiasm on their side, came as a breath of fresh air. John Gielgud, for instance, was a mere twenty-five when he first attempted Hamlet at the Old Vic in the 1920s.

It must indeed have been frustrating to have been an ambitious but young player with companies where the actor-manager always hogged the attention and the lead-roles. It is perhaps not surprising that a violent reaction against the actor-manager tradition should come from Edward Gordon Craig, son of Irving's leading-lady at the Lyceum, Ellen Terry. Craig had undergone a nine-year spell as a junior actor with Irving's company. On tour lead roles had come his way but once he had shaken off the dust of those nine years (and briefly directed his mother in Shakespeare) Craig was to depart for a life-long stay in Europe where he published seminal books on theatre – *The Art of the Theatre* in 1905 and *Towards a New Theatre* in 1913.

Craig's theories have been criticised for reducing the actor to the role of puppet (had he longed to make a marionette of Irving in his youth?). The early Old Vic Shakespeare companies were entirely without the means to put Craig's grandiose scenic theories into practice – indeed few organisations were to put them to the test. But his violent rejection, from the safety of his home abroad, of the London actor-manager traditions must be placed, along with the works and the writings of Poel and Granville Barker, as a factor in the climate of 'new thinking' about Shakespeare production when the Old Vic Shakespeare Company was beginning to acquire an international reputation.

Lilian Baylis' frequently quoted remark that, not being able to get any more clean pictures for the Old Vic, she turned from cinema 'in despair' to Shakespeare is as amusing and as inaccurate as many of the more colourful stories told about her. Far from turning 'in despair' to Shakespeare, Lilian Baylis very much resented the Old Vic Governors' allowing Shakespeare to be staged at the Old Vic in the spring of 1914. This was partly because she saw it as a rival and a threat to her then

best-loved opera company. In particular, however, she deeply resented
the fact that 'her' Old Vic was being used by Rosina Filippi to stage
Shakespeare as part of a Filippi-led campaign on behalf of 'People's
Theatre'.

The Filippi season was in fact a débâcle. But it did help to plant in
Lilian Baylis' mind the idea of opening her own Shakespeare company
at the Old Vic. As Richard Findlater succinctly puts it in his biography
of Lilian Baylis, 'The Governors had spoken firmly in support of
Shakespeare and more materially, Lilian seems to have decided that
there were several points in his favour – as long as Rosina Filippi was
not making them. He was cheap to stage, if produced in the right way,
he provided a good deal of moral uplift. There were, it seems, plenty
of actors eager to act in his plays, who could be persuaded to do it
"Mainly as a labour of love", as all things should be done at the
Vic . . .'

The awesome prospect now opens up of chartering the development
of play direction at the Old Vic in the sixty-two years that elapsed
between the setting up of the Old Vic Shakespeare Company in 1914
and the moving out of the Old Vic of the National Theatre Company in
1976. Obviously, in a comprehensive book of this kind, any attempt at
a detailed chronological examination of the intervening seasons would
be the surest way of obliterating the sight of the wood for the trees. A
clearing through the jungle of productions that constitute the Old Vic's
twentieth-century dramatic history must, however, somehow be
made.

Perhaps a starting point in this operation may be made by looking at
the artistic directors whose régimes break up this history into its
constituent phases. A broad indication of the personality of these
directors and the way it shaped their approach to the productions
ought, at least, to provide some guidelines.

As far as the forty-nine years of the Old Vic Company itself are
concerned, probably the best way of coming to grips with the directors
involved is to see them as two groups – those that worked under Lilian
Baylis' management from 1914 to her death in 1937 and those directors
who enabled her enterprise to survive from 1937 to 1963. Finally, there
must be a coda on direction at the Old Vic from 1963 to 1976 when the
National Theatre Company were tenants of the Old Vic.

First, back then to 1914 and Lilian Baylis' conversion to Shakespeare – so long as Rosina Filippi were not in charge. Philip Ben Greet became in the autumn of 1914, when in his fifty-sixth year, the first of the Old Vic directors. His was an infinitely different world from the consciously innovating reformists – whether they were in the practical mould of a Poel or a Granville Barker or the more flamboyantly theoretical format of an Edward Gordon Craig. Greet had learned his Shakespeare business the hard way, touring Shakespeare in England and North America, in the most primitive conditions that any hard-working actor-manager could expect to contend with. The emphasis had often been on the pastoral open-air presentation of Shakespeare today associated with London's Open Air Theatre in Regent's Park which Greet in fact helped to establish.

This long experience had ensured that Greet knew his Shakespeare inside out. It also ensured that he took the most calamitous of disasters as a necessary professional hazard. He made heroic efforts to establish the continuity of a Shakespeare Company at the Old Vic in the First World War years of 1914-18. For this white-haired, blue-eyed, High Church actor-manager, the Old Vic work was his contribution to the war work. He made no attempt to dabble in the then fashionable theories of neo-Elizabethan staging or to restore the traditional cuts in Shakespeare's texts. Sitting on stage with a bag of sweets in his hand, Greet would put his rehearsal cast through time-honoured bits of business and was satisfied so long as the actors got through the evening and the public accepted the make-do sets and costumes (some permanently borrowed from the actor-manager, Matheson Lang). If the productions seemed reformist compared to the splendours of Irving or of Tree's Shakespeare, it was due to a combination of the pastoral staging tradition and sheer lack of money with which to embark on anything fussier.

Greet was fortunate to have at the head of his company, Sybil Thorndike who had trained at his own 'Academy' and had toured North America with him. She was not at that time a star. But her willingness to play male as well as female parts, her vitality and her good relationship with Lilian Baylis ensured that she was a pillar of strength in what were afterwards to be described as 'the dark days of the Old Vic'.

A second distinction of Greet's régime was the inauguration of what was to become an Old Vic ritual – a gala Shakespeare programme on Shakespeare's supposed birthday of 23 April. The first of these was in April 1915. In the following years as the Company grew more famous and prestigious, this Shakespeare Birthday Programme grew into a marathon presentation in which former stars returned to contribute a celebratory scene or monologue. Such an event could not claim to contribute anything so lofty as the emergence of an Old Vic house style. But it had a lot to do with the style of the house – the family feeling that grew up between the audience regulars and the artists who appeared on the Old Vic stage. The return of former Old Vic artists to ritual celebrations helped to underpin this feeling of belonging to 'a family'. Another ritual – the cutting of the Twelfth Night Cake in a ceremony attended by generations of former players – continued into the 1970s and was promoted by the Vic-Wells Association, even though both the Old Vic and Sadler's Wells had by then ceased to be occupied by an Old Vic or a Sadler's Wells Company.

Perhaps the most valuable legacy from the Greet Old Vic régime was the establishment of the tradition of giving matinee performances for schools. In the 1960s and 1970s the sophisticated use of drama in education does make the crocodile formations of schools filing up to see special Shakespeare matinees appear, retrospectively, a crude form of drama education. And these matinees before noisy bun-devouring children were certainly not popular with the actors whose job it was to keep the young audiences held by the plays. But the work was valuable in establishing the reputation of the Old Vic as a national centre of culture. More to the point, these matinees helped the Baylis management to balance its always shaky books.

First notice of these schools' matinees appears in the Old Vic General Report for the 1914–15 season which remarks:

Special matinees of some of the plays have been given on Wednesdays for schoolchildren and the Management have endeavoured to produce those which the various schools are reading and taking for examinations. Attendances were highly gratifying. . . . *As You Like It* was given and the demand from the LCC schools was so great that two extra matinees had to be arranged. Over 4,000 children witnessed the play that week.

That, by any standards, was an impressive start. So it is hardly surprising that Lilian Baylis looked upon Greet's work in providing Shakespeare matinees for the London County Council Schools after he had left the Old Vic in 1918 as a form of rivalry.

After Greet's departure there were short seasons under the direction of G. R. Foss and, jointly, under the actors, Charles Warburton and Russell Thorndike. Though these seasons were interesting in as far as actors alternated in roles like Othello and Iago, they really kept the enterprise going until Robert Atkins was demobilised and able to take up his four-year appointment as the Shakespeare director from 1920 to 1925. In these four years the Old Vic was to become both a nationally and an internationally recognised institution.

By the time he came to direct the fortunes of the Old Vic drama company, Atkins was a seasoned thirty-four-year-old actor whose apprenticeship had been served touring with the Ben Greet and Frank Benson companies. He had also made an impression during a wartime season at the Old Vic in the year 1915-16, playing roles requiring an actor of stamina and sturdiness, like Richard III, Sir Toby Belch, Caliban and Lear. There was nothing willowy or palely poetic about Robert Atkins.

His fiery temper, his foul language, his heavy drinking and womanising may suggest that the Old Vic had a philistine rather than an artistic innovator at the helm in the early 1920s. And Atkins was certainly no university-educated intellectual like the post-Baylis Shakespeare directors such as Tyrone Guthrie, Hugh Hunt and Michael Benthall. Moreover his relationship with Lilian Baylis was, if anything, more acrimonious than the one that had existed between Ben Greet and the Vic's lady Manager. Atkins was later to suggest that Lilian Baylis in fact kept the job of Shakespeare director open to him on the basis of his ability in running the Old Vic Company's 1916 visit to Stratford-upon-Avon when Greet and Baylis were not even on speaking terms. When that job did come his way for four extraordinary years, 'rowing terms' would be an apt description of the stormy relationship between the Vic's drama director and its Manager.

But just as Greet had been the right man to keep the Shakespeare Company ticking over in the war years, so Atkins was the best choice to thrust the venture forward at a time when it still lacked elementary resources like proper dressing rooms and workshops.

Unlike Greet, Atkins was in favour of restoring much of the original Shakespeare texts instead of accepting the status quo of the then standard cuts. More importantly, he plumped firmly for the nearest possible approximation within such a theatre of Elizabethan staging by forcing Lilian Baylis to agree to the installation of a false proscenium and moveable platform over the orchestra. He benefited from the fact that Russell Thorndike had had the courage to remove the ancient grooves on which the old melodrama sets had been assembled. But Atkins was anxious to go much further in pushing the action of the play over into the lap of the audience. His platform-type settings began the very necessary process of speeding up the pace of the presentation of the plays. Atkins' lighting effects were at the time much admired, however primitive the resources with which he achieved them.

The celebrity that the Old Vic was now beginning to acquire rested to some extent on Atkins' choice of plays as well as on the new ways in which he sought to present them. To stage such rarely revived Shakespeare plays as *Titus Andronicus* and *Troilus and Cressida* as well as directing the first public production in English of Ibsen's *Peer Gynt* helped to ensure that drama critics now started to regard productions at the Old Vic as essential viewing – however unwilling Lilian Baylis may have been to provide them with free seats.

Confirmation of the Old Vic's growing status came in two ways under the Atkins régime. The first occurred early on when the Old Vic Company made the first of what, over the years, were to be world-wide visits abroad. At the invitation of the Belgian Minister for the Arts, the Old Vic represented Britain at a short season in Brussels in June 1921. 'The Old Vic', the General Reports notes with obvious pride over this visit, 'seems to be regarded by experts as a theatre where Shakespeare plays are presented in the right way'.

What really helped to focus attention on the Old Vic's shoestring Shakespeare work was the 7 November 1923 production of *Troilus and Cressida*. With this presentation, the Old Vic could claim to be the first theatre to have presented the complete cycle of Shakespeare plays in the

First Folio. This, of course, had not been a conscious aim when the Company first came into being in 1914. But it did illustrate how much Shakespeare had been given. In the 1950s Michael Benthall was to repeat this achievement and though he too had to complete the job under difficulties worsened by a dwindling Arts Council subsidy, his resources were infinitely better than those of the early Old Vic directors. Throughout the Greet régime and for the better part of Atkins', the Old Vic was without workshops and dressing rooms until Morely College was rehoused in its own premises. And both directors had to share the theatre's woefully inadequate resources with an opera company.

Unlike Andrew Leigh, Harcourt Williams and Tyrone Guthrie who were to follow him, Atkins could not claim to have launched a major star or to have basked in the glory of the successful visit of an established one. Actors of the magnitude of John Gielgud and Edith Evans were to come into their own on the Old Vic stage later. But with the return of Ernest Milton, one of the most famous of the Vic's early Hamlets, and with companies that included Ion Swinley and John Laurie, Atkins obviously had a talented company to bring to bear on the reforms he was determined to make.

Despite the verbal hit and run relationship that existed between drama director and manager, it is clear from the Annual General Reports that Lilian Baylis was well aware of the importance of the work being done for her by Robert Atkins. In the Report for the 1921-22 season for example the following extract is revealing:

Unquestionably the amazing success of *Peer Gynt*, given with practically the whole of Grieg's music, has been the distinguishing feature of the season. Produced with great trepidation and with what was, for the Vic, a very great expense, entirely against the advice of experts, *Peer Gynt* has been the means of bringing a still wider public to the Old Vic . . . once more the method of production used at the Old Vic (that is, the use of the 'apron stage' and self-coloured curtains rather than cumbersome 'sets') has vindicated itself. How many theatres would have had the courage to present the play with the swift simplicity that is essential if the tangled thread of the story is to hold the stage?

Extracts from the 1922-23 season make it clear that Atkins was alive to the need for producing Shakespeare plays in a related way as well as giving the Vic public important works like *Peer Gynt*:

> A special feature of the season has been the predominance of History Plays. It has long been the ambition of Robert Atkins, the producer, to give the chronicle plays from *King John* to *Henry VIII* in succession. And if he has not attained this idea, he has at any rate got very near it. . . . For ease and coherence in these History Plays, and to obviate delay in changing scenes, a third stage was projected over the orchestra pit, at a slightly lower level than the 'apron stage', so that the Old Vic resembled, as far as was compatible with a modern structure, the Elizabethan stage of Shakespeare's own day. . . . Unfortunately the lesser-known histories, which surely every student and indeed citizen of London ought to see, where not too well supported by the public.

The Report for the 1924-25 season succinctly records the passing of Atkins' remarkable five-year stint as the Old Vic's director and, in ringing out the old director, rings in the new one.

> It was with the keenest regret that the Governors received in March the resignation of their producer for the Shakespeare plays, Robert Atkins, who has acted in that capacity at this theatre since 1920. In June of that year Mr Atkins, who had already been stage-manager at the Old Vic, was given the opportunity of trying his mettle in the matter of production, to prove that he could carry out the ideals he had already expressed. After five years at the Old Vic, his name has become practically world-famous where Shakespeare is concerned . . . Andrew Leigh, who had a hand in the first Shakespeare productions here, and has always been ready to help when a principal comedian was required in the Shakespeare Company, has been appointed to fill Robert Atkins' place.

If the Greet and Atkins régimes had been notable for the stormy relationship that existed between directors and management, that of Andrew Leigh from 1925 to 1929 was, on the contrary, remarkably calm. Leigh earned the nickname 'Merry Andrew' and it seems to have been bestowed with good reason for, when the time came for Leigh to hand over in the 1929-30 season to Harcourt Williams, the Report remarks, of Leigh, 'he never lost the friendship and goodwill of a single one of those who have worked with him'.

A gentle and easy-going personality is not necessarily the hallmark of a good or of a great director. It might, therefore, be pardonable to wonder if Leigh's four years were something of an anti-climax after the stormy whirlwind of activity when Atkins presided over the transformation of well-meaning shoestring local enterprise into a still impoverished one that nonetheless claimed international attention. Leigh was fortunate in that he started his period as Old Vic director by engaging two already established stars to lead the company – Edith Evans and Balliol Holloway. As the Report puts it:

> To speak of the producer as new is in one sense incorrect, but Andrew Leigh has had to adapt himself to very different conditions from those of the gas-lit, hand-to-mouth days of 1914. Moreover, the Old Vic departed to some extent from its established policy of engaging comparatively unknown artists. This, at any rate, is true with regard to the two principals, one an exceptional experienced and admirable Shakespeare actor, the other an inimitable English actress whose established fame has certainly been enhanced by the parts she has played so brilliantly at the Vic during the past season.

The runaway success of Edith Evans in the 1925-26 season ensured that the first post-Atkins season was anything but an anti-climax. The addition to the non-Shakespeare repertoire of Dekker's *The Shoemaker's Holiday* may not have carried the *éclat* of an Ibsen première, but it did show that the new director was not to rely solely on stars winning an enthusiastic public exclusively in the best-known and best-loved Shakespearean works.

If an anti-climax was felt then it came the following year. Thanks to the box-office appeal of Edith Evans, business had been excellent. The 1926-27 Report remarks that up to Christmas the takings had hardly diminished by comparison, but subsequently they had suffered, chiefly owing to a bad patch struck unexpectedly in the early spring.

The momentum was bound to fall off again the following season when the theatre was closed for re-building and the drama company had to take itself off for a period to the Lyric Theatre, Hammersmith. As the Report for 1927-28 puts it:

> The activities of the Shakespeare Company for the past year fall naturally into three divisions: the first comprising the season at Hammersmith, the second that at the Old Vic and the third the short tour, which included a visit to Scotland.

The Old Vic Company was fortunate to have the use of the Lyric, Hammersmith, while its own theatre was being rebuilt. But the smaller stage and resources of the Lyric meant that plays which needed big crowd scenes and the swiftness of action provided by the Vic apron stage could not be attempted. Notwithstanding these difficulties, Leigh managed to add another non-Shakespeare play to the repertory, *The Two Noble Kinsmen*, attributed to Shakespeare and Fletcher. It had not been publicly performed since Shakespeare's day, the Report proudly pointed out.

The Report for the 1928-29 season admirably sums up the Leigh régime. It notes that he was the first director to benefit from the theatre's rebuilding in 1927. But it also notes that he paid the price for it with the decentralisation caused by the move to Hammersmith. That his first, Edith Evans, season was the most successful ever, in financial terms, is remembered. But so is the fact that in his four years at the Old Vic he directed no less than thirty-eight plays, twenty-three of which were by Shakespeare. Among the others the innovation of introducing *The Shoemaker's Holiday* and *The Two Noble Kinsmen* is recalled. And, as the Report gratefully brings down the curtain on Leigh, it raises it on his successor, Harcourt Williams. Announcing Williams' appointment, which was also to last four years, it is remembered that his 'wife's family having such old and close associations with this theatre, her mother, Antoinette Sterling, having been perhaps the most beloved of all the great artists who gave their services to Emma Cons'. Harcourt Williams at that time had little experience of directing. It was said that Lilian Baylis took him up on the strength of his directing a matinee of children's plays presented by Antoinette Sterling's daughter.

Like Andrew Leigh, Harcourt Williams was to reverse the process of confrontation with Lilian Baylis that had marked the eras of Ben Greet and Robert Atkins. And he was to accelerate the pace of productions. Time-honoured 'business' was to be thrown out, as were the vestiges of the Victorian actor-manager delivery of the verse. In this respect, Williams was fortunate in securing the services as lead player of John Gielgud, who had been a mere walk-on in the days of Robert Atkins. Gielgud's mercurial Shakespearean verse-speaking has become so legendary that his engagement seems, retrospectively, to have been as auspicious for the Williams' régime at the Old Vic as Edith Evans' début at the same theatre had been for Andrew Leigh's. There was to be a difference, though. Edith Evans remained for a season. John Gielgud stayed for several. And he became as much Harcourt Williams' co-director as his leading man.

The venture got off to a difficult start. The gallery regulars resented the speed with which Shakespeare's verse was delivered, or as they saw it, 'gabbled'. The opening productions – *Romeo and Juliet* and *The Merchant of Venice* – had bad notices. In despair, the gentle Harcourt Williams went to Lilian Baylis' office to tender his resignation. Instead of the haughty female adversary Greet and Atkins had found in that office, Harcourt Williams discovered instead a mothering friendly soul who was prepared to back him up – whatever the critics and the regulars might say. It was to take her much longer to overcome her suspicion of Harcourt Williams' successor, Tyrone Guthrie. When the regulars complained of *his* innovations, in 1933, she listened. And Guthrie temporarily departed after a single initial season. Only later did she come back to him and even prepare to think of Guthrie as her successor.

As far as Harcourt Williams was concerned, Lilian Baylis' confidence in him and his lead player proved to be justified. The opening season progressed from the shakey *Romeo and Juliet*, through *Macbeth* to an 'entirety' sell-out Hamlet that helped to establish John Gielgud as a new leader of his profession on the classical stage. Much to the management's satisfaction, improved notices were matched by improved takings which began to rival the by-now legendary box-office success of the 1925 Edith Evans season. And with his production of *A Midsummer Night's Dream*, Harcourt Williams had a personal success as a director.

Temperamentally, Harcourt Williams was not well suited to the exhausting demands of being an Old Vic director. These were made even harder after January 1931 when drama productions alternated between the Old Vic and what Lilian Baylis hoped would be a north London Old Vic, Sadler's Wells Theatre. But, though Williams lacked the physical stamina and the aggressive personality of a Robert Atkins, he was sufficiently in touch with the Shakespeare reformers to go further than Atkins in bringing Old Vic Shakespeare up to date. In his book on his work at the Old Vic, *Four Years at the Old Vic,* he frankly acknowledges his indebtedness to Granville Barker's *Shakespeare Prefaces.* And Gordon Craig wrote to him that 'the producers are going to save the English stage and have already begun'. With fifty productions to his credit, either as director, co-director or leading actor, Williams could justly claim to have made an impressive 'beginning'.

The Annual General Report for the 1930–31 season show Williams as keen to introduce the intimacy of the Elizabethan stage to Sadler's Wells as Robert Atkins had been to ensure its presence at the Old Vic. The Report notes:

> The producer's fondness for using the orchestra pit as a means of exit and entrance, as a simple experiment for imitating the three stages of Elizabethan days, has left its mark on the structure of Sadler's Wells. There two broad and beautiful staircases communicate with the orchestra pit and enhance the proscenium in place of the rather makeshift wooden stairs at one end only of the stage which have to be used at the Old Vic.

There was a characteristically Baylis economy measure in this device which clearly reflected managerial approval in the words 'this method is particularly useful where armies have to be represented, for the tops of several lances showing above the edge of the stage proper make a great effect without the employment of a vast 'crowd' . . .

The Old Vic's reputation as the nursery for the major British actors of the twentieth century was to be consolidated under the Williams' régime. Quite apart from John Gielgud, this director also had the good fortune to recruit Ralph Richardson, Peggy Ashcroft and Malcolm

Keen to his company. And the return of Edith Evans, as Viola and Emilia in *Othello*, ensured that the Old Vic audiences were able to enjoy the faster-paced Shakespeare executed by some of the greatest artists of the twentieth century, some of them at the start of their classical careers. The partnership of John Gielgud and Ralph Richardson under Harcourt Williams' direction in the early 1930s is particularly fascinating. In 1975 the same two actors were again working together at the Old Vic in Harold Pinter's *No Man's Land*, this time with the National Theatre Company.

When Harcourt Williams decided to conclude his fourth and final season with the Vic-Wells Company by playing Prospero in *The Tempest* he told the last night audience at the end of the performance, 'I hand my baton to the coming man, Tyrone Guthrie' and broke his Prospero staff on these words. It is doubtful if Harcourt Williams could have known how far into the distance this 'coming man' was to carry that baton.

The wholesale innovation that the thirty-three-year-old Guthrie inaugurated in his first 1933-34 season smacked of iconoclasm. For his attack was not so much directed at the last vestiges of Victorian actor-manager Shakespeare but at the cheeseparing conditions under which previous directors had been obliged to attempt reform. Charles Laughton made it a condition of his joining Flora Robson to lead Guthrie's new company that he would be professionally costumed. For this purpose he secured a grant from the Pilgrim Trust to ensure a higher standard of set and costume design than had been previously seen at the Old Vic. At least that was the intention. Unfortunately the then still inexperienced Guthrie employed an eminent architect to design a permanent set that Guthrie himself subsequently admitted was not only impractical but also intrusively contemporary – no matter how much ingenuity was used in re-painting and lighting it.

Lilian Baylis was also prevailed upon to employ a company of stars including Athene Seyler and Ursula Jeans as well as Flora Robson and Charles Laughton. Though their salaries were pitifully small by West End standards, they were enormous by Baylis reckonings. So much reform in so short a time ensured that Guthrie's new broom lasted for a single season only. The first of the non-actor university-educated directors at the Old Vic made what proved to be a temporary departure.

For the following two seasons, 1934-35 and 1935-36, Lilian Baylis turned to Henry Cass who had made a considerable reputation with a company in Croydon and promised to bring a new vitality to the Vic-Wells company. In 1976, with a not inconsiderable career as a film director behind him, Cass was the only surviving Baylis director available for consultation. He was quick to state that like Harcourt Williams, on whose recommendation he came to the Old Vic, the sheer workload of a Shakespeare repertory company alternating between the Vic and the Wells made demands beyond his stamina. Neither did he claim to be on the same intellectual wavelength of a Guthrie. An inspection of what Cass in fact achieved in those two years make his recollection of his work at the Old Vic in the mid-1930s seem unnecessarily modest. Of the twenty plays he presented at the Old Vic there were a number interesting non-Shakespeare dramatists like Shaw, *St Joan* and *Major Barbara*, Ibsen, *Peer Gynt*, Chekhov, *The Three Sisters* and Sheridan, *The School for Scandal.*

A special feature of this régime was that Cass persuaded Lilian Baylis to back him to the hilt in presenting a brand new play chronicling the last days of Napoleon, *St Helena*, by R. C. Sheriff and Jeanne de Casalis. This, in itself, was remarkable. For, just as the English Stage Company at the Royal Court from 1956 was famous for the presentation of new plays, the Old Vic Company from 1914 had achieved its reputation on the contrary for sticking to Shakespeare and the classics. Apart from the Christmas presentation of plays by Lilian Baylis' confessor, Father Andrew, the Old Vic Company had no reputation at all as a company anticipating the work of the English Stage Company in promoting the writings of new young English dramatists. In the event, *St Helena* had a terrible press and played to empty houses until Winston Churchill wrote to *The Times* on its behalf. In this way, a two-week flop was turned in a matter of a days into a profitable six weeks run and even managed a West End transfer.

In the autumn of 1936 Lilian Baylis and Tyrone Guthrie were reunited and the manager seems to have bowed to Guthrie's becoming her successor. This time he was allowed to get away with dismantling time-honoured Old Vic procedure and still remain on the staff. The first thing Guthrie sensibly did was to ensure that drama remained at the Old Vic and that the ballet and opera companies settled into Sadler's Wells

Theatre. The confusion in the public's mind about what opera, ballet performance or drama production was on at which theatre was thereby overcome. This helped Guthrie also to kill off the sacred 'Green Leaflet' – a publicity handout printed on green paper in which the season's details were distributed from the company's earliest days. The trouble with that Green Leaflet was that it did not allow for flexibility. The announced programme had to be adhered to whether or not a production turned out to be a success and ought to have an extended run – or, on the contrary, was a flop and should be withdrawn. Guthrie's first season with a smaller company led by names as talented as those of Edith Evans, Michael Redgrave, Alec Guinness and Laurence Olivier ensured that what was to be the last season under Lilian Baylis's management was also one of that management's most exciting.

The post-1937, post-Lilian Baylis years at the old Vic are mainly a chronicle of the work of university-educated professional directors like Guthrie himself, Hugh Hunt, Michael Benthall and Michael Elliott. This course was to be interrupted only by a return to an enlightened actor-manager era when Laurence Olivier, Ralph Richardson and John Burrell were the triumvirate of directors who ran the Old Vic Company from 1944 to 1949 in exile at the New Theatre (now Albery) pending the re-building of the Old Vic, damaged in the blitz of 1940.

Before turning in more detail to the post-Baylis Old Vic, it would be as well to glance at an outside factor which was to have repercussions on performances of Shakespeare in the Waterloo Road, since Shakespeare was to remain the Company's chief dramatist.

Hitherto the reform in Shakespeare production had emanated from the teachings of Poel, Granville Barker and, to a limited extent, Craig. It was concerned with the speeding up of the delivery of the verse and the pace of the staging on some approximation to the simplicity and intimacy of the Elizabethan stage. In 1925 quite a new influence was to be felt with the arrival in London for a season of Shakespeare by the Birmingham Repertory Company run by the wealthy theatrical benefactor, Barry Jackson. What Jackson brought to Shakespeare was the performances of the plays in modern dress. In the mid-1920s this, when applied to *Hamlet*, had caused a sensation and a flurry of controversy. It was to be characteristic of Guthrie's spirited but irreverent attitude to Shakespeare that he was to be the first Old Vic director to bring 'modern dress Shakespeare' to the Old Vic in 1938 when a twenty-four year old Alec Guinness played the Prince of Denmark in its entirety in contemporary clothing.

Guthrie's lighter-hearted régime was to be reflected in his first season's choice of non-Shakespeare plays. Wycherley's *The Country Wife* was, in 1937, a much smuttier Restoration masterpiece for the Governors of the Old Vic to accept than Congreve's *Love for Love* which Guthrie had included in the repertory of his first season back in 1933. With the Wycherley play there was a head-on. clash with the Governors. But the play remained intact. The combination of a lewd classic like Wycherley's play and Shakespeare in modern-dress indicated that the spirit of moral uplift that marked Emma Cons' Royal Victoria Hall and for many years still pervaded Lilian Baylis' Old Vic was, under Guthrie, to make way for a theatre with a freer and a more flexible policy. The commitment was still to provide drama cheaply. But the generation that started to go to the Old Vic in the late 1930s would not have relished having themselves described, as the Old Vic Charter classified them, as 'labourers and artisans'.

When the Old Vic Company under Guthrie's direction was invited to stage its production of *Hamlet* at Elsinore in 1937 in the last months of Lilian Baylis' life, torrential rain forced the improvised staging of the play in the ballroom of Elsinore's Kronborg Castle. The in-the-round, arena type staging necessary was to be a prologue to Guthrie's later work in this form of staging. His work was to stretch as widely as the use of Edinburgh's Assembly Hall for his famous production of *The Three Estates* to his founding, in North America, of the Stratford Ontario Theatre and the Guthrie Theatre in Minneapolis.

It was sad that Guthrie could not have explored this radical change of staging from the Old Vic itself. As a Regency playhouse with its proscenium arch, it did not lend itself to the return to Elizabethan staging on the scale that Guthrie was to foster after he had left the Old Vic's permanent administration. Had he been able to do so, it would have seemed a logical development of the work begun on the same stage by Robert Atkins at the beginning of the 1920s. However, only two years after Lilian Baylis' death in 1937, Guthrie, as her successor, was to see her achievements dispersed and to some extent dissipated as a result of the onset of the Second World War. Guthrie had the thankless task of overseeing the work of the Old Vic from the safety of exile in the Lancashire town of Burnley where, under austerity war-time conditions, regional tours were set up. The climate was not right for further reform and radical experiment with a return to arena staging. The most that could be hoped for was survival. It was achieved – but at the cost of the Baylis Opera and Ballet Companies becoming permanently disengaged from the Old Vic Shakespeare Company.

It would however, be misleading to suggest that Guthrie's work at the Old Vic should be summarised as that of a thwarted disciple of a William Poel and the Elizabethan Stage Society. The fustiness of that Society had no part in Guthrie's witty and inventive personality. He wore his scholarship lightly and his productions were never solemn. On the contrary, even his most fervent admirers could not help noticing that this director's lively sense of fun resulted in some of his productions being so restlessly full of irrelevant but amusing stage business that attention was sometimes distracted from the verse itself. Was this because the director seemed to have a lack of confidence in it? How else, they asked, could one explain the need to invent staging that kept the audience entertained. Such a director, however inventive, must suspect that the regulars would find over-familiar Shakespeare tedious if not decked out in new directorial clothes. It was a point of view that grossly oversimplified Guthrie's faults, though there was a foundation of truth in it.

Michael Benthall, who was to be one of Guthrie's successor's after the Old Vic Company returned to the Old Vic Theatre in 1950, learnt his business as an actor with Guthrie and as co-director, in the 1944 revival of *Hamlet* starring Robert Helpmann at the New Theatre. Benthall, also was to be censured for being waywardly inventive in some Shakespeare revivals. But there was to be an essential difference between Guthrie as mentor and Benthall as pupil. Guthrie, once he had left the Old Vic's permanent staff was repeatedly to explore the open staging of Shakespeare with scenery reduced to a few essential props. Benthall, behind the proscenium arch of the Old Vic and, in particular, with the collaboration of the designer, Leslie Hurry, was to place the Shakespeare business in a painterly, often gorgeously costumed world where it could be said to have been as much choreographed as directed.

This diversity of taste can be most readily confirmed by consulting

Guthrie's biography, *A Life in the Theatre*. After regretting that Sadler's Wells Ballet broke away from what had been the Baylis Empire at the end of the Second World War, Guthrie deals with its re-emergence at the Royal Opera House where it was to be eventually the Royal Ballet. Revealingly, Guthrie remarks, that 'without content, ballet has no right to the pretension that it is an art on an equality with opera or drama'. And he dismisses the Royal Opera House as 'an artistic graveyard: its cubic capacity is enormous but it holds a comparatively small audience' and then rounds off his dismissal of ballet as 'a mere sweetmeat on the theatrical menu'.

Guthrie was to return to the Old Vic for the 1951-52 season of which the highlight was Donald Wolfit's performance in the title-role of *Tamburlaine*. But after his exhausting war-years with the Old Vic Company, his future was to be in staging Shakespeare and other writers in new open-stage theatres where the proscenium frame was an anathema.

For Michael Benthall, neither ballet nor the proscenium arch were an anathema; he would not have otherwise survived nine years at the Old Vic with its modified picture-frame stage from 1953 to 1961. Nor would he have collaborated so closely and often, so rewardingly, with a former leading ballet dancer, Robert Helpmann.

The post-Baylis Old Vic fortunes cannot, however, be simplified into the mere divergence of direction taken by Guthrie and Benthall. Before those fortunes were over with the winding up of the company in 1963, there had been a most important resurgence of the company in exile at the New Theatre from 1944 to 1949 under the Olivier/Richardson/Burrell triumvirate and that resurgence had a lot to do with a revival of actor-manager theatre and much less with the austerities of Elizabethan staging or the painterly riches of proscenium-arch style presentation.

In 1944 Guthrie had been able to persuade the Admiralty to release both actors from war service on the grounds that they could do much more valuable morale-boosting work by keeping the Old Vic flag flying in central London. The triumvirate, for such it was to become when the young John Burrell joined the two famous actors, began brilliantly. The period is remembered in terms of star names giving star performances – Olivier's doubling-up in a single evening of

Oedipus in *Oedipus Rex* and Mr Puff in *The Critic* being the most striking.

Despite the acclaim that was heaped on performances like Olivier's Richard III and Richardson's Falstaff in the early years of the triumvirate régime, all was far from well with it. Guthrie, in his biography, puts his finger on what went wrong. He writes, 'The Shakespeare Company was now being operated by a triumvirate – Olivier, Richardson and John Burrell. I had agreed to the arrangement and already had misgivings about it. Burrell, considerably younger and less experienced than the other two, could not be expected to have the authority and the weight to stand up against their towering personalities.' Guthrie, in consequence, blames himself for what happened. The star actors tried to have their cake and eat it. They made films, toured north America and Australia and still remained Old Vic director-managers. Increasingly John Burrell had the burden of administration and direction heaped upon him. Towards the end of the 1944-49 triumvirate the strain began to show. It was perhaps unfortunate that it had begun with such brilliance in terms of star performances because the Old Vic Company public at the New Theatre had exacting standards by which to judge the company.

At the close of the five-year period when the contract of the triumvirate expired, the Old Vic Governors appointed in their place a director who had emerged with much promise from the Bristol Theatre Royal which had been re-opened as the Bristol Old Vic. By name, Hugh Hunt, he was to direct the final season at the New Theatre and the opening seasons of the Old Vic Company's return to the Old Vic, beginning in November 1950.

The complications in the fortunes of the Old Vic Company at this period are made harder to charter because of important though eventually abortive attempts to widen the scope of the organisation. One of these was the founding of the Old Vic School in January 1947 under the direction of Michel Saint-Denis which made use for a time of the damaged Old Vic Theatre. A Young Vic Company, under Michel Saint-Denis, Glen Byam Shaw and George Devine was also set up as a complementary organisation both to offer work to promising young actors and to play for young people and to tour. The Old Vic School was wound up in 1952, the Young Vic having been disbanded a year earlier. Clearly the formation and premature demise of two such important enterprises involves internal dissension within the organisation which it is beyond the scope of this book to discuss.

On the surface, the initially brilliant and acclaimed work of the 'triumvirate', with the backing up in the late 1940s of an Old Vic School and a Young Vic Company should have ensured that the Old Vic Company's return to the Old Vic Theatre in 1950 would carry the entire enterprise to even greater heights. Instead the early 1950s marked the ending of both the Old Vic School and Young Vic Company – and the early departure of the new director, Hugh Hunt.

The Hunt régime is fully described in Hugh Hunt's admirably honest book, *Old Vic Prefaces.* These are based on blueprints of lectures that Hunt had given his cast before getting down to the business of day to day rehearsing. Clearly, in this scholarly atmosphere, the Old Vic had come a very long way indeed from the sweet-munching days of Ben Greet. And just as Andrew Leigh had the good fortune to begin his régime with Edith Evans, and Harcourt Williams his with John Gielgud, so Hugh Hunt for the Old Vic's final New Theatre Season had a star of the magnitude of Michael Redgrave to inaugurate his.

The beginning looked auspicious whatever rumblings of discontent may have been going on in the wings over the Young Vic and Old Vic School. But as far as Hugh Hunt's own work is concerned, a key to its drawbacks may be discerned in the Postscripts the author has had the candour to round off his Prefaces with. The careful reader will see that there was a considerable discrepancy between the ideas outlined by Hunt at the start of the production and their carrying out for the first night and the critics. Although Hunt had the advantage of having Peggy Ashcroft to lead his Old Vic Company back into the Old Vic in 1950 (as Viola in *Twelfth Night*), it soon became clear that the beginning of the 1950s was not to make a highlight in the Old Vic's history. In his book Hunt himself takes responsibility. In the postscript to his final production at the Old Vic, *Julius Caesar* in 1953, he even goes so far as to apologise to his cast for exposing them to criticism for which he alone was to blame.

The sequel was the arrival of a new Old Vic administrator, Alfred Francis from 1953 to 1958, and the artistic directorship of Michael Benthall which lasted from 1953 to 1961. In the face of a shrinking Arts

Council subsidy, Benthall pressed ahead with his Five Year Plan for the presentation of all thirty-six Shakespeare plays in the First Folio. Benthall himself was compelled to undertake the direction of many more of the plays than he had intended to. The fact that the Old Vic formed second touring companies meant that the organisation's resources were stretched to the limit. But money was made on these overseas tours, so funds began to be available to add to a grant from the City Parochial Fund for the building and opening of the Old Vic Annexe in 1958. This brought the old theatre workshop resources beyond the wildest dreams of Lilian Baylis and directors like Greet, Atkins, Williams and Cass. In order to survive, the Old Vic had to secure the services of name artists not associated with Shakespeare and the classical theatre. The engagement of Ann Todd as Lady Macbeth in 1954 and of Frankie Howerd in 1957 to play Bottom in *A Midsummer Night's Dream* are good examples. These artists were brave to risk their professional reputations for a modest salary by making their Shakespeare debuts in a theatre associated with artists whose classical training had been long and arduous. Risks of this kind kept the Old Vic Company alive. But the foundations for an ensemble such as Michel Saint-Denis, George Devine and Glen Byam Shaw had had in mind in the late 1940s can hardly be said to have been achieved in the season-to-season experiments that the Old Vic Company had to make to carry out its Five Year Plan.

The final years of the Old Vic Company were enlivened by the guest appearance of a director like Franco Zeffirelli, whose 1960 production of *Romeo and Juliet* brought excitement and critical attention to a theatre and to a company that had seemed through the late 1950s to be losing its vitality. In the circumstances, Michael Elliott's period as the last Old Vic director for the 1962-63 season cannot have been easy in the light of the imminent transformation of the Old Vic theatre to the National Theatre under Laurence Olivier. Wisely, Elliott surrounded himself by a nucleus of artists who had been associated with his pioneering work with the 59 Company at the Lyric Theatre, Hammersmith, some of whom were to re-join him for the 69 Company to be established in Manchester in 1969.

When Laurence Olivier took over the direction of the National Theatre Company in 1963 it would have been easy for him to fall into the trap of making the new company a re-constituted version of the Old Vic Company he had directed with Richardson and Burrell at the New Theatre. Wisely he brought into the new organisation names associated with the new movement begun at the Royal Court in 1956 with the English Stage Company's première of John Osborne's *Look Back in Anger*. The critic who had done most to boost the new movement, Kenneth Tynan, was appointed Literary Manager. Royal Court directors, John Dexter and William Gaskill were made Associate Directors. They certainly ensured that the new company housed at the Old Vic did not begin with the museum-like trappings and bureaucratic administration that had blighted the work of some of the long-subsidised German municipal theatres – not to mention more venerable institutions like the Comédie Française and the Moscow Art Theatre.

But thirteen years is a long time to wait for the completion of your own home. By the time the National Theatre Company came to leave the Old Vic for its new South Bank Theatres in 1976, the strain of leading the National Theatre Company as actor with performances on the scale of Othello, Edgar in *The Dance of Death*, and Shylock as well as directing plays and administering the theatre, meant that even Sir Laurence's health was overtaxed and the direction of the National Company had passed to Peter Hall.

Perhaps one of the highest compliments that could be paid to the pioneering work done by Lilian Baylis' directors and their successors was that only when the National Theatre Company left the Old Vic did many people realise that the National Theatre and the Old Vic were not one and the same thing.

VIII   *Some Actors*

In the twentieth century, the two words 'Old Vic' have become synonymous with great acting, particularly in the plays of Shakespeare. Is it possible to define the qualities that constitute an 'Old Vic' actor? Does the term simply mean *any* actor who has happened to appear on the Old Vic stage at some time between the forming of the Shakespeare Company in 1914 and the winding up of the Old Vic Company in 1963? Should it even be extended to include all actors who appeared with an Old Vic Company, perhaps on a regional or an overseas tour, but who did not necessarily appear on the Old Vic stage itself? Ought the term to be further widened to include National Theatre Players who appeared at the Old Vic during the National Theatre Company's tenancy of the theatre from 1963 to 1976?

So very many actors have allied, in the public mind, the words 'Old Vic' and 'great acting'. Their quantity makes the task of defining their art all the more difficult. It would certainly help if the principal actors were the product of a single school that had shaped their technique and influenced their approach to the interpretation of Shakespeare and other great dramatists performed on the Old Vic's twentieth-century stage.

No such help is forthcoming. It is true that Lilian Baylis proudly announced the founding of an Old Vic Dramatic School in 1933. But, as one of its leading teachers was a conjuror engaged to teach actors 'quick thinking', it is hardly surprising that this academy has been and gone without leaving more than a footnote to theatrical history. It certainly failed to impart an Old Vic housestyle.

The Old Vic Theatre School, founded by Michel Saint-Denis in April 1946, at first looks considerably more promising. In his book,

Theatre: The Rediscovery of Style, Saint-Denis explains that the over-riding aim of this school was to provide both student actors and student technicians with a sense of ensemble, since they aimed to be what he called 'ensembliers'. It might seem logical, therefore, to expect that this school would provide the parent company at the Old Vic with certain definable qualities. But Saint-Denis' training organisation was disbanded soon after the Old Vic Company returned to its home theatre in 1950: it cannot help us very much in our enquiry.

Careful consultation of the Old Vic General Reports are. not particularly helpful either. Though successive Old Vic drama directors are welcomed in these pages on arrival – and also praised and thanked on departure – actors are more rarely mentioned. This in itself points to a consistent policy towards actors: they were not billed in this theatre as stars appearing in a particular season of plays. The *star* was the Old Vic Company itself. It is true that during the 1944 to 1949 period, when the Old Vic ran for five years in the West End under the triumvirate direction of Olivier, Richardson and John Burrell, audiences for a period did think more in terms of star actors giving star performances. But the tradition in the Waterloo Road itself was quite different.

Since the Old Vic Company was never able to pay well – or even tolerably well – by West End commercial standards, it is quite natural that once an actor made his reputation in the Waterloo Road, he was soon obliged to accept more lucrative offers coming from Shaftesbury Avenue managements and from film companies. The permanent billing 'Old Vic Company' did, therefore, give a misleading sense of continuity. In fact it was a seasonally re-employed *ad hoc* company. With the bait of the show-pieces in the Shakespeare canon, the loyalty of some of the great names of the twentieth-century British stage was commanded. Sometimes these names remained for successive seasons during their formative years. Later they occasionally returned to lead the company – rather in the manner of guest artists returning to what was once home ground.

In the circumstances, it seems wise to abandon any attempt to define an Old Vic actor in terms of an acting 'style' – or even in terms of the evolution of an acting style. What may be more rewarding is to glance at the careers of some of the most famous actors whose work has ensured the association of the Old Vic Theatre with this vague term 'great acting'. Inevitably, this means ignoring the industry of many hundreds of actors who did excellent work on the Old Vic stage for a very poor salary. But the well-intentioned jumbling together of deserving names will not make an already jumbled picture any clearer.

A theme does, however, exist that may enable some of the jigsaw to be pieced together. It concerns the range of characters tackled by some actors on the Old Vic stage compared to a certain specialisation in roles on the part of others.

The term 'Gentleman and Players' belongs to the world of sport. The borrowing of it here, in an attempt to categorise some of the work of the Old Vic's most famous actors, is bound to seem a snobbish intrusion. The fact remains that the Waterloo Road stage has seen successive generations of actors whose work can fairly be described as that of a 'Gentleman player'. On the other hand, there have been some outstanding artists whose performances have ranged beyond such aristocratic confines to merit the term a 'Player player'.

These two separate groups were not adversaries. If they were taking up a challenge at all, it was the challenge of the plays themselves, in particular, that offered by the works of William Shakespeare.

Six celebrated actors who were to take on Shakespeare in the Waterloo Road and thereby add to the Old Vic Company's fame were all born in the first fourteen years of the twentieth century – before the Company was even formed in the autumn of 1914. First, in 1902, arrived Ralph Richardson and Donald Wolfit. John Gielgud came along in 1904 with Laurence Olivier following in 1907. Michael Redgrave was next in 1908 with Alec Guinness completing the group with his birth in April 1914. They form a 'group' in the sense that they had all made their debuts before Lilian Baylis died in 1937 and therefore belong to the Baylis era to the extent that their careers with the Old Vic began in her lifetime. They are further linked in as far as they were all to become actor-knights. But they are not placed together here for that reason. It is just that their gifts are better known than most. These are also so varied that they offer as good a mosaic of the physical, mental and spiritual forces that helped shape the Old Vic's reputation as any other half dozen actors.

John Gielgud was the first of the knightly sextet to come to the Old Vic. In fact, his professional debut was made on its stage as the Herald amongst the spearcarriers in *Henry V* in 1921 when this actor was just seventeen. Although he remained with the Company for a time at the beginning of Robert Atkins' five-year régime, it was too soon to judge for certain then whether he was to be a Gentleman player or Player player. Between his leaving the Waterloo Road in 1922 and his return seven years later in 1929, John Gielgud twice took over roles from Noël Coward – in *The Vortex* and *The Constant Nymph*. Retrospectively, the clipped Coward-like inflections that Gielgud then commanded would seem to have made him a natural choice as leading man for Harcourt Williams' first 1929-30 season. This director arrived at the Old Vic with the avowed intention of speeding up the delivery of Shakespeare's verse as well as continuing the process, begun by Robert Atkins, of accelerating and simplifying the staging of the plays. Could there have been an actor better suited to collaborate in these reforms than John Gielgud who, in that first Harcourt Williams season, was assigned the parts of Romeo, Richard II, Oberon, Orlando and Hamlet?

In his autobiographical book, *Four Years at the Old Vic*, Harcourt Williams shows himself to be understandably proud of his discovery. 'I was never in any doubt about my leading man,' he writes. 'I had seen John Gielgud play a Butterfly in Nigel Playfair's production of *The Insect Play* at the Regent . . . I was not greatly impressed at that time as he had a strange body carriage from the heels backwards. But I had heard of his success under Komisarjevsky at the Barnes Theatre, and when I saw him as Oswald with Mrs Patrick Campbell in *Ghosts* and in *The Lady with the Lamp*, I realised that here was a very different person. Artistically, he had grown out of all knowledge and the fact that he had so grown appealed to me.'

Harcourt Williams goes on to relate how the negotiations to employ Gielgud nearly collapsed since Lilian Baylis was determined to knock ten shillings off the salary of Gielgud's leading lady, Martita Hunt. Then the writer goes on to remark, apropos Gielgud's signing his contract, 'that drop of ink saved Gielgud six years of toil, for it would certainly have taken him at least that time to put himself where two years at the Old Vic did'.

Gielgud was fortunate to be taking on leading roles at the Old Vic with a director whose personality was as relatively gentle and amiable as that of Harcourt Williams. Had the director possessed the explosive disposition of Robert Atkins, Gielgud might not otherwise have become unofficial co-director as well as leading man. This experience was to stand him in good stead when he himself became director as well as leading actor outside the Old Vic. And, in this context, it is interesting that Gielgud has described his conception of a director as an 'umpire'. He sees himself neither as dictator to the artists nor entirely as their servant. Rather, he envisages himself as someone able to give, what he hopes, is fair and reasonable advice to a cast of experienced actors naturally needing to consult him – however well they know their business. Yet Gielgud himself has been unafraid of putting his talents and reputation in the hands of an ultra-experimental director like Peter Brook who has a quite different conception of the director's role. A notable example of this Brook/Gielgud collaboration was to be seen at the Old Vic itself when John Gielgud appeared in Peter Brook's production of the Seneca *Oedipus* for the National Theatre Company in 1968. For the history-conscious this event was particularly fascinating because it represented a reversal of the Harcourt Williams/John Gielgud collaboration on the same stage in the 1930s when, on the contrary, the actor tended to predominate in the actor-director relationship.

Although Gielgud's Romeo at the start of the Williams/Gielgud season was unsuccessful, business and critical appraisal so picked up as the months went by that Gielgud finished the first year with his first attempt at Hamlet. By then it certainly was clear that this leading man was to be an aristocrat among players. His Prince of Denmark was even seen in the West End – at the Queen's in 1930. A second 1930-31 Old Vic season followed, when the Old Vic Company alternated between the Old Vic and the newly-opened Sadler's Wells. It consolidated his growing reputation for being a prince amongst players – a reputation that was to be established with the general West End theatregoing public through the long-running success at the New Theatre of *Richard of Bordeaux*.

John Gielgud himself has admitted his inability to play 'common'. He has in his time, appeared as a servant – most notably in the film, *Murder on the Orient Express*. But this cameo was, revealingly, as a gentleman's 'gentleman'. On stage, John Gielgud's immensely subtle and flexible delivery of verse has not extended to the successful assumption of characters with strong regional or cockney accents. Nor has his strong suit in the theatre been as an acrobatic actor or one who has delighted in the eccentricities of wild and lurid make-up.

These qualities did not work to his advantage in the mid-1950s with the advent of what was called the 'New Drama' by its admirers, or 'Kitchen Sink Drama', by those less enthusiastic about the new generation of dramatists emerging, in particular, from the Royal Court Theatre. Gielgud was, for a time, forced to retreat into the one-man recital world of an anthology programme like *The Ages of Man*, compiled from Shakespearean parts, many of which Gielgud had first played at the Old Vic.

Among these was Prospero, a 'father' role Gielgud first tackled at the Old Vic in 1940. It was a part he was to keep in his repertoire for a longer period than his world-famous Hamlet. He was, in fact, still playing this part when into his seventies and had returned to appear in Peter Hall's production of *The Tempest* for the National Theatre Company at the Old Vic in 1975. He had not appeared with the Old Vic Theatre Company in exile at the New Theatre from 1944 to 1949 during the Olivier/Richardson/Burrell directorship. And his only appearance with the Company when it had returned to the Waterloo Road was as Cardinal Wolsey in *Henry VIII* in 1958. This was a prestige production to mark the conclusion of Michael Benthall's Five Year Plan in staging all the plays in the First Folio.

In the circumstances, John Gielgud's appearances with the National Theatre Company at the Old Vic at a time when Laurence Olivier was its director came as a matter of some disappointment. The promised appearance together of Olivier and Gielgud – they had not been seen in the same play since they alternated Romeo and Mercutio in the West End in 1935 – did not materialise. Gielgud was given Orgon and not the title-role of *Tartuffe* in the 1967 Molière revival at the Old Vic. And Peter Brook's production of the Seneca *Oedipus* attracted more attention for the experimental nature of the production than for Gielgud's performance in it.

It was, therefore, fortunate that John Gielgud was able to return to the Old Vic before the National Theatre Company moved to its South Bank home in 1976. By 1975, Peter Hall had become Olivier's successor with the National Theatre Company. Hall's production that year of *The Tempest* was in the form of a masque in which some felt

Gielgud's Prospero remained rather isolated. But his appearance, also under Peter Hall's direction, in Harold Pinter's *No Man's Land* was a triumph and an award-winning performance at that.

It was a triumph shared with Ralph Richardson who co-starred in this four-handed Pinter play. Young theatregoers recalled the brilliant partnership of these two veteran players in David Storey's *Home* at the citadel of the New Drama, the Royal Court Theatre. This had taken place as recently as 1970. Older theatregoers, whose longer memories made them more history-conscious, realised that this partnership went considerably further back than 1970.

In the late 1920s, Harcourt Williams had spotted Ralph Richardson at Barry Jackson's Birmingham Repertory Theatre and had been impressed by his performance as Pygmalion in Shaw's *Back to Methuselah*. It was typical of Richardson, even in those days, that, when interviewed to join the Old Vic company in 1930, he spoke of his 'feeling doubtful about his usefulness in a round of Shakespeare parts'. And Gielgud, now into his second Old Vic season and Harcourt Williams' adviser and confidant, also questioned the advisability of taking on Richardson. It would be quite unworthy of Gielgud to attribute this reservation to the fear of the arrival of a scene-stealing rival. And, in any case, there were no grounds for fearing competition on Gielgud's own territory. For, if Gielgud was essentially a Gentleman player, Richardson was manifestly a Player player. Being of a heavier weight, he was cast, significantly, as Caliban and not Prospero in *The Tempest* and as Enobarbus and not Antony in *Antony and Cleopatra*. And when Sadler's Wells was opened in January 1931 as the north London Old Vic, he played the down-at-heel Sir Toby Belch to the Malvolio of Gielgud and not the love-sick nobleman, Orsino.

Further evidence of Richardson's physique placing him in the 'player' category came in the 1937-38 Old Vic season. In this he played Bottom in *A Midsummer Night's Dream* and also Othello. The latter was a role that Gielgud was to be conspicuously unsuccessful in when he attempted it, many years later, at Stratford-upon-Avon. Richardson's verse-speaking has never been as mercurial as Gielgud's. But his having a less aristocratic demeanour has meant that a greater variety of parts, particularly in Shakespeare, have been open to him. And he has been fortunate that he has found in the plays of J. B. Priestley and Robert

Bolt roles that have given scope for his ability to find the touch of poetry in the seemingly ordinary and not immediately colourful man-next-door.

Richardson's early years of harsh apprenticeship with regional touring companies and also with the Birmingham repertory, make him less a product than Gielgud of the Old Vic nursery. But his long-term association with the Old Vic Company has, if anything, been closer. His co-directorship, with Olivier and John Burrell, of the Company in its five years at the New Theatre ensured that. And his performances as Peer in *Peer Gynt*, Falstaff in *Henry IV Part I* and *Part II*, and the title-role of *Cyrano de Bergerac* go down in theatre history.

The Olivier/Richardson partnership was never renewed. Richardson did return to the Old Vic towards the end of Michael Benthall's Five Year Plan to play, in 1956, the title-role of *Timon of Athens*. But, whilst Olivier was director of the National Theatre from 1963 to 1974, Richardson did not come back to the Waterloo Road. Only when the directorship of the National had passed to Peter Hall did he make a return. Then it was to play an Ibsen title-role, *John Gabriel Borkman*. The joint appearance soon afterwards with John Gielgud in *No Man's Land* provided a fascinating reversal of roles. Pinter had written parts that enabled Gielgud to create a seedy writer whilst it was Richardson's turn to be the gentleman host, albeit an alcoholic one.

In life, too, Gielgud's and Richardson's mode of living have been very different. Gielgud's recreations have been essentially a part of his life in the theatre and have involved stage designing and music both of which were to be useful to him when he came to direct opera at Covent Garden. Richardson's interests have been well away from the theatre and he has found the theatrical cocktail circuit that accompanies touring abroad an especially burdensome course to travel.

His life-style, in fact, has been something of a paradox. He has been an enthusiastic rider of fast cars and motor-bikes and, when in his seventies, took delivery of a brand-new motor-cycle on which he turned up to rehearsals in crash helmet and goggles. Yet he has also been a lover of gently-paced gracious living in a semi-rural rather than in a modish metropolitan setting. His town houses, overlooking Hampstead Heath and Regent's Park, show their owner to be a lover of green open spaces. His study, redolent of good books and good wine, has an aroma of the gentler England of eighteenth-century Georgian clubland. Yet the twentieth century has afforded this actor the opportunity to court with death on the road and in the air at speeds which have quite literally taken away the breath of both driver and passengers.

It would be easy to create a wrong impression by concentrating on the inherent comedy in the contrast between the formal eminence of Richardson as an actor-knight and the informal figure he cuts as a speed freak. This would mean overlooking an important aspect of his character. Harcourt Williams wrote, perceptively, of Richardson as 'an actor whose mind demands material data and is wont to shy at the metaphysical in nature'. And Williams' description of Richardson 'foxing' his way through rehearsal is probably as apt a description of the man's approach to life itself. Richardson has always been a canny observer of the theatrical scene and the acuteness of his observation is easily masked by the apparent disparity he shows in conversation between his thought and speech processes.

A third actor-knight, who was also to become the first actor to be a baron as well, did not begin his long association with the Old Vic Company until the very close of the Baylis era. Laurence Olivier's *Hamlet* did not open at the Old Vic until the last year of her life. Indeed, the postponement of Olivier's *Macbeth*, under Michel Saint-Denis' direction, has been credited with being a major factor in causing the series of heart attacks which brought about Lilian Baylis' death in November of 1937. In the fullness of time, Olivier was to experience the physical toll taken by the awesome responsibility of directing the National Theatre Company at the Old Vic.

Like Richardson before him, Olivier had done his apprentice work with Barry Jackson's Birmingham Repertory Company. But when Olivier did join the company the variety of parts he was offered by Tyrone Guthrie showed that here was another Player actor rather than a new Old Vic member of the Gentleman's team led by a Gielgud. Apart from the Hamlet and Macbeth, the parts that came Olivier's way in the 1937-38 season spanned Henry V, Iago and Caius Marcius in *Coriolanus*.

Although his arrival at the Old Vic was some sixteen years after Gielgud's debut in the Waterloo Road, Olivier's career was to be such that he was to be even more closely associated with the organisation.

His five-year co-directorship of the Old Vic Company itself, combined with his directorship of the National Theatre Company at the Old Vic from 1963 to 1974, meant that seventeen years of Olivier's career were to be spent as an Old Vic director, or as a director of a company occupying the Old Vic Theatre.

The sheer wear and tear of being associated for so long a period with one theatre has probably produced a love-hate relationship between Olivier and the Old Vic. On the one hand, when he returned to the Waterloo Road as National Theatre director in 1963, he made Lilian Baylis' former office his dressing-room. And, out of sentiment, he got her old office desk out of store and installed it in what became known as the Baylis Room. On the other hand, when he first came to the Old Vic in the late 1930s, he found the extreme parochialism of the Baylis-era audiences alien to him. Constituted as they were from the ranks of Vic-Wells Association, they were friends who had known one another for more years than many of them cared to remember. They seemed, however unfairly, to complement the place's fusty atmosphere of 'dead cats and boiled eggs', all too redolent of its parish hall beginnings under Emma Cons.

Yet the Old Vic's glory has been raised to unparalled heights, thanks to the acting of Laurence Olivier. Quite apart from the pre-Second World War Hamlet, Macbeth and Caius Marcius, there were the performances for the Old Vic Company at the New Theatre in the 1940s which have become as legendary as his major performances for the National Theatre Company at the Old Vic itself. It is perhaps difficult for the generation whose theatregoing began in the 1960s and early 1970s to realise that the feverish excitement generated by Olivier nights at the Old Vic had been anticipated by an earlier generation with Olivier nights in the 1940s.

For those whose playgoing got underway after the setting up of the National Theatre in 1963, such Olivier evenings meant his 1964 Othello, his 1966 Edgar in *The Dance of Death*, his 1970 Shylock and his 1971 James Tyrone in O'Neill's *Long Day's Journey Into Night*. But, for those who conceived a passion for great acting in the 1940s, the place to go for release and fulfilment was the New Theatre. There Olivier's greatness could be marvelled at in Old Vic Company productions which featured him as the Duke of Gloucester in *Richard III*, King Lear,

Sir Peter Teazle in *The School for Scandal* as well as the amazing double-bill which encompassed the howling tragedy of Oedipus in *Oedipus Rex* and the mannered comedy of Mr Puff in *The Critic.*

Much less of the 'Gentleman' player than Gielgud and much more of a play director than Richardson, Olivier has embodied the theatre theatrical. He has delighted in elaborate make-up, whether in the vein of his long-nosed Richard Crookback or that of his negroid Othello, necessitating his arrival at the Old Vic hours before curtain-up. Yet he has avoided a return to the rhetorical grandeur of the Victorian actor-managers which, in mid-twentieth century, would be instantly derided as 'ham'.

Far from harking back to the days of Irving and Tree, he has been alertly aware of the need to renew his art with each new generation of audiences and of writers. And the renewals in his private life, reflected in his marriages to Jill Esmond, Vivien Leigh and Joan Plowright, have been paralleled in his professional life with the need to divorce his art from forms of theatre that are passing from the vanguard into history.

When the 'New Drama' came along in the late 1950s he did not turn away from it as John Gielgud at first was compelled to do. Nor did he take Richardson's safer course of plumping for a new writer acceptable to a commercial management like Robert Bolt whose *Flowering Cherry* saw Richardson safely through the critical years of 1957 and 1958. Olivier went straight for the generator of the new movement and, with his Archie Rice in John Osborne's *The Entertainer* at the Royal Court in 1957, found himself riding the crest of the New Wave. And, when he returned to the Old Vic in 1963 as the new National Theatre's overlord, Olivier wisely incorporated in his staff key figures associated with the New Drama.

Kenneth Tynan, most influential critic in promoting the New Drama, arrived as Literary Manager. And the Royal Court's two most celebrated directors, John Dexter and William Gaskill, joined as Associate National Theatre directors. The latter pair however, unlike Tynan, were not to remain with the National for the entire period that Olivier was its supremo.

Olivier has always been an essentially practical man of the theatre. His superabundant vitality has therefore led him to admire a director like Tyrone Guthrie who preferred to get to pragmatic grips with the problems of staging a play, rather than to theorise overmuch. In the 1930s, Michel Saint-Denis rehearsed Olivier's *Macbeth* clutching sheaves of elaborate notes and the result was the inevitable and unfortunate postponement of the first night. In the 1970s, William Gaskill, a much-admired studio exercise man and Brecht disciple, rehearsed Olivier as Brazen in *The Recruiting Officer*. But afterwards he said that he did not feel his methods of improvising to gain a sense of ensemble got very far with this particular actor. Perhaps a clue to Olivier's difficulties here lies in the particularly English, no-nonsense interpretation he puts on the word 'professionalism'. Certainly his brand of thorough-going professionalism has ensured that his name has become the most famous of the Player players.

Of the three remaining actor-knights who came to the Old Vic stage towards the close of the Baylis era, one belongs quite distinctly to the 'Gentleman's team' and the other two must be sided with the 'Player players'. Michael Redgrave is the aristocrat here. And, in totally dissimilar ways, Alec Guinness and Donald Wolfit have been the men for all seasons.

If Olivier has inherited the mantle of Garrick and Irving as recognised leader of his profession, it was Donald Wolfit who proudly took on their roles as actor-managers in the old-fashioned and unfashionable sense of the term. His apprenticeship for the stage had been served in the early 1920s with the Charles Doran and Fred Terry touring companies before he joined the Old Vic for Harcourt Williams' first 1929-30 season. Still a relatively unknown twenty-seven-year-old, he played Claudius that season to Gielgud's first Hamlet.

It is fascinating that these two future stars should have crossed the theatrical firmament at the particular time. For, though Gielgud was to remain longer in the Waterloo Road, his true public probably lay in the West End with the audiences who flocked to his classical seasons at the Queen's and Haymarket theatres in the 1930s and 1940s. Wolfit, on the other hand, was to find a bedrock for his reputation by stomping the country with his unsubsidised Shakespeare troupe, playing for an enthusiastic regional public. Wolfit shared with Lilian Baylis an endearing sense of his own importance and, like her, a rich source of theatrical anecdote has tended to obscure the real achievements of his enterprise, despite the tattiness which touring and shortage of money inevitably forced upon him. As well as the Claudius to Gielgud's first Hamlet, Wolfit was also to tackle during that first 1929-30 season at the Old Vic, a whole range of secondary parts such as Tybalt, Cassius, Touchstone and Macduff. It showed him at once to be one of the Players. And, more to the point, he was to be a Player player bent on bringing great drama to ordinary people and therefore very much more in the Baylis mould than other actors who became more closely identified with her enterprise and her theatres as the years went by. Wolfit was not, in fact, to return to the Old Vic until 1951 when Tyrone Guthrie also briefly returned to fill in the gap between the ending of Hugh Hunt's artistic directorship of the company and the beginning of Michael Benthall's in 1953. Although Wolfit had in the meantime frequently appeared in the West End, his reputation did not lie with the smart set in Shaftesbury Avenue. It was built up on his regional and world tours, his brave lunchtime Shakespeare seasons in the blitzed London of the Second World War, and above all, on the impact made in the 1940s by his playing of King Lear.

The Guthrie/Wolfit season opened promisingly with the actor in the title-role of Tamburlaine. And it was followed, even more promisingly, with Wolfit as the foppish Lord Ogleby in *The Clandestine Marriage.* Although these contrasting roles were not played on the same evening, they made something of the same impact of Olivier's double-bill of *Oedipus Rex* and *The Critic.* Alas for the Old Vic, there was a disagreement in mid-season and a new generation who hoped in the 1950s to see the Lear that Wolfit had rendered so famous in the 1940s never materialised. The result was that, compared to a Gielgud, Wolfit's associations with the Old Vic were comparatively short-lived. But he deserves his place in the history of this Waterloo Road theatre because his independence, his wayward guts and the sheer size and magniloquence of his verse-speaking all formed part of the raw material upon which Lilian Baylis first built her Shakespeare company.

The close of the Baylis Old Vic era was to be marked by the Waterloo Road debuts of two future stars whose gifts have made a fascinating contrast. Michael Redgrave, like John Gielgud before him, was to make his professional debut on a London stage when he joined the Old Vic Company in September 1936 at the age of twenty-eight. Also like Gielgud, he was to be on the side of the Gentlemen. Alec Guinness, then only twenty-three, arrived in the same season. Redgrave, a former schoolmaster, would have put in a much earlier appearance but for some characteristic Baylis haggling over the small change of salary when Redgrave first auditioned in the mid-1930s. The result was that Redgrave's professional grounding in the theatre had been with Liverpool Repertory Company for two years. Guinness, on the other hand, had three years' professional experience in London behind him in a number of small parts, some of them Shakespearean. His rise with the Old Vic Company was to be meteoric. He was to graduate from playing Osric in the *Hamlet* of the 1936-37 season to taking on the title-role in its entirety and in modern-dress in the 1938-39 season.

Redgrave had set his seal as a Gentleman player with his handling of parts like the outrageous Mr Horner in *The Country Wife*, Orlando in *As You Like It* and Laertes in *Hamlet*. Guinness quickly showed his forte as a Player player with his inventive interpretation of Shakespearean eccentrics like Osric and Boyet in *As You Like It*. If Guinness lacked the physical weight and size to compete with a Richardson or a Wolfit, there was a quicksilver originality about this actor that enabled him to investigate quaint areas of human behaviour inaccessible to others.

Neither Redgrave nor Guinness were to follow up their promising Old Vic debuts by returning to the same theatre in the full glory of their maturity. After playing Ferdinand in the 1940 *The Tempest*, Guinness in fact never returned to the Waterloo Road either with the Old Vic Company after the theatre's re-opening in 1950 or with the National Theatre Company. And Redgrave's return in 1963 to join the newly-formed National under Olivier's direction was nearly as disappointing as Gielgud's first season with the same Company. In the title-role of Chekhov's *Uncle Vanya* Redgrave was able to demonstrate his unique ability to play wounded, vulnerable and soul-torn heroes that has made him a Gentleman player of a different sort to Gielgud. But Redgrave's attempt to play 'coarse and common' with the National Theatre revival in 1964 of *Hobson's Choice* in which he appeared as the North Country bootmaker, Henry Hobson, was not a success. Retrospectively, it seems to confirm Gielgud's wisdom in restricting his appearances in the lower orders of society to a gentleman's 'gentleman'. Though Redgrave had had a success far outside the aristocratic milieu with *Uncle Harry* (in the West End in 1944), tormented professional men like his schoolmaster in *The Browning Version* have been a speciality of his career. It was surprising, therefore, that Redgrave was not seen at his best in the National Theatre Company's revival of *The Master Builder* in 1964 when he played Halvard Solness.

Both Guinness and Redgrave had had a closer link with the Old Vic when the company was playing at the New in the 1940s. In fact Guinness was with the organisation for nearly two years, from early 1946. Rather overshadowed by Olivier and Richardson, he played the Fool to the former's Lear and the Comte de Guiche to the latter's Cyrano de Bergerac. He did come into his own, however, with the title-role of Richard II and with the bizarre role of the Dauphin in *Saint Joan* which particularly suited his gifts for elaborating on the quirky. And Hlestakov in *The Government Inspector* gave full scope to his individual turn of comedy playing. Later, like his contemporaries, he had to pick his way through the post-1956 New Wave Drama. With Ionesco's *Exit the King* he found an impressive role with which to ride the wave. It was therefore unfortunate that his willingness to risk his reputation in the William Gaskill-directed *Macbeth* at the Royal Court in 1966 proved a daring rather than a successful venture. And it seems even more unfortunate that, of the surviving actor-knights whose careers began at Lilian Baylis' Old Vic in the 1930s, Guinness is the only one not to have returned to this theatre as a National Theatre player.

Redgrave's return to the Old Vic Company at the New was at the end of this era in the company's history. Hugh Hunt had taken over from Olivier and Richardson in 1949 when Redgrave moved in to lead the company with his Berowne in *Love's Labour's Lost*, his Marlow in *She Stoops to Conquer* and his Rakitin in *A Month in the Country*. All were parts very much in the compass of a Gentleman player and helped to round off the New Theatre era before the Old Vic Company hit a low spot on its return to its own theatre.

Perhaps the 1950s at the Old Vic would have had more highlights to it had Redgrave been persuaded to return to the Vic to pursue his Shakespeare career there instead of at Stratford-upon-Avon. In losing him at that time, the Old Vic lost one of the nation's greatest Gentleman players when in maturity. In this connection it is interesting that Gielgud has the reputation for being an intellectual, though Redgrave's books – *The Actor's Ways and Means* and *Mask or Face* published in the 1950s – give him a more substantial claim to be recognised as such. Gielgud has been seen to be an absorbing source of theatrical reminiscences and anecdotes, but Redgrave's published work reveals more of the actor theorist and the scholar. Although nearly four years Gielgud's junior, Redgrave's career in his late sixties has not been as rewarding as his colleague's. As Gielgud and Richardson in Pinter's *No Man's Land* renewed the partnership begun in the 1930s at Lilian Baylis' Old Vic in the new National Theatre on the South Bank, it is a pity that a further 'Gentleman and Player' partnership could not somehow have been effected by combining the contrasting artistry of Michael Redgrave and, say, Alec Guinness.

The Second World War, which began when these two actors were still at the beginning of their careers, was to have wide-ranging and long-lasting effects on the Old Vic organisation. The bombing in 1940, and consequent closure until 1950 of the theatre as a public playhouse, was to mean that the Waterloo Road for a decade ceased being a modestly-paid showcase for a new generation of Gentleman or Player players. With the Company's war-time retreat to Burnley in Lancashire and its commitment to regional touring, it was certainly in no position to provide a metropolitan shop-window for young actors to follow in the steps of a Gielgud, Richardson, Wolfit, Olivier, Redgrave and Guinness. And the New Theatre seasons are remembered chiefly for the magnificent acting of established names rather than for the emergence of new talent. But at the very end of the New Theatre seasons from 1944 to 1949 a thirty-two-year-old actor joined the company and was to prove a long-stay artist. Although this actor, Paul Rogers, had not received anything like a knighthood by the time the National Theatre Company had grown out of the cocoon of the Old Vic, he was to perform yeoman's service for the Old Vic Company and return to the Old Vic as a National Theatre player. If the term 'yeoman's service' gives an impression of humdrum and plodding work, that is quite unintentional. It is apposite in as far as Paul Rogers was to belong to the category of Old Vic Player players.

When Paul Rogers joined the Old Vic Company under Hugh Hunt's direction at the New for the 1949-51 season, neither he nor the Company could have foreseen that he was to remain with the organisation, on and off, for a decade. If a yardstick for placing an actor in the 'Player' category lies in the variety of parts attempted, there certainly could be little difficulty in placing Paul Rogers in the right team. His bullish and rather heavy-weight presence were to make him ideal casting for roles like Bottom in *A Midsummer Night's Dream*, the Falstaff of *Henry IV* and *The Merry Wives of Windsor*, and Cauchon in *Saint Joan*. But his talents extended very far beyond what nineteenth-century stock companies called 'the Heavy Man'. He tackled, with a great measure of success, lighter-weight parts like Mercutio in *Romeo and Juliet* and Touchstone in *As You Like It*. And, if this were not ample evidence of his versatility, there were the lead roles of Shylock, Macbeth, Leontes and King Lear that came his way. The hard-pressed, overworked and underpaid conditions with which Michael Benthall's Company had to contend with in the 1950s did not always make for an ideal showcase for work of such an astonishing variety. When Paul Rogers later joined Peter Hall's Royal Shakespeare Company at Stratford-upon-Avon, he was better placed, for this was a Shakespeare Company that also offered an actor a London home and the chance to play in new plays by modern authors. But even at the Old Vic in the 1950s, Paul Rogers was fortunate enough to appear in one of the company's rare excursions into new drama – *The Other Heart* in which he won the Clarence Derwent Award for his performance as William Villon.

Perhaps Paul Rogers' good-natured acceptance of the need to be a good company member and take a bash at all manner of parts has worked against his stature being recognised as soon and as widely as it should have been. In this respect, it was unfortunate that his return to the Old Vic as a National Theatre player in the mid-1970s should have been in a disappointing new play from Peter Nichols, *The Freeway*. But Paul Rogers has contributed so much to the survival of the Old Vic Company, from which in many ways a National Theatre has grown, that his long-term admirers can only hope that this Player player will have an opportunity to make as much a contribution to the South Bank as he has to the survival of an Old Vic Company in the Waterloo Road.

Unlike his contemporaries at the Old Vic in the 1950s, John Neville and Richard Burton, Paul Rogers did not have the sort of good looks that help to provide an initial passport to stardom. A RADA-trained actor, Neville was twenty-eight when he joined the London Old Vic for the 1953-54 season after three consecutive seasons with the Bristol Old Vic. Burton was the same age when he joined the company for the same season. But he had something of a West End career behind him, both before and after going up to Oxford University. Although both were of an age when their careers were liable to be interrupted by National Service, they were luckier than Paul Rogers. His stage career was just starting up when five years' naval service in the Second World War brought it to a long temporary halt.

With John Neville and Richard Burton installed as Old Vic lead players in the 1950s, the Old Vic stage was set to see the partnership of a Gentleman and Player player much on the lines of the one John Gielgud and Ralph Richardson had first formed in the same theatre in the 1930s. Although the senior couple were to see their careers criss-crossing over a longer time span, the parallels between John Gielgud and John Neville on the one hand as 'Gentlemen' players and Ralph Richardson and Richard Burton on the other as Player players does seem worth a little investigation.

As far as Neville was concerned, there had been a brief prelude to the Waterloo Road seasons in the 1950s. He had walked on in 1947 with the Old Vic Company at the New Theatre when Alec Guinness had been playing the title-role of Richard II. This had been one of the parts in which Gielgud had shone at the Old Vic in the 1930s and it was one to which Neville was to bring distinction on the same stage. Indeed his refined and sensitive features and slender build seem to make him the natural inheritor of the Gielgud aristocratic tradition. And, in the 1950s, roles like Hamlet, Romeo and even the smaller comedy part of Sir Andrew Aguecheek showed him to be Gielgud's heir. Unlike Gielgud, however, he did not have the good fortune to find a *Richard of Bordeaux* to consolidate his career at this point with a smash-hit in the West End. Nor, by the late 1950s, was the West End the place for long-running Shakespeare productions or seasons such as Gielgud had enjoyed in the 1930s.

In many respects, however, John Neville's career shows many signs of an actor deliberately casting off the unwelcome mantle of a latter-day Gielgud. After leaving the Old Vic in the early 1960s, he turned his back on a West End career to become a founder-director of the new Nottingham Playhouse. Although the appointment ended amid controversy, John Neville's work showed a strong commitment to the promotion of a strong regional theatre in Britain to offset the dominating position held by London's West End and, potentially, by a centralised National Theatre complex in the capital.

When John Neville played the cockney Don Juan in the title-role of Bill Naughton's *Alfie* at the Mermaid in the early 1960s, he seemed, both deliberately and successfully, to make a break with his usual image. During the National Theatre's tenancy of the Old Vic, John Neville did not return to the scene of his triumphs with the Old Vic Company in the 1950s – except for a brief period as a Governor of the theatre.

If a commitment to the promotion of strong regional theatre in Britain through his work with the Nottingham Playhouse (and the Prospect Theatre Company) was to take John Neville away from the Waterloo Road in one direction, his former partner there, Richard Burton, was to be lost to the Old Vic and London theatre for quite other reasons. Superstardom in the cinema and marriage to one of Hollywood's most durable divas, Elizabeth Taylor, ensured that his last performance with the Old Vic Company was in 1956 when Burton and Neville alternated the roles of Iago and Othello. The partnership, if it may be so called, had begun in 1953 with Neville playing Fortinbras to Burton's Hamlet. In the intervening seasons, Burton's sturdier physique and resonant Welsh voice ensured that his path at the Old Vic lay with the 'Player' roles.

When Burton appeared as the Bastard in *King John*, Sir Toby Belch in *Twelfth Night*, Caliban in *The Tempest* and Caius Marcius in *Coriolanus*, he showed himself to have as wide a range as Ralph Richardson had displayed on the same stage in the 1930s, often with the same characters. Certainly, in the seasons that John Neville and Richard Burton led for the Old Vic Company in the early 1950s, there was a feverish excitement in the gallery reminiscent of the best days of the Baylis era with swooning gallery girls needing to be ticked off much as Lilian Baylis had once instructed her Vic opera audiences to hold back with the applause and the enthusiasm in the 1920s. Considering the fervour Burton and Neville aroused, it is sad that this short-lived acting partnership has not been renewed in the way that the

Gielgud/Richardson partnership has survived so rewardingly into the 1970s. Somehow the Gielgud/Richardson generation has found a more successful means of pursuing a theatre and a film career without one destroying the other.

It will be some time before John Neville and Richard Burton are into their seventies. But it would be nice to think that both might survive the more hectic pace of the second half of the twentieth century to renew something of the glories these two actors brought to the Old Vic in the 1950s. By the time the National Theatre opened in 1976 neither had appeared with that company (or indeed with the Royal Shakespeare Company played very much less Shakespeare on the Sean Kenny ciated the qualities of both actors as Old Vic Company members will watch the way their theatre careers are eventually shaped with particular attention to see which of them remains the Gentleman and which the Player player.

Once the National Theatre took over the Old Vic for thirteen years in 1963, the most immediate discernible difference was that the new Company played very much less Shakespeare on the Sean Kenny's restyled stage. It is true that the venture opened with Laurence Olivier's production of *Hamlet* with Peter O'Toole as guest star in the title-role. It is also true that some of the highlights of the National Theatre Company's tenancy of the Old Vic were with Shakespeare, notably the Zeffirelli-directed *Much Ado About Nothing* and Olivier's appearances as Othello and Shylock. The fact was, however, that the new Company played a repertoire of international classics and new plays with better pay and working conditions than the Old Vic Company had been able to offer. In the circumstances, it might have been expected that a further young generation of actors would follow in the steps of Gielgud, Richardson, Olivier, Guinness, Redgrave, Neville and Burton. Curiously, surprisingly few of the most promising actors of the 1960s and 1970s came up with the new company, or at least few stayed with it for very long.

Tom Courtenay, one of the most promising actors to come to the fore in the 1960s was also the one to stay with the National Theatre Company for the shortest period. He had made his professional debut on the Old Vic stage with the Old Vic Company in 1960 as a twenty-three-year-old Konstantin in *The Seagull* directed by John

Fernald who had been Principal of the Royal Academy of Dramatic Art when Courtenay was a pupil there. Courtenay's gritty, north country voice placed him firmly in the group of new young actors to emerge from the English regions like Albert Finney and Nicol Williamson. He was, therefore, far from the 'Gentleman' player lineage of the Gielgud/Redgrave/Neville tradition. Unfortunately his appearance in the single role of Andri in Max Frisch's *Andorra* with the National Theatre Company in 1961 hardly gave Old Vic audiences an opportunity to judge whether he belonged either to the Gentleman or Players team. Judgement had to be deferred until his appearances with the Manchester 69 Company and with West End managements enabled them to gauge the diversity of his talents.

Courtenay's RADA contemporary, Albert Finney, also appeared with the National Theatre Company with disappointing rarety and certainly he cannot be said to have grown up with it during Laurence Olivier's directorship of the company. Finney's groundwork had not even been with the Old Vic Company in the 1950s. Instead he had gone to the Birmingham Repertory Company where he had remained for two years. It was playing the title-role in John Osborne's *Luther* at the Royal Court that gained him international recognition rather than the parts he played initially with the National Theatre Company in the mid-1960s: Don Pedro in *Much Ado About Nothing*, Jean in *Miss Julie* and the farce roles of Harold Gorringe in Peter Shaffer's *Black Comedy* and in a revival of Feydeau's *A Flea in her Ear*. These, together with John Armstrong in John Arden's *Armstrong's Last Goodnight*, certainly revealed the versatility of a Player player. So it was perhaps not surprising that in a theatre famous for the greatness of the aristocratic Hamlet of John Gielgud, there were difficulties for some in appreciating the greatness in the Salford-born Hamlet that Finney offered at the very end of the National Theatre's Company's stay in the Waterloo Road in 1976.

Another major theatre actor at the beginning of an ascendent in the 1960s was Ian McKellen. He, too, was with the National Theatre Company for an all-too-brief period. His Claudio in the 1965 production of *Much Ado About Nothing* showed all the princely demeanour of the Gentleman player, even in Zeffirelli's Italianate production. Since McKellen was born in Lancashire and educated in

Bolton, this actor showed that it was possible to keep up the elegant Gielgud traditions and still hail from the north country, however snobbishly some metropolitan audiences tended to classify actors coming from anywhere remotely north of Camden Town. Perhaps McKellen's subsequently becoming a founder-member of the Actors Company, dedicated to a total democracy in the running of the organisation, helps to explain why his stay with a necessarily hierarchical establishment like the National Theatre Company was so brief. It was a sad loss to the Old Vic at the time – though both the Prospect Theatre Company and the Royal Shakespeare Company were to benefit later from the services of this democratically-minded aristocrat of players.

The National Theatre Company at the Old Vic was fortunate in securing the long-term services of two actors previously associated with the New Wave writers at the Royal Court Theatre. Both Frank Finlay and Robert Stephens had appeared in an early John Osborne play, *Epitaph for George Dillon* and both went on to appear in the later 1950s in Arnold Wesker plays at the Royal Court. Their appearance with the National Theatre at the Old Vic helped to dispel any doubts that this was to be a museum, doubts already lulled by the employment of other artists associated with the avant-garde of the time.

Of these two actors, Frank Finlay was to remain with the National for the longer period. His debut was as First Gravedigger in the 1963 inaugural production of the O'Toole Hamlet and he was back with the company at the close of its Old Vic era in John Osborne's *Watch It Come Down*, premièred in 1976. In the interval he had, perhaps, been a little overshadowed by Olivier during the period that the latter was artistic director. When, for example, Olivier played Othello in 1964 it was inevitably the star in the title-role that the public came to see. And there was no alternating of Othello and Iago as there had been in the 1950s with Burton and Neville. But Finlay was given much on which to exercise his wide talents on as a Player player, like Willie Mossop in *Hobson's Choice* and Dogberry in *Much Ado*. Finally, he came into his own with the 1974 production of *Saturday, Sunday, Monday* in which he shared leading roles with Joan Plowright and with Olivier offering a small cameo study in the original Old Vic production before this

Ralph Richardson as Peer Gynt (John Vickers).

Sybil Thorndike as Constance in *King John*.

Donald Wolfit as Tamburlaine.

Donald Wolfit in *The Clandestine Marriage* (John Vickers).

Robert Helpmann: *The Merchant of Venice.*

...ard Burton and Claire Bloom: *Hamlet* (Angus McBean).

Judi Dench and John Stride: *Romeo and Juliet* (Houston Rogers).

Richard Burton as Iago (Ang McBean).

John Neville as Othello with Rosemary Harris as Desdemona (Angus McBean).

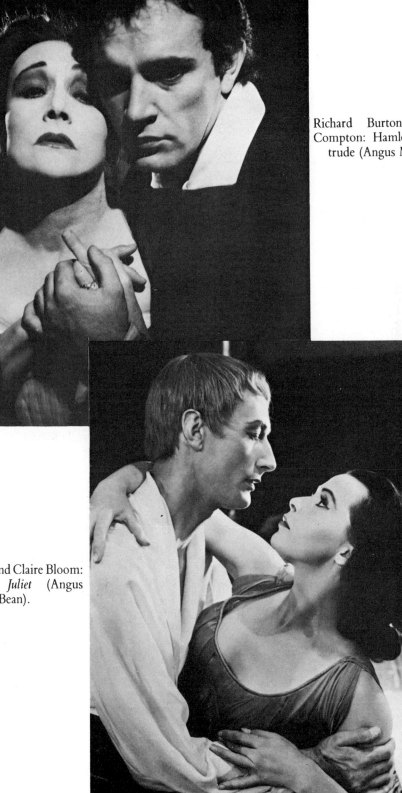

Richard Burton and Fay Compton: Hamlet and Gertrude (Angus McBean).

n Neville and Claire Bloom: *meo and Juliet* (Angus McBean).

Richard Burton as Coriolanus (Angus McBean).

Richard Burton as Sir Toby Belch (Angus McBean).

Zeffirelli-directed Eduardo de Felippo Neapolitan comedy transferred to the West End.

Robert Stephens was more fortunate in that he had more spectacular parts in which to shine. He too had begun with the inaugural *Hamlet* production in which he appeared as Horatio. But he went on to play a big showcase part like the Inca ruler, Atahuallpa, in Peter Shaffer's *The Royal Hunt of the Sun* in which he was partnered by another ex-Royal Court actor, the 'Player player' Colin Blakely who was to prove another long-stay National Theatre artist. Although Robert Stephens easily commanded a vein of aristocratic melancholy which served him well as Jacques in *As You Like It* and Vershinin in *Three Sisters*, he had the added stage dimension of an actor half-hesitant, half-ingratiating that makes the Gentleman label stick to him a little uneasily. He was certainly fortunate to have the title-role of *Tartuffe* when Gielgud joined the company and played Orgon. And his appearances with the National Theatre Company at the Old Vic will probably be remembered less in terms of a Gentleman and Player player partnership (such as was offered when he played Atahuallpa to Colin Blakely's gruff Spanish soldier, Pizarro) and more in those of the partnership with his then wife, Maggie Smith, with whom he was seen as Benedick to her Beatrice, Francis Archer to her Mrs Sullen in *The Beaux Stratagem* and Loevborg to her Hedda Gabler.

A player of the younger generation who made his London debut at twenty-five as Leartes in the inaugural 1963 production of *Hamlet* was Derek Jacobi. A number of good parts came his way at the Old Vic which seemed to suggest that the company was nurturing at least one major player in the course of the first decade of its existence. With roles as varied as Simon Bliss in *Hay Fever*, Touchstone in *As You Like It* and the King of Navarre in *Love's Labour's Lost* confirming his early promise, it was sad that when a major lead role, Myshkin in *The Idiot* was given to him in 1970 it was in a production that was insufficiently successful to establish Jacobi as a lead National Theatre Player.

But the theatre is very often a disappointing place. And the greater the triumphs, the more sad the setbacks. Perhaps the saddest of them all came one Monday afternoon in March 1976 when a figure slipped anonymously into a seat to watch Peggy Ashcroft open the National Theatre on a downbeat note with the transfer from the Old Vic of her performance of Winnie in Beckett's *Happy Days*. The anonymous figure was Laurence Olivier whose work with the Old Vic Company and with the National Theatre Company at the Old Vic had done so much towards ensuring the belated opening of the National Theatre building he helped design. That he was no longer fit enough to open it spectacularly with a *King Lear* seemed as unfortunate as the fact that nobody had thought to name one of the National's three theatres after Lilian Baylis, the Company's gruff godmother whose monument was the Old Vic Theatre down the Waterloo Road.

Some Actresses

Considering that Shakespeare wrote no part for an actress, since all his female characters had to be created by young men, it is surprising how full the Old Vic annals are of leading ladies who have made or consolidated their classical reputations in Shakespearean plays.

Of course such reputations could not be forged on the mighty anvil of the female equivalents of a Hamlet, a Lear, an Othello or a Prospero. Shakespeare, understandably, has been unable to provide them. And, indeed, confronted with a play like *Julius Caesar* where the ratio of two meagre parts for actresses is to some thirty for actors, the ladies would be justified in envying their French counterparts who have a classical dramatist like Racine to place them fairly and squarely in the centre of the stage in a part like that of, say, Phèdre.

A superficial glance at the plays included in 'The Complete Works' seems to substantiate the view that the absence of actresses in the Elizabethan theatre has ensured that a Shakespeare Night is hardly a Ladies' Night. Of the thirty-seven plays listed, only two not particularly well thought of – *The Taming of the Shrew* and *The Merry Wives of Windsor* – actually feature women characters in their titles, if not by name. And, of the remaining thirty-five plays, only three others refer to female lead roles and then in tandem with the gentlemen who are mentioned first – *Romeo and Juliet, Troilus and Cressida* and *Antony and Cleopatra*.

And yet the extraordinary fact is that a dramatist who was writing for a company as exclusively male as a rugger team, has peopled his plays with a great variety of female parts. In the circumstances, all that might reasonably be expected is a series of explorations in that androgynous territory where female characters spend a good section of the evening passing themselves off as young lads. Viola in *Twelfth Night*, Portia and Nerissa in *The Merchant of Venice* and Rosalind in *As You Like It* manage to do this in scenes resonant with poetry of such melting tenderness that it would seem churlish to expect much more.

Yet consider the sheer diversity of female Shakespeare characters who never for a moment slip into a pair of breeches. For actresses still young and attractive enough to explore what used to be called ingénue roles, there are the 'daughter' parts ranging from the fatally vulnerable Ophelia to the rewardingly bright Anne Page of *The Merry Wives of Windsor* and from the tragically destined Juliet and Cordelia to the more happily favoured Imogen and Miranda.

For the more mature Shakespeare actress, still wishing to play women in love, there is the wittily provocative Beatrice of *Much Ado About Nothing* and the fatally seductive Egyptian Queen of *Antony and Cleopatra*. And for those actresses whose years no longer allow them to venture on these lines without holding themselves open to ridicule, there still remains a rich store of 'mother' parts from the sensual but weak-willed Gertrude of *Hamlet* to the proud and defiant Volumnia of *Coriolanus* and from the bawdily loquacious Nurse in *Romeo and Juliet* to the wise and reserved Countess of Rousillon in *All's Well That Ends Well*.

So brief and so selective a catalogue necessarily omits mammoth roles like Margaret of Anjou who bestrides Shakespeare's account of The Wars of the Roses in the History Plays. And there is a whole gallery of smaller and lighter roles as diverse as Titania in *A Midsummer Night's Dream* and the quick-witted Maria of *Twelfth Night*. Moreover, on an inferior social level, there are some amusing lower depths to be relished ranging from the bawds of the History Plays to the gormless rustic sexpots of the country comedies, personified by Audrey in *As You Like It*.

Did Shakespeare himself grow impatient at so wide a spectrum of women having always to be created by men in what today we would call 'drag'? If the Head of State for the first part of Shakespeare's writing career could be a woman taking a lively interest in the theatre, why should a true-life woman actor be such an unthinkable depravity? Elizabeth I's courtiers protected the players from the impending avalanche of anti-theatre puritanism by their patronage. But, had there been Elizabethan predecessors to the Restoration actresses, it would seem that even such exalted defence against the violent prejudice directed at the public playhouses of Tudor England would have been unavailing. Old Vic actresses of the twentieth century must have been thankful that this did not inhibit Shakespeare from writing so rewardingly about women. For an actress signing up to join the Old Vic Company was committing herself to an organisation where, for nearly fifty years, more than the lion's share of the drama was to be taken up with the presentation of Shakespeare's plays.

Two actresses whose careers dominate the first three quarters of the twentieth-century English theatre prove also to be the indispensable caryatids supporting even the most cursory account of the performance of Shakespeare and the classics in the same period by the Old Vic Company. Dame Sybil Thorndike and Dame Edith Evans have been these caryatids. Such an architectural description of them may perhaps however be unfortunate, implying similar, static and somewhat decorative pillars of the Old Vic. It would be hard to think of more dissimilar leading ladies. And, whatever else they have been in the Waterloo Road, they have never stood still there or merely adorned the plays that they have appeared in.

From the Old Vic point of view, the fundamental differences between these two Dames have been the date of their first appearances with the Shakespeare Company and their status in the theatrical firmament at the time of their Waterloo Road debuts. Dame Sybil arrived first, at the very beginning, to join the newly-formed company under Ben Greet's direction in the autumn of 1914. Though already thirty-two and with seasons in North America and with Miss Horniman's pioneering Manchester Theatre behind her, Dame Sybil was not yet a 'West End star'.

Dame Edith, delaying her arrival until the 1925-26 season, was already a 'big name', and into her thirty-seventh year. Robert Atkins, by then, had been and gone, leaving the Old Vic with an international name and a reputation for being able to provide invaluable shop-window experience for artists with classical aspirations.

Dame Edith, under Andrew Leigh's direction, said that she had come to the Old Vic to learn how to play Shakespeare. Having in her earliest theatrical years worked with William Poel and the Elizabethan Stage

Society, for whom she played Cressida, Dame Edith was not quite the novice her modest avowal made her seem. Nonetheless, she was offered an extraordinarily wide repertoire of Shakespeare leads in which to consolidate her career in his plays with the general public. They ranged from Portia in *The Merchant of Venice* to Katharine in *The Taming of The Shrew* and from Mistress Page in *The Merry Wives of Windsor* to the Nurse in *Romeo and Juliet.* Dame Edith's success with these roles was to render her name even more famous than before. And her appearances that season at the Old Vic were to be a great asset to its Manager, Lilian Baylis, in terms of sell-out box-office business.

Dame Sybil's Old Vic baptism in 1914 had not been quite the same. In the wartime seasons, from 1914 to 1918, she had been offered an even greater range of parts. This, of course, was partly because she was with the company for a longer, four-year period. It was also because the absolute necessity at the time of turning every able-bodied actor into a soldier meant that Dame Sybil had to help to keep things ticking over by playing male as well as female roles. Later she was to recall how much she had enjoyed doing this. She had always envied actors the greater opportunities available to them in Shakespeare.

So Dame Sybil's First World War Old Vic repertoire included Rosalind *and* Launcelot Gobbo in *The Merchant of Venice,* Lady Macbeth *and* the Fool in *Lear,* Beatrice *and* Ferdinand in *The Tempest,* Viola *and* Puck in *A Midsummer Night's Dream.* To recall that Dame Sybil sometimes played to audiences so small that it hardly seemed worth ringing up the curtain at all is to suggest that her début was not quite the success Dame Edith's was to be in the mid-1920s. But that is to misunderstand the two decades entirely. Dame Sybil's work under Ben Greet in the 1914–18 years was an astonishingly bold move to set up a Shakespeare Company in the Waterloo Road with totally inadequate resources. Dame Edith was fortunate (and wise) to come along when Robert Atkins' five-year stint as Shakespeare director had added prestige to an enterprise than had previously been obliged to depend more on brave 'make-do' measures than on any striving after artistic refinement. And Dame Edith's 1925-26 season only added to the process of achieving prestige for the enterprise, especially as she was able to coax a special wardrobe out of Lilian Baylis without resorting, as

Charles Laughton was to do later, to getting a special grant to ensure a professional standard with regard to costumes.

When both Dame Sybil and Dame Edith, then respectively ninety-one and eighty-six, appeared in the May 1974 presentation of *Tribute to the Lady* as part of the Old Vic's contribution to the Lilian Baylis Centenary Festival, the historically-minded could hardly help but reflect on how far beyond their Old Vic debuts these actresses had gone on over the years to renew their ties with the Old Vic Company. Neither of them had come to the Waterloo Road early enough to essay, as later generations of Old Vic actresses were to do, the most tenderly young roles of a Juliet or an Ophelia. But their enduring careers in the theatre ensured that both were able to render, in their own individual ways, a good half-century's service to the Old Vic in most of Shakespeare's best-known female roles.

Would it be too gross an oversimplification to see the careers of these actresses as the female complement to those of John Gielgud and Laurence Olivier? Although married, Dame Edith had no family and there has always been a great fastidiousness – even hauteur – that would seem naturally to ally her art closely to the bachelor and gentlemanly dedication that Gielgud has brought to his art. Dame Sybil's generous and outgoing personality, thriving on a large family with umpteen grand- and great-grandchildren, would seem to bring her personality more into the orbit of Olivier whose children also span several generations and whose performances have always crackled with a certain theatricality and panache.

When Sybil Thorndike came to play Jocasta in 1946 to Olivier's Oedipus in the golden days of the Old Vic Company's tenancy of the West End New Theatre, there seemed to be a natural renewing of a professional partnership which had worked well in 1938 when Thorndike had been the Volumnia to Olivier's then thirty-one-year-old Caius Marcius in *Coriolanus*.

But the parallels do not survive close scrutiny. Dame Sybil, a dedicated Churchwoman with a consequent special understanding of Lilian Baylis, believed that once you married that was for ever, come what may. Although Olivier has found family life and the generations of children he has sired a vital complement to his life in the theatre, his domestic life has involved three marriages to three actresses – Jill

Esmond, Vivien Leigh and Joan Plowright. If the professional partnership of Sybil Thorndike and Lewis Casson and Olivier and his wives could be analysed in a way that would throw meaningful light on their respective services to the Old Vic, this line of enquiry might be worth pursuing. But all the evidence points to the folly of attempting to dovetail the professional and private lives of artists, except where it can be done thoroughly in a biography.

When Dame Sybil returned to play for the Old Vic Company from September 1927 to January 1928, she had become very much more the recognised star than she had been on leaving the Old Vic in 1918. Her appearances in the title-role of the first London production of *Saint Joan* in 1924 had seen to that. It was characteristic of Dame Sybil's generous loyalty to the Old Vic that while the theatre was being re-built she should lead the company in exile at the Lyric Theatre, Hammersmith. Her now well-established celebrity and her special appeal with Old Vic devotees helped to ensure the success of the difficult Hammersmith season in which Dame Sybil played, in her forty-second year, Katharine, Portia, Beatrice and both the Chorus *and* the Princess in *Henry V.*

Two years later, at forty-four, Dame Sybil was playing 'mother' Shakespeare roles – Gertrude in a production of *Hamlet* staged at the Lyceum to raise funds for a 'second Old Vic' – Sadler's Wells Theatre. Her brief return to the Old Vic itself in 1932 was in a non-Shakespeare role, the Citizen's Wife in Beaumont and Fletcher's *The Knight of the Burning Pestle.* By the time of the next return in 1938 to play Volumnia to the Olivier Caius Marcius in 1938, Lilian Baylis was dead and Tyrone Guthrie had begun the régime that was to see the break-up of the triple Baylis empire of drama, ballet and opera companies with the onslaught of a Second World War.

In that Second World War, Dame Sybil was to do as much to keep the Old Vic banner flying as she had to help to establish it in the first place in the First World War. She toured the Welsh mining villages as Medea, Shaw's Candida and as Lady Macbeth as well as acting from the Old Vic's regional base in Burnley. Further work on these lines followed in 1945 when Dame Sybil toured Europe with an Old Vic Company helping to entertain troops not yet demobilised. The rigours of war-time touring of the classics were rewarded when Dame Sybil joined the Old Vic Company under the triumvirate of Olivier, Richardson and Burrell during that illustrious period of the Company's history at the New Theatre where Dame Sybil's Mistress Quickly to Richardson's Falstaff and Jocasta to Olivier's Oedipus made a particular impression.

Until they both appeared in the 1974 Gala Evening of *Tribute to the Lady* Dame Edith and Dame Sybil were not seen together in an Old Vic production at the Old Vic itself. History-conscious admirers of the Company had to wait until the 1950 première of *Waters of the Moon* by N. C. Hunter at the Haymarket to see these divas of the Waterloo Road together in the same long-running play. And Dame Edith was indeed as much as Dame Sybil a 'Queen of the Old Vic Company'. It is true that after that brilliant 1925-26 season, she did not return to the Old Vic until the 1930s. But she was then to surprise and delight her admirers by successfully playing Shakespearean ladies in love at an age when it might have been expected that an actress would have to put them behind her.

In 1932, at the age of forty-four, her Viola was warmly received. And, more surprisingly still, in 1936 at the age of forty-eight, she proved a radiant and winning Rosalind to the Orlando of the then twenty-eight-year-old Michael Redgrave, making his London début with the Old Vic Company. This was only three years before Dame Edith first essayed the aristocratic gorgon, Wilde's Lady Bracknell, with which she was to be indelibly associated for the remainder of her career. No doubt, such success with a Rosalind in her forties, enabled Dame Edith to have the courage to beguile London playgoers with her fifty-eight-year-old Cleopatra in the West End, only two years before rejoining the Old Vic Company at the New Theatre to play 'mature' classic roles such as Lady Wishfort in *The Way of the World* and Madame Ranevsky in *The Cherry Orchard*.

When the Old Vic Theatre itself was repaired from its wartime bombing and ready to be re-opened, Dame Edith flew back from New York to speak the specially written prologue for the occasion in November 1950. Sadly, Dame Edith's explorations of the Shakespeare matrons – Volumnia and the Countess of Rousillon – were to belong exclusively to Stratford-upon-Avon's theatre history. Dame Edith did, however, return to the Old Vic in 1958 to play Queen Katharine in

Henry VIII to mark the completion of Michael Benthall's Five Year
Plan to stage the whole of the First Folio plays.

The appearance in the same programme of Dame Sybil and Dame
Edith in the 1974 Baylis Centenary presentation of *Tribute to the Lady*
may have prompted some veteran Old Vic playgoers to attempt to
define the different art of these two great actresses. How would they
have gone about it? Perhaps they would have begun by making the
point that although Dame Sybil was an actress of medium height, she
had the personality and especially the voice to create an impression of
being always an imposing and dominating presence. This would
account for Dame Sybil's long-standing success in Greek tragedy
which was not a sphere suited to Dame Edith's talents. The fact
that Dame Sybil's voice was so essentially a *theatre* voice helped to
reinforce her conviction that she had never mastered the art of the
cinema and disliked seeing herself on the screen.

Dame Edith, on the other hand, made a most successful film career in
her later years. But in the theatre she had an asset that could never be
adequately captured in the cinema. By some alchemy known only to
herself, she could 'will' an audience into believing her the epitome of
beauty and youth. Other members of the company that she happened
to be appearing with at the Old Vic may in fact have been younger and,
off-stage, might have been considered, in conventional terms, more
attractive. Yet they lacked the magic quality of being able to project
into the audience the indefinable essence of youthful radiance and
irresistible beauty.

The Old Vic Company's presentation of Shakespeare and of other
classical writers would have been immeasurably the poorer without the
services of these two great actresses. But in admiring their long-term
achievements with the Company, it would be wrong to overlook the
many other artists who appeared with them without capturing the
public attention so enduringly.

In the 1930s, another contrasting pair of leading ladies began what
were to be long-term associations with the Old Vic. If Dame Flora
Robson's debut in the Waterloo Road was delayed until her thirty-first
year in the Old Vic Company's 1933-34 season, this was no fault of her
own. She had applied to join the Company twelve years before
immediately on leaving the Royal Academy of Dramatic Art in 1921.

Although she had successfully auditioned for Robert Atkins (who was eager for her to join his Company), the future Dame Flora was sent away by Lilian Baylis with characteristic lack of grace and the advice to get some training and experience before presuming to think that she could come to the Old Vic to perfect her art.

Dame Peggy Ashcroft was more fortunate. Under Harcourt Williams' direction, she was allowed to join the Old Vic Company in lead roles when still only twenty-five. Her first, 1932-33 season, saw as many Shakespearean riches come her way as had fallen in the paths earlier of Dame Sybil and Dame Edith. Among the treasures were Cleopatra, Imogen, Portia, Perdita and Juliet as well as the non-Shakespearean roles of Kate Hardcastle in *She Stoops to Conquer* and Lady Teazle in *The School for Scandal.*

Both Dame Flora and Dame Peggy too were, years later, to return to the Old Vic in the 1974 gala performance of *Tribute to the Lady.* Dame Peggy, then sixty-six, played Lilian Baylis herself and Dame Flora, seventy-two, offered a delicate reading of Miss Prism in *The Importance of Being Earnest.* As with Dame Sybil and Dame Edith, the evening provided an opportunity for Old Vic playgoers with long memories to take a bird's eye-view of their long and distinguished careers. In the case of Dame Peggy, this was expanded in February 1976, when *Tribute to the Lady* was repeated as the National Theatre Company's final performance at the Old Vic.

Dame Flora, having been rudely shooed away from the Old Vic at the beginning of the 1920s, came back in 1933. She had become a star, having made a spectacular West End career playing roles that had been studies in hysteria and in madness. Tyrone Guthrie's first innovatory 1933 season at the Old Vic was initially built round Dame Flora. At that time, one of her closest friends was Charles Laughton. Just then his career was at a zenith as a film star and he was eager to join Dame Flora at the Old Vic and at Sadler's Wells. In that first controversial Guthrie season Dame Flora and Charles Laughton were consequently seen together in the leading roles of *Henry VIII, Measure for Measure* and *Macbeth.*·

Fresh from his success with the film, *The Private Life of Henry VIII,* Laughton was in a strong position to obtain a special grant from the Pilgrim Trust to ensure that his Old Vic début was in less make-do sets and costumes than had necessarily been the rule in the past. This hardly endeared him to Lilian Baylis. And Tyrone Guthrie's account of the Manager's tactless handling of Laughton after the first night failure of his Macbeth explains why the Baylis-Laughton relationship was not a cordial one.

Years later Dame Flora admitted that Laughton's training had not equipped him with the skill to handle the Shakespeare verse and to disarm criticism from the, by now, conservative regulars in the Old Vic gallery. Dame Flora also explained that her own training probably made her seem more formal and versified in contrast. By the end of the season, the artists had been working together long enough to begin to make an impression as a company. But before its close Lilian Baylis had decided to part with Guthrie, though at that point she was not to realise that this was only for the time being. From Dame Flora's point of view, however, this experience at the Old Vic was disappointing for an artist eager to explore the classical field and escape the West End stereotype casting of female hysteric *par excellence*. She did not return to the Old Vic again in the 1930s.

Dame Peggy was also an absentee from the Old Vic for the remainder of the 1930s. When she returned, briefly, to play Miranda in *The Tempest* in 1940, the bulk of her classical playing had been with John Gielgud at the Queen's Theatre. And this association was to be continued outside the Old Vic Company at the Haymarket Theatre in the mid-1940s. By this time, of course, the Old Vic Theatre itself had been bombed and it was not to be re-opened for public performances by the Old Vic Company until 1950 when Dame Peggy appeared in Hugh Hunt's revival of *Twelfth Night* as Viola.

The fact that this actress was still playing Viola – however successfully – when already forty-three was an indication of the way her career had developed. She had so remarkable a reputation in lyrical roles that she found herself playing near-ingénue classical parts long after actresses of her searching intelligence had gone off to explore comedy roles like the Nurse in *Romeo and Juliet* or the more vicious of Shakespeare's ladies like Goneril, Regan and Lady Macbeth. Her ability to sound the harsh as well as the sweet Shakespeare note was not fully realised until Katharine the Shrew and the marathon role of Margaret of Anjou was assigned to her at Stratford-upon-Avon with the Royal

Shakespeare Company's presentation of *The Wars of the Roses* in the 1960s. And, even after this achievement, Lady Macbeth never came her way on stage.

When Dame Peggy returned to the Old Vic as a guest artist with the National Theatre in the mid-1970s it would therefore have been especially interesting to see her tackle a Shakespeare villainess in a theatre where her lyrical artistry had first been established. But her appearances in the National Theatre Company's revival of *John Gabriel Borkman* and the virtuoso role of Winnie in Beckett's *Happy Days* ensured that these were happy evenings for her Old Vic admirers. That so lyrical an artist as Peggy Ashcroft should play the far-from lyrical Lilian Baylis herself at the National Theatre Company's final performance at the Old Vic in February 1976 was a source of special fascination to history-conscious visitors to that theatre.

Dame Peggy's appearance in *Happy Days* had a special significance, too, for twentieth-century students of the British theatre. Unlike a number of actresses whose reputations were made in the 1920s and 1930s, Dame Peggy had showed herself alertly receptive to the New Drama of which Beckett formed so vital a part. Between Dame Peggy's appearance at the re-opened Old Vic in 1950 and her return there with the National Theatre Company under Peter Hall in 1975, she had appeared in new plays by Pinter, Albee, Günter Grass and Marguerite Duras as well as taking in Ibsen and Chekhov revivals.

Dame Flora's return to the Old Vic was in November 1958 when she was seen as Mrs Alving in *Ghosts*. Unlike Dame Peggy, her career in the 1950s and 1960s had not embraced the new writers. And those who treasured her performance in the intervening years in Shakespeare *The Winter's Tale*, Wilde *The Importance of Being Earnest* and Henry James, an adaptation of *The Aspern Papers*, may have been saddened that these had to take place away from the Old Vic. But it would be wrong to suppose that Dame Flora remembered the Old Vic as the theatre where Lilian Baylis had sent her away with a flea in her ear and had then involved her in the Laughton/Baylis tensions of Tyrone Guthrie's innovatory 1933-34 season.

When Dame Flora unveiled the plaque on Lilian Baylis's south London home in 1974 she spoke with warmth both of Lilian Baylis and in particular of the responsive Old Vic gallery public. She had been delighted especially with the story of an Old Vic gallery woman, wife of a costermonger, who had emerged from a performance of *Hamlet* remarking with sympathetic concern, 'them 'amlets did have a deal of trouble in the family, didn't they?'

In private life there have been certain superficial resemblances with the earlier generation of lead Old Vic Shakespeare actresses, Dame Sybil and Dame Edith. Dame Peggy, three times married, has, like Dame Sybil, had a family life to fall back on and has also seen some members of this family enter the theatre. Dame Flora has never married and her family life has been with caring for her sisters rather than bringing up children. Both Dame Peggy and Dame Flora, though never living their private lives publicly, have used their names to forward public issues of merit – Dame Peggy on behalf of artists hounded by totalitarian régimes, Dame Flora on behalf of raising money for charitable organisations, especially those concerned with the welfare of the young. Though Dame Flora has never been a mother herself, she has indirectly mothered very many children.

The lean years of the Second World War when the Old Vic Company, bombed out of its historic London home, was obliged to lead a life half-way between that of gypsy and evacuee, were not propitious for the promotion of the careers of a new generation to follow Sybil Thorndike, Edith Evans, Flora Robson and Peggy Ashcroft. But two years before the declaration of that war, an actress who first played Ophelia for the Old Vic Company in 1937 was to have a career that became inextricably bound to the Company.

Vivien Leigh was a mere twenty-three-year-old when she played Ophelia at Kronborg Castle, Elsinore, to the Hamlet of her then future husband, Laurence Olivier. Breathtakingly beautiful and clearly a future star herself, she might have been expected to outlive a Thorndike, an Evans, a Robson or an Ashcroft to be present as a Dame in the theatrical establishment at the time of the opening of a National Theatre on the South Bank in 1976. But she had died in her early fifties at an age when Edith Evans was still playing Cleopatra and with decades of theatrical achievement ahead of her.

Is it better to be able to cast a spell of irresistible beauty, as Edith Evans has done, or is it the greater asset to be the possessor of remarkable good looks? Is it an advantage or a hindrance to be married to a great actor like Olivier? Does such a marriage leave an actress exposed to the spiteful claim that roles and prestige accrue to her through her husband rather than as a result of her own talents and ability? If, as has been asserted, Dame Sybil Thorndike's indefatigible energy was 'too much' for her husband, Lewis Casson, might not it also be argued that Laurence Olivier's standing in the theatre was 'too much' for Vivien Leigh? Finally, when an actress is a film star of the magnitude that Vivien Leigh became, does she not have to work doubly hard to overcome a prejudice against film stars so many of whose careers depended on sex appeal as much as on acting ability?

There is no simple and unequivocal answer to these questions. Those for whom the name Vivien Leigh is synonymous with Scarlett O'Hara in the film version of *Gone with the Wind*, should, however, be reminded of the scope of her classical assignments and the extent of her services in Shakespeare – to the Old Vic Company in particular. Those who were initially struck by Vivien Leigh's attractiveness may have thought that her Titania in *A Midsummer Night's Dream*, which was revived at the Old Vic in the autumn of 1937, along with her Ophelia, represented the extent of her Shakespeare repertoire. Although she did not live long enough to essay the matrons like a Volumnia or a Countess of Rousillon, Vivian Leigh's range was to prove considerably wider than that. Although her Juliet to Laurence Olivier's Romeo in New York in 1940 was in a production that flopped, this set-back fortunately did not put an end to the husband and wife partnership in Shakespeare.

At first that may have seemed what had happened. But it was a personal success in a Thornton Wilder play which prevented Vivien Leigh from being free to join Olivier at the beginning of his five-year stint as joint-artistic director and lead actor with the Old Vic Company from 1944 to 1949 at the New Theatre. But, towards the end of that period, Vivien Leigh was able to join her husband in Australia and New Zealand to head a touring Company which included a repertoire that enabled her to play Lady Anne in *Richard III* and Lady Teazle in *The School for Scandal*. She was seen in these roles in London at the New Theatre at the beginning of 1949 and added the name part of Anouilh's *Antigone* to her credits then.

From the point of view of outlining Vivien Leigh's career after that season in terms of the Old Vic Company, it is unfortunate that 'The Oliviers', as they were then called, left the organisation. Vivien Leigh's Cleopatra to her husband's Antony was under the Olivier management at the since-demolished St James' Theatre. And when Olivier joined the Shakespeare Memorial Theatre in Stratford-upon-Avon in the mid-1950s, so did Vivien Leigh. The result is that her first Viola, her Lady Macbeth and her Lavinia in *Titus Andronicus* belong to the history of Stratford-upon-Avon and not the Waterloo Road.

However, after the breaking up of their marriage, Vivien Leigh returned to the Old Vic organisation whilst her husband founded the Chichester Festival Theatre as a seeming dress-rehearsal for his appointment as artistic director of the National Theatre Company at the Old Vic. This Vivien Leigh never joined. Her last services to the Old Vic, therefore, were back in Australia where she headed an Old Vic Company to play Viola in *Twelfth Night,* Paola in Giraudoux's *Duel of Angels* and the consumptive heroine, Marguerite, in *The Lady of the Camélias.* These productions did not come to the Waterloo home. By the time the tour was completed Michael Elliott was preparing the Old Vic Company's final season under his direction before the enterprise was wound up to make way for the National Theatre Company.

It would probably be fair to sum up Vivien Leigh's work at the Old Vic or for the Old Vic Company as an illustration that to have beauty, intelligence, a world-wide film reputation and a colossus of the British theatre as your husband are not necessarily in themselves the combination of good fortune that they would seem. They did help to ensure that Vivien Leigh's name will never be forgotten when the Old Vic Company's history is studied. But her own career would undoubtedly have been a longer one if her many gifts had been accompanied by robust health.

Two other actresses whose careers were to be cut tragically short through ill-health made a considerable reputation with the Old Vic Company in the 1940s. By the time she came to play Ophelia at the age of twenty-six to Robert Helpmann's Hamlet at the New in 1944, Pamela Brown already had considerable experience behind her as a result of Shakespeare seasons in the late 1930s at Stratford-upon-Avon, the Regent's Park Open Air Theatre and at the Old Vic itself. And Margaret Leighton had gained some varied experience at the Birmingham Repertory Theatre before joining the Old Vic Company at the New Theatre for a three-year period from 1944 to 1947. Both, however, were to consolidate their careers with the Old Vic, Margaret Leighton by remaining for those three years with the London Old Vic; Pamela Brown by taking lead roles at the Bristol Old Vic.

Since Margaret Leighton's London and New York debuts were with the Old Vic Company, hers was the career that was perhaps more closely identified with the Vic organisation. For her the New Theatre days were certainly a rewarding time with parts as varied as Regan in *King Lear* and Roxane in *Cyrano de Bergerac* affording her nearly as wide a range of roles as Dame Sybil had enjoyed in the Company's infancy. Once again from the point of view of the Old Vic's history, her subsequent Shakespeare career was to belong to other theatres – her Ariel and Lady Macbeth belonging to the Stratford-upon-Avon Festival seasons of the 1950s and her Cleopatra to the Chichester Festival season of 1969. Even so, the fact that before her death in 1976 her last London appearance was with another actor whose career had been initially forged on an Old Vic stage seemed somehow appropriate. It was with Alec Guinness in *A Family and a Fortune* in 1975.

Once the Old Vic Company was able to give up its tenancy of the New Theatre and return, in 1950, to its home in the Waterloo Road, the stage was set for yet another generation of actresses to follow in the footsteps of Thorndike and Evans, Robson and Ashcroft and their Second World War successors.

Disappointingly few of the new young actress leads came from the Old Vic satellite organisations like Michel Saint-Denis' Old Vic Theatre School or the Bristol Old Vic Theatre School which survived whilst the London establishment was allowed to waste away. The first of the new generation of actresses to be acclaimed on the reconstructed Old Vic stage was Claire Bloom, who had in fact trained at the Guildhall School. Unlike the early days of Sybil Thorndike and Edith Evans, the Old Vic was now recruiting future major actresses while they were still very young. Claire Bloom was a mere twenty-one when she was acclaimed as Juliet and Jessica in the 1952-53 season. But though so much younger than Edith Evans when making her Waterloo Road debut, Claire Bloom, like Dame Edith before her, came to the Old Vic with some previous Shakespeare experience and West End stardom behind her – the former gained at Stratford-upon-Avon and the latter as Isabelle in *Ring Round the Moon*. In the minds of the press and the general public; however, she was above all a film star for the simple reason that she had recently made *Limelight* with Charlie Chaplin.

In the 1953-54 season Claire Bloom's repertoire was to include Ophelia, the Helen of *All's Well That Ends Well* and Viola. And, in 1956, she was back at the Old Vic in June to repeat her performance as Juliet before touring with the Old Vic Company in this role in North America. At that time, it must have seemed that her career would follow the pattern of an actress like Peggy Ashcroft with regular returns to Shakespeare and the British festival companies that staged his plays. Surprisingly, her appearances in the late 1950s and the 1960s were either in the West End, in a Sartre play, or at the Royal Court, in Chekhov, to be followed, in 1971, with *A Doll's House* which came via New York to the Criterion in Piccadilly Circus. Those of her admirers in the early 1950s at the Old Vic who might have hoped that when this actress reached her fifties, she would have been seen as the Beatrice of *Much Ado* or the Rosalind of *As You Like It* with an ensemble like the Royal Shakespeare Company or the National Theatre Company at the Old Vic were to be disappointed. Films and two marriages have claimed much of her time and creative energies. But so moving was the wounded and aching beauty that Claire Bloom brought to her Juliet and to her Ophelia, the hope must remain that in the fullness of time the Shakespeare cycle will be filled and that a Gertrude in *Hamlet* or perhaps a Countess Rousillon in *All's Well That Ends Well* will come her way and enable her to round off the Shakespeare cycle of women roles.

Had Claire Bloom not cornered Shakespeare's younger heroines at the Old Vic at the beginning of the 1950s, another actress doing little more than walking on with the company at that time would certainly have made these parts her own. Dorothy Tutin was also a mere twenty-one when she joined the London Old Vic in 1951 after training at the Royal Academy of Dramatic Art and spending a year with the Bristol Old Vic in 1950. Here was another major classical actress at the start of her career and one whose art has been less swallowed up by work overseas and filming than Claire Bloom.

At the Old Vic, Anne Page in *The Merry Wives of Windsor* and the Princess of France in *Henry V* were the best parts that came her way. So the Bristol and London Old Vic can only claim to have provided a shop window for an actress who was to become a West End star with *The Living Room* and *I Am A Camera* before going on to Stratford-upon-Avon and the Royal Shakespeare Company and exercising her velvet-textured voice on the lyric raptures of a Juliet and a Viola.

Another major actress whose career began in the 1950s can even more justifiably claim to have been launched into the theatrical firmament by the Old Vic since her first-ever professional appearance on stage was with this company when, at twenty-three, she played Ophelia to John Neville's Hamlet. The actress was Judi Dench and the year was 1957. Like Dame Sybil Thorndike at the start of the Old Vic Company, Judi Dench was to remain with the organisation for four years – the years that led up to its close to make way for the National Theatre Company at the Old Vic. She was to take over the lyrical roles previously played by Claire Bloom. And she was to play so many others as well that one is reminded of the variety of parts Dame Sybil undertook, even if Judi Dench's repertoire did not quite encompass male as well as female parts.

The highspot of Judi Dench's first professional years with the Old Vic Company was undoubtedly her Juliet in Zeffirelli's famous 1961 production of *Romeo and Juliet.* But her four years at the Old Vic established that she was that rare combination: an actress capable of successful excursions into the realms of poetic tragedy, represented by an Ophelia and a Juliet, and also capable of triumphing in comedy parts ranging from Cecily Cardew in *The Importance of Being Earnest* to Anne Page in *The Merry Wives of Windsor* and Kate Hardcastle in *She Stoops to Conquer.* It is revealing that, at this stage in her career, Judi Dench was cast as Maria in *Twelfth Night* and not Viola.

Like Claire Bloom before her, Judi Dench was to move on to the Royal Shakespeare Company at Stratford-upon-Avon. That she was eager to play Shakespeare's harsher portraits of women was shown later when she joined her former Old Vic partner, John Neville, to play Lady Macbeth to his Macbeth at the Nottingham Playhouse. This production was seen, under British Council auspices, in West Africa but not at the Old Vic or indeed anywhere in London. Although Judi Dench has ventured into the cinema, she is one of the few major leading actresses to remain, like many of the early Old Vic actresses, primarily a theatre artist. It is very much to the credit of the Old Vic Company's direction that at the start of her career she had the opportunity to demonstrate in the Waterloo Road that she was both a lyrical actress *and* a comedienne.

The Old Vic Company had got off the ground in the 1914 to 1918 years in part because an actress like Sybil Thorndike was prepared to remain with it for four consecutive seasons and play almost every role under the Shakespearean sun, including some male characters. An actress who was to show similar loyalty and an equal willingness to carry the responsibility for a challenging repertoire of Shakespeare roles was Barbara Jefford. Hers was the distinction of leading the Old Vic Company in its final years and remaining with it for five consecutive seasons from 1956. A RADA-trained actress who had made a stunning impression at Stratford-upon-Avon in the early 1950s, she was still only twenty-six when she made her Waterloo Road debut.

Although she was not obliged to take on parts normally played by men, Barbara Jefford was to outdo even a Sybil Thorndike in the variety of roles she undertook in those five seasons. They ranged from the comedy leads of Viola in *Twelfth Night*, Beatrice in *Much Ado About Nothing* and Rosalind in *As You Like It* to the heavy tragedy roles of Queen Margaret in the three parts of *Henry VI*, Regan in *King Lear* and Lady Macbeth on the company's North American tour. And, outside the Shakespeare repertoire, she switched from the elegant comedy of Wilde's *The Importance of Being Earnest*, in which she played Gwendoline Fairfax, to the obsessional passion of the title-role of Shaw's *Saint Joan*.

An actress who was so prodigal with her talents as Barbara Jefford on the Old Vic's behalf probably needed a part like a new Saint Joan to consolidate her reputation outside the Old Vic, much as Shaw's heroine had consolidated Sybil Thorndike's in the 1920s. Barbara Jefford's post-Old Vic Company career has taken her on world tours and has involved her opening the London Mayfair Theatre, in Pirandello with Ralph Richardson, as well as appearing with the Royal Shakespeare Company at the Aldwych. But her own Saint Joan role has still to be navigated.

The actress who at first improbably provides the neatest link between the Old Vic organisation itself and the National Theatre Company which was to occupy the Old Vic from 1963 to 1976 is Joan Plowright.

The word 'improbably' is inserted because, when Joan Plowright came to the National Theatre in 1963 as Laurence Olivier's wife and a leading member of his company, she epitomised in the public mind the New Drama established at the Royal Court Theatre. Her appearances with the English Stage Company in plays by Ionesco and, in particular, her performance of Beatie Bryant in Arnold Wesker's *Roots* ensured that she was closely identified with the new movement.

Like Albert Finney, who also hailed from the north of England, there was a regional quality to her acting personality that seemed ideally suited to a number of the dramatists being promoted by the Royal Court Theatre. The difference was that, being born in 1929 and therefore six years Albert Finney's senior, Joan Plowright's preparation for a stage career had been rather different from Finney's. He studied at the Royal Academy of Dramatic Art whilst Joan Plowright's grounding for the theatre had been at the Old Vic Theatre School with Michel Saint-Denis, Glen Byam Shaw and George Devine. Her first professional engagements were with the Bristol Old Vic and on tour with the London Old Vic Company in the early 1950s. So, however much Joan Plowright's celebrated creation of Beatie Bryant in *Roots* would make her appear a quintessential interpreter of the Royal Court established New Drama, in fact her own theatrical roots went back to the Old Vic Theatre and the Old Vic Company.

If Vivien Leigh's debut in Shakespeare at the Old Vic focused attention on the doubtful assets of striking beauty and eventual film stardom, Joan Plowright, at the same theatre had to take into account prejudice of a different sort before attempting Shakespeare in the Waterloo Road. A residual regional accent was an essential part of her stage personality and a valuable string to her bow in comedy and also in moments of strong emotion. But the Old Vic theatre that had accommodated the tradition of speaking Shakespeare as a Gielgud or a Redgrave spoke the verse was a difficult house in which to introduce a north country warmth to his leading-ladies. This was a problem that was to beset other actors of the same generation – notably Nicol Williamson with his Roundhouse Hamlet and Albert Finney with his National Theatre Hamlet of 1976. Those who had been brought up to the verse speaking of John Gielgud and Edith Evans might be expected to resist the new flattened delivery of the lines much as an early generation who had grown up with a certain rhetorical grandeur of an Ernest Milton or an Ion Swinley were to resist the speedy and informal delivery of Charles Laughton's 1933 Macbeth.

As it turned out, most of Joan Plowright's appearances in the first years with the National Theatre Company at the Old Vic were in roles where a sturdy regionalism was in fact desirable – notably in the title-role of Shaw's *Saint Joan,* Sonya in *Uncle Vanya* and Maggie Hobson in *Hobson's Choice.* Her assumption of the role of Beatrice in the Zeffirelli-directed *Much Ado About Nothing* was a wise choice for an actress who was as much a comedienne as she was a tragedienne. It boded well for her later National Theatre Shakespeare appearances such as her Rosaline in the 1968 *Love's Labour's Lost* and her Portia in the 1970 revival of *The Merchant of Venice.*

Already into her mid-thirties by the time the National Theatre came into being, Joan Plowright was not ideally placed to take on the romantic heroines like Ophelia, Juliet and Viola, since the Claire Bloom, Dorothy Tutin and Judi Dench generation of leading ladies had established a tradition of playing these roles much younger than had prevailed when Sybil Thorndike and Edith Evans were in their heyday. More to the point, these were not roles that intelligent admirers of Plowright's artistry would have wanted to see her tackle.

And indeed there was no need for her even to consider taking them on. The arrival of the National Theatre Company at the Old Vic meant the end of the forty-nine years of the Old Vic Shakespeare Company with its chief commitment to the presentation of the Bard. From the point of view of a National Theatre Company actress, as opposed to an Old Vic Company actress, this meant a number of things. It meant rather better working conditions in as far as the new organisation was better subsidised. It meant a far wider choice of plays to explore in repertoire – as opposed to short repertory runs. It meant a chance to take on a contemporary play like Natalia Ginzburg's *The Advertisement* in which Joan Plowright appeared in 1968. It also meant the opportunity to devise and to direct the 1970 National Theatre season of uncompromising plays by woman writers – a venture which both Emma Cons and Lilian Baylis would certainly have encouraged – even though their Victorian sensibilities may have been thankful that this enterprise took place outside the Old Vic at the Jeannetta Cochrane Theatre.

Although Joan Plowright was actress-wife to the National Theatre's director, Laurence Olivier, such an enterprise was clearly not a husband and wife company in the sense that the Laurence Olivier and Vivien Leigh enterprise at the St James' Theatre in 1951 had been. If such a National ensemble could have been considered to have a leading lady that role would have to be assigned in the National's early years to Maggie Smith. This was the actress who played Desdemona to Laurence Olivier's Othello in the National Theatre Company's first Shakespeare production in 1963. And Maggie Smith was certainly to benefit from the greater variety of parts a National Company could offer an actress. Roles that she played included characters as diverse as Hilde Wangel in *The Master Builder* and Beatrice in *Much Ado About Nothing*, not to mention Mrs Sullen in *The Beaux Stratagem* and the title-role of *Hedda Gabler*.

If the regional component in Joan Plowright's personality had been a source of interest to some, others may at first have speculated on how Maggie Smith's previous reputation as an intimate revue artist with her consequent mannered delivery would be used in what was a company committed to playing a repertoire of international classics as well as new plays. Such speculation would have had to ignore the fact that, however celebrated the Kenneth Williams-Maggie Smith revue partnership had been in the 1950s, this actress had already shown her ability to work well beyond the confines of revue at the Old Vic itself when she joined one of the last Old Vic Companies in the 1959-60 season to play Celia in *As You Like It*, the Queen in *Richard II*, Mistress Ford in *The Merry Wives of Windsor* as well as the heroine of Barrie's sentimental *What Every Woman Knows*. It would be difficult to think of the last in terms of the quicksilver sophistication of intimate revue.

Another artist whose reputation had first been established in the West End as a comedienne, in light comedy rather than revue, was Geraldine McEwan. By the time she came to join the National Theatre Company at the Old Vic in 1965 she, too, had already demolished convictions that her slender frame and idiosyncratically incisive voice must preclude her from attempting the classical Shakespeare parts as a result of her success in them in the late-1950s at Stratford-upon-Avon. Geraldine McEwan arrived in the Waterloo Road with Shakespeare roles as varied as Beatrice in *Much Ado About Nothing* and Ophelia in *Hamlet* behind her to demonstrate that a voice that seemingly pointed straight at comedy and revue could in fact also be brought to the service of Shakespeare and the classical theatre.

Once the initial prejudice of critics and public in pigeon-holing artists in the light comedy category in which their reputation was first made had been overcome, the techniques acquired could be deployed on tragedy too. So, like Maggie Smith, Geraldine McEwan was to reap the benefit of the catholic nature of a National Theatre Company's repertoire. Her success in the Feydeau farce, *A Flea in her Ear*, was to be as great as her accomplishment in playing the wife to Olivier's husband in Strindberg's grisly picture of marriage in *Dance of Death*. The lesson to be drawn both from Maggie Smith and Geraldine McEwan's work with the National Theatre Company is that it is unwise to write off young artists who make their initial impact as comediennes, as incapable also of taking on tragedy.

Is it possible to discern anything in common at all between these actresses? Can a bird's eye-view be taken of artists who played mainly Shakespeare for the Old Vic Company as well as those who went on to feature in the international repertoire of a National Theatre Company at the Old Vic? Even from such a necessarily selective glance compiled from the hundreds of actresses who have helped to make the Old Vic famous, some tentative conclusions may be reached.

Firstly, it must be obvious that conventional beauty is no passport to success in Shakespeare and the classics. This is not an indirect way of suggesting that leading ladies at the Old Vic have had the misfortune to have the type-casting appearances of Macbeth's Weird Sisters. If Old Vic actresses who have had enduring careers in the theatre have certainly not been witches in appearance, neither have they arrived in the Waterloo Road as mere beauty queens. The careers of Dame Sybil Thorndike and Dame Edith Evans at the Old Vic demonstrate that, in the long run, there are qualities far more important than just conventional good looks. Of these qualities perhaps the most important are those of having the guile, energy, intelligence, will-power and authority to be able to project an illusion of size, grandeur and beauty. And lovely Ophelias will not stay the course to grow into impressive

Gertrudes, if they do not also have the stamina, good-health and sheer perversity to ride out the fashionable tides of theatrical taste.

Fay Compton, who was an enchanting thirty-year-old Ophelia to John Barrymore's controversial Hamlet in 1924, survived to play Gertrude in 1953 to Richard Burton's Old Vic Hamlet when this actress was approaching sixty. Perhaps her enduring and enormously wide-ranging career on the stage may provide a clue to the *sine qua non* to success in a theatre devoted in particular to Shakespeare. Apart from her Ophelia of the 1920s, Fay Compton's beauty inspired Barrie to write the play *Mary Rose* for her. With the passing of the years, Fay Compton could no longer continue to repeat her performances of that play on stage. But such was the beauty of her voice that she could still play on radio youthful parts when the actress herself was already in middle-age. This is not meant to advocate a return to senior citizen playing the Shakespeare heroines, and a stage peopled with elderly actresses passing themselves off as ingénues for a nostalgically minded audience. The point is that to survive in the theatre, an actress must, in Shakespeare at least, have a 'theatre' voice as opposed to a 'theatrical' voice. However many years may pass, an artist will survive and have a valuable contribution to make so long as the gifts that she has brought to bear may still be effortlessly relayed to the farthest reaches of the house without alarming those fortunate enough to be sitting closest to the stage.

Sometimes, as in the case of Dame Peggy Ashcroft, this enduring voice may have a lyrical quality that makes it hard for her to be given some of the harsher characters that might interest her. And sometimes, as in the case of Claire Bloom, the vulnerable quality in that voice seems to have militated against her tackling the mature comedy roles that her colleagues have found rewarding. Sometimes, as in the case of Judi Dench, a sunniness of disposition is reflected in that voice that enables it to take on the comic as well as the tragic roles. The work of Maggie Smith and Geraldine McEwan for the National Theatre Company at the Old Vic has certainly demonstrated that voices that would seem custom-built for comedy can in fact be rewardingly used in tragedy.

But it is the voice, coupled with the ability to bewitch an audience into believing an actress looks as she would have her public believe she looks, that in the end is of paramount importance. And no actress is going to bewitch an audience in Shakespeare unless she has the voice with which to cast the spell. Harley Granville Barker said it all with a dictum that points to the overall importance of the voice and the use of the voice in Shakespeare. What he said was, 'Verse and prose were Shakespeare's sword and dagger. Let these rust or let them be ill-wielded and no defensive armouring of a performance by scenery, costume, or even well-thought acting will avail.'

Postscript

'And what is going to happen to the Old Vic next?' This is a question a lot of people suddenly began to ask themselves in March 1976. The National Theatre Company had at last begun its much-postponed departure for its new South Bank home. The Old Vic closed its doors and, ominously, 'went dark'.

The unthinkable thought of the Old Vic being pulled down seemed even more unthinkable at the beginning of 1976 as builders moved in, set up scaffolding and began the work of restoring the ancient building to tip-top condition. Under the terms of its lease of the theatre, the National Theatre Company had to leave the Old Vic and its Annexe properly repaired and maintained. It was hard to believe that an army of workers should repoint the venerable brickwork and undertake repairs to the roof and the chimneys only to move out so that the theatre should then be closed down and eventually demolished.

Yet it was certainly worrying that the news of the National Theatre Company's departure was not immediately followed by an announcement of future plans. It was not, after all, as though the Old Vic Governors had been idle in the early 1970s as the National Theatre Company announced its departure and then postponed the move as hoped-for completion dates of its own home came and went.

A scheme whereby the English Stage Company would operate both at the Royal Court and at the Old Vic was investigated. For some, the prospect of a company with such a fine reputation for promoting promising young dramatists allying itself to a theatre with such a long record of promoting promising young actors must have seemed an exciting proposal. But, although the scheme was gone into with some care, nothing in the end came of it.

Other companies, or company directors, showed a keen interest. Among them was Joan Littlewood's Theatre Workshop Company, which shared the Old Vic's tradition of providing theatre for the people and needed a temporary home whilst the Theatre Royal at Stratford East underwent major repairs. Frank Dunlop's Young Vic Company also saw itself as a natural heir to the Old Vic for similar reasons.

Formed in 1970 as an off-shoot of the National Theatre Company, at a time when Dunlop was a National Theatre Associate Director, the Young Vic had, by 1976, become an independent organisation offering intimate arena staging of classics and new plays at 'student prices'. Although there may at first have been misgivings that a Young Vic Company at the Old Vic might conceivably have wished to impose a democratic arena staging on the hierarchical seating and proscenium stage of the Old Vic, the claims of this company were carefully mooted. The Young Vic's home – a converted butcher's shop just down the road – was a temporary structure and when the short lease on this building expired, the Young Vic's application to move into the Old Vic had an added urgency to recommend it. The result was an announcement in May 1976 that the following year the Young Vic would in fact take over the Old Vic tenancy – with an Arts Council subsidy.

The scheme that had been looked into over a greater period of time was one whereby the Old Vic would return to its late 1920s role as a home for drama, opera and ballet. This had been known as the 'Tri-Partite' plan involving the opening up of the old orchestra pit that the farewell visit of Dame Nellie Melba had once done so much to enlarge. The Tri-Partite scheme was that the Old Vic and its Annexe should be shared during a working year by Prospect Theatre Company, the touring section of the Royal Ballet and the English Music Theatre Company. The Arts Council went as far as setting up a relevant Lyric Theatre Enquiry to look into the needs and resources of the lyric theatre in London. It was found that the Tri-Partite plan did, in fact, have much to recommend it. But the Arts Council also found that, in 1976, they had insufficient subsidy to back such a potentially expensive sharing arrangement of the Old Vic – however worthy.

Things had now begun to look very gloomy. The freehold of the Old Vic was vested with the Charity Commission. It may well have been that the Commissioners would now feel that it could best meet the original charity intentions in the 1970s by allowing the Old Vic to be sold off and the money used to provide scholarships for needy students or by subsidising tickets for needy theatregoers. As these thoughts crossed the minds of one or two people, a London evening newspaper reported the sighting of the ghost of Lilian Baylis – a truly terrifying spectacle by all accounts.

Dame Ellen Terry had threatened to haunt Miss Baylis had she allowed certain structural alterations to change an Old Vic to which Dame Ellen had become particularly attached. Now it looked as though Miss Baylis, Companion of Honour, had returned from a far better place to put in a discreetly publicised spectral appearance at a time when the future existence of the entire building was temporarily in doubt.

Early in 1976 there had been talk of Glenda Jackson heading an American-financed company somewhere in London, with support from former Royal Court artists like the director, William Gaskill and the dramatist, Edward Bond. In April 1976 it was prematurely disclosed that Miss Jackson's Company would in fact be the first to re-open the Old Vic in August that year with a revival of *The White Devil*. Other companies would follow to keep the Old Vic alive until it could commence its own rejuvenated life as the 'Young Vic at the Old Vic'.

The shadow of the late Miss Baylis was not spotted again once these tidings were made public. It must now be hoped that the lady may be allowed to rest in peace untroubled by the Old Vic's future. If this book's outline of the theatre's history in some way helps to ensure this, it will have served its purpose.

Recommended Reading

Booth, John *The Old Vic 1816-1916* Stead's 1917
Booth, Michael *English Melodrama* Herbert Jenkins 1965
Clarke, Mary *Shakespeare at the Old Vic Vols I-V* Hamish Hamilton 1953-1958.
Dent, Edward J. *A Theatre for Everybody* T. & V. Boardman 1945
De Valois, Ninette *Come Dance with Me* Dancebooks 1975
Fagg, Edwin *The Old 'Old Vic'* Vic-Wells Association 1936
Findlater, Richard *Lilian Baylis, The Lady of the Old Vic* Allen Lane 1975
Guthrie, Tyrone *A Life in the Theatre* Hamish Hamilton 1960
Guthrie, Tyrone *In Various Directions* Michael Joseph 1966
Hamilton, Cicely and Baylis, Lilian *The Old Vic* Cape 1926
Hunt, Hugh *Old Vic Prefaces: Shakespeare and the Producer* Routledge & Kegan Paul 1954
Marshall, Norman *The Producer and the Play* Macdonald 1957
Marshall, Norman *The Other Theatre* John Lehmann 1947
Newton, H. Chance *The Old Vic and its Associations* Fleetway Press 1923
Thorndike, Sybil and Russell *Lilian Baylis* Chapman & Hall 1938
Williams, Harcourt *Four Years at the Old Vic* Putnam 1935
Williams, Harcourt *Old Vic Saga* Winchester Publications 1940
Williamson, Audrey *Old Vic Drama 1934-1947* Rockcliff 1948
Williamson, Audrey *Old Vic Drama 1947-1957* Rockliff 1957

REFERENCE

The Oxford Companion to the Theatre edited by Phyllis Hartnoll
Who's Who in the Theatre Vols I-XV Pitman
The Old Vic Annual General Reports 1905-1963
The Old Vic Magazine 1919-30

Index